BUDDHISM AND DALITS
SOCIAL PHILOSOPHY AND TRADITIONS

Buddhism and Dalits Social Philosophy and Traditions

C.D. Naik

KALPAZ

Published by

Kalpaz Publications
C-30, Satyawati Nagar,
Delhi – 110052
Ph.: 011-47034999, 9811692060
www.kalpazpublications.com
E-mail: kalpaz@hotmail.com

Distribution Network
gyanbooks.com
India, USA, Canada, UK, Australia, France

ISBN: 978-93-5722-515-1 (PB)

First Published, 2024

Printed at: Gyan Press, Delhi.

Budhism and Dalits Social Philosophy and Traditions
Author: C. D. Naik

Contents

Preface

Buddhism is nothing if it is not social. A man from Kapilavastu on the border of Nepal saw the interaction of interests among individuals, associations, kingdoms and general folks with murderous hunt for enthronement, cut-throat competition between kins, rule of might over meek from a corner of Uruvela forest and found the way leading to the end of this misery and professed and propagated his vision of new and fresh dispensation by words of mouth while treading the rugged lands from east to west and north to south on foot for forty five years and breathed his last at the age of eighty years in Kusinagar. This was Siddhartha Gautama the Buddha whose legacy is transmitted to the world through Buddhist countries and missionaries who cared it more than their own and passed it on to us at present.

Buddhism as philosophy appealed to the rational and as art to the artists. In the later half of the 19th century the attention of European scholars was drawn to the study of the Buddha and his religion. The story of Buddhism in India extended to Far East with its ramifications into different schools and sects, its literature, its education, its rulers and writers, during the fifth and seventh centuries A.D., its art, its revival and its present status in the world.

The most compassionate feature of Buddhism was its adoption of Dalits as its own and rendering service to uplift them on par with generality. Dr. Ambedkar, the 14th Dalai lama, Ven. Thich Nhat Hanh, Sulak Sivaraksha and alike belonged to this social stream of Buddhism. They have always espoused the cause of the most degraded and downtrodden sections of society and set them free from the thraldom of social slavery, economic exploitation, educational backwardness and political subjugation.

Out of 14 million Dalits in India none falls above ultra poor or poverty line poor. As such they suffer from poverty including deprivation of food, income and employment and, being socially disadvantaged group Dalits suffer from backwardness in education, discrimination in employment, atrocities and suppression in social, cultural and religious matter. Needless to stress that compared to SCs and STs, let alone OBCs and General category the Buddhist group in Maharashtra has greatest incidence of poverty. No radical change is possible without Dalit participation in the midst of capitalist privatized corporate market economy neglecting human labour and its contribution for new products and new order of humanity.

Ambedkar was not a person, he was an institution. This single man shook the whole empire of injustice and inequality and brought on par with every other dignified human being in the civilized world the century long perished untouchable. That is why Suriyabongse, Malalasekere, Vijayavardhane, Ledi Sayadaw, U Ba Swe, Sankrityayan, Csoma de Korosjkeda, Soka Gakkai, Yamada Mumon, Buan-an,Kausalyayan, Sangharakshita, Shosan Suzuki, Phrakhru Aduu, Buddhadasa and such others stand closer to Buddha and Babasaheb as well as social philosophy than any other Father and Prophet as well as philosophy without social context.

Modern education is an effective instrument of occupational and social mobility in individual's life, but not in social life, particularly in India. Tantric teachers, living on cremation grounds, taking outcaste women as their tantric consorts, and using skulls as drinking vessels, expressed with their behavior their transcendence of conventional action, and reactions against the unreasonable aspects of the caste discrimination of Brahmanism at that time. Social Buddhism in Tantric form made the opposite ends of sansara and nirvana meet and the incalculable span of time required for practice of perfection by Bodhisattva reduced to a snap. The style of our life has changed in the last decades, but the hearts of men have remained the same. No less strong than the urge for prosperity, joy and progress, is the longing for a glance beyond into the realm of the timeless.

For the preservation of society marriage institution was devised by man from the time immemorial. Which marriage and which method of marriage can preserve the associated mode of life in a better way? Over and above the Brahma and Asura marriages there is a method of civil marriage and Buddhist marriage system wholly endorses it within its framework. So simple, so time saving, so economic, so natural and so rational a method Buddhist marriage really presents a superb model for every social section. Its golden rule is, "Never let passion override compassion".

Its succession Act 2007 as put forth in this book follows its preceding Act 1925 and provides any Buddhist to dispose of his or her property by will or other testamentary disposition in accordance with its provisions.

For Dalits of modern day India Deeksha Bhoomi has become a centre of organization, unity and solidarity and no less holy for the Dalits and Buddhists than Mecca and Madina for the Muslims. This is the modern Kasi for them as has been Benares for the Brahmins. This is the stronghold of the Neo-Buddhists as Aligarh has been for the non-Buddhists. The days are not distant when the Dalits will create their own university as the Hindus and Muslims had theirs already. The struggle for management of Bodh Gaya Buddha Vihara sprang from this centre and became known to all quarters. The Fourth wheel of Dhamma was turned here at the hands of Babasaheb Ambedkar and it will not come to an end come what may.

The ruling deity of Indian national life is from Buddhist fold- the wheel at the centre of tri-colour flag, the lion capital on the currency, the motto on the wall above the speaker's seat, the dome on the Raj-Bhavan and Parliament House, the envious number of Ambedkar Statues, Buddha parks and villages and towns named after great men of Buddha's mind and so on give the living impression of the bygone golden era of our nation.

Not only this but even the non-governmental organizations adopted the principles of Ambedkar and social life such as liberty, equality and fraternity in their respective modus operandi and functioning across the country with slogan of educate or each one teach one, agitate or change for better and organize or generate better mode of social life. This will perhaps be the torchlight for coming generation to see through dimness of past glory and dazzling of present momentary name and fame.

It is our responsibility to take Dr. Ambedkar's thoughts to every common man of this country, then only our nation will be strong enough to face the challenges of 21st century and will become a developed nation.

Finally I am inclined to remind the readers that one who knows Pali needs no light from outside.

C.D. Naik

Acknowledgements

Let me express my deepest gratitude for greatest services rendered by Bodhishree, Nirvan, Preeti in preparation of this manuscript. I owe a word of gratitude to Shri L.R. Bailey, Editor of Bheem Patrika, Jullundur for giving me and my Institute a visit as chief guest in the national seminar and delivering his lectures on the theme that enlightened our minds. I cannot forget dear Prof. Andrea for inviting me at International conference in Kolkata and Shantiniketan on Tantra and Buddhist hermeneutics, which has inspired me to write a paper on this theme as included in this book. The organizer of national seminar in the department of social work in Sayaji University, Baroda also deserved my heartfelt thanks for organizing my keynote speech and giving good response. During the process of preparing this manuscript I was benefitted by the company of Chairman, vice-chancellor, professors, research scholars and friends whose names are too famous to be mentioned here. Lastly but not in the least I give my hearty thanks to Kalpaz Publication and its team of editors for bringing this manuscript to refinement and publication.

C.D. Naik

Introduction

Buddhism and Dalits: Social Philosophy and Traditions is the latest issue of the author. It has eleven chapters based on research papers, projects and articles prepared by the author earlier. The chapter (I) on *Rise and Decline of Buddhism: History* gives historical outline of how Buddha introduced the revolutionary system of society and how his descendents continued that spark of life through vicissitudes of reactionary forces and rising and falling tides of time. Chapter (II) on *Globalisation and Dalits* tells the story of the effect of privatization and marketisation of goods and services on the state role and Dalits' fate falling more and more apart from each other as helpless victims of corporate power and its empire across the globe. It is a research paper of the author focusing on the wild spread economic speculation at the cost of public work, welfare and will. Chapter (III) on *Social Message of Buddhism* highlighted the Buddha's Dhamma meant not only for individual perfection alone but also for sublime service to mankind as a whole. It traced contributions of Dr. Ambedkar and the significance of Buddhism for the Asian world to lead the humanity in the footprints of the Bodhisattvas and uproot the socio-economic-political-religious-ethnic-religious suffering by selfless service to the world community through Buddhist spirit.

Chapter (IV) on *Sociological Aspects of Buddhism* reflected relevance of Dr. Ambedkar's thought to the contemporary social principles and practical realities of working in and for society. This paper was presented in National Seminar of the Sayaji University Department of Social Work, Vadodara as key note and was appreciated very much by the audience as it set the real note of modern social needs and remedies.

Chapter (V) on *Buddhist Tantra* is a research paper presented at International symposium in Kolkata and Shantiniketan in last March 2009. It analysed the Buddhist tantrism as social Buddhism, which is both easy and broad for the lay society to aspire and elevate for Buddhahood with concern and compassion for transformation of world into a Buddhafield for the establishment of living nirvana on the face of this planet.

Chapter (VI) on *Buddhist Marriage and Method* is perhaps a new and ideal feedback for a Buddhist society in India and abroad for its material is culled from scriptures and canonical principles and it gave a critique to the tradition both in letter and spirit of life. A sequel to this is chapter (VII) contributed by the Government of Maharashtra's Hon'ble State Minister, Shri Nitin Raut's on Buddhist Marriage and Succession Act 2007, which is based on the notes of the Hindu Code Bill of Dr. Ambedkar, who had tried his best to lead it through the Parliament with the favour of the then Prime Minister Shri Jawahar Lal Nehru so that the parity and equality of men and women in matters of marriage, right to inheritance, succession, adoption, divorce and such other related things should be established in Indian society, but, alas! neither the Prime Minister nor the Hindu intellectuals of the time including the Hindu progressive ladies supported the bill, nor showed an iota of concern for the fair sex that resulted in the resignation of Law Minister Dr. Ambedkar from the Cabinet in 1951.

Chapter (VIII) on *Deeksha Bhoomi of Ambedkar* is based on the research project of Buddhist minority in Nagpur, conducted by this author himself in 2006. It highlighted how the Buddhist and scheduled caste population lumped together for census purposes and were deprived of their size-wise share of representation in Lok Sabha and State Legislature seats due as per their combined population figure, with Government turning the deaf ear to their grievances.

Chapter (IX) on *Ambedkar's Spirit of Constitution and Social Organisation* reflected how Fundamental rights of a citizen and directive principles of state are obligatory and how spirit of constitutional framers was lost in the verdict of Supreme court and high courts. It offers synoptic view of Dr. Ambedkar's brilliant and lucid definitions of intricate knotty issues of Indian national and social life.

It has also supplemented with the functioning of the social organizations today in the context of application of Ambedkar's thought to them in the districts of Madhya Pradesh.

Chapter (IX) on *Educational Policies and Programmes for Dalits: Present* gives an exposition of Government policies for higher education and scholarship with appreciation and criticism offered by its author Prof. Katkar, Chandrapur, who had presented it in the National Seminar on *Dr. Ambedkar's Social Philosophy: Educational and Economic Development of Weaker Sections* held in the Institute, Mhow on 27-28 February, 2009.

Lastly the Chapter (XI) on *Pali Grammar* is a contribution of Dr. Ambedkar to Pali Vyakaran in making this abstruse subject simplified and accessible to the non-Pali background seekers of knowledge of Buddha's diaglogues recited in Pali in day-to-day lay Buddhist routine incorporated in his Bauddha Puja Path and Dictionary in Marathi, Gujrathi, English and Pali of Volume sixteen published under the Writings and Speeches of Babasaheb Dr. Ambedkar by Education Department, Government of Maharashtra, Mumbai.

Thus this book is useful for common educated circle and intellectual academic classes including students of Indian politics, social science, history, ethics, religion, law and literature.

If any errors are found in elucidating the matter in this volume the author will humbly submit to it and rectify it at the earliest next opportunity. Any benefit derived from the reading of this book by the user will be taken as a gain to the author himself.

C.D. Naik

List of Contributiors

Dr. Nitin Raut was awarded the degree of Ph. D. from Nagpur University in the year 2008 on his thesis related to family planning in the context of Dr. Ambedkar's view on it. Prof. C.D. Naik as external examined of his thesis approved his work and recommended Doctorate award for the same. Shri Nitin Raut has been the member of Legislative Assembly (North Nagpur) continuously and is now holding the port folio of Minister in the State of Maharashtra.

Prof. Satyapal Katkar is M.Sc. (Psychology), M.A. (Dr. Ambedkar Thought), M. Ed.; P.G.D.P.R.; D. Hindi and in teaching profession at Gadiward, Rajura, Dist. Chandrapur (M.S.).

*Dr. C.D. Naik is Professor and Head of the Division of Dr. Ambedkar Thought and Philosophy and Dr. Ambedkar Chair (Additional Charge) at Dr. Babasaheb Ambedkar National Institute of Social Sciences, Dr. Ambedkar Nagar, A.B. Road, Dongargaon, (Madhya Pradesh)-453 441 (India).

1

Rise and Decline of Buddhism : History

C.D. Naik

Religious violence in India includes acts of violence by followers of one religious group against followers and institutions of another religious group, often in the form of rioting. Hinduism, the largest religion in India, accounts for 80 per cent of the population; Islam, the second largest religion, accounts for 13 per cent of the population; Buddhism, Jainism, and Sikhism taken together account for 3 per cent of the population; and Christianit accounts for 2 per cent of the population. Other religions such as Zoroastrianism and Judaism, although not popular, have a centuries long history in India. Religious fundamentalism is considered a major driver; with Hindu nationalism, Sikh separatism, Christian Evangelism, and Islamic Fundamentalism acting as catalysts or as primary forces for outbreaks of violence. Despite India's secular and religiously tolerant nature, broad religious representation in various aspects of society including the government, the active role played by autonomous bodies such as National Human Rights Commission of India and National Commission for Minorities, and the ground-level work being carried out by non- governmental organizations, sporadic and sometimes serious acts of religious violence tend to occur as the root causes of religious violence often run deep in history, religious activities, and politics of India.

Along with domestic organizations, International human rights organizations such as Amnesty International and Human Rights Watch publish reports bringing embarrassing attention to acts of religious violence in India. Foreign government organization such as United States Department of State have also published similar, but controversial, reports which have largely been dismissed in India as interference in internal affairs.

The Rise, Fall and Revival of Buddhism

According to Prof P.V. Bapat, Buddhism is a religion of kindness, humanity and equality. The Sramanas who lived a life of retirement in the forests and gave themselves up to philosophical speculation did not sympathize with sacrifices involving the slaughter of animals. Indeed, the Brahmans had subsequently to modify their position and substitute for live animals images made of corn-flour (pista-pasu). Buddhism denounced all claims to superiority on the ground of birth as the Brahmanas claimed. It threw open the doors of organized religious life to women and men alike. The institution of a band of disciplined, selfless workers was at the very foundation of the Buddhist organization, to which he instructed "Let not two of you go in one and the same direction—*Ma ekena dve agamittha*".

Popularity of the Buddha and his religion largely depended upon his method of approach to the masses. The Buddha had asked his disciples to preach his doctrine in the people's own speech (sakaya niruttiya). Though Gautama Buddha belonged to an aristocratic family, his life and work were those of a democrat. When it came to voting, marked sticks (salakas) were used and a responsible officer was appointed to keep watch over the voting. During his lifetime, the Buddha allowed things to be decided democratically by the Sangha; and after his death, too, he did not want to restrict the freedom of the Sangha by appointing his own successor. He wanted the Dhamma and Vinaya to be its guides after his death and anything which was not authorized by the Dhamma and Vinaya was to be rejected by the Sangha. The Sangha drew its inspiration from small oligarchies (ganarajya) like those of the Vajjis or Licchavis of Vaisali and of the Mallas of Pava or Kusinara.[16] At one time the Sakyas also enjoyed a similar form of government, but they seem to have lost it long before. The Buddha showed great admiration for the Vajjis or Licchavis when, in the Mahaparinibbana-sutta, he likened the Licchavis to the thirty-three gods (Tavatimsa). He also warned Ajattasastru's Minister. Vassakara, saying that the Vajjis would remain invincible as long as they adhered to the seven rules governing their conduct (satta apparihania dhamma), namely, (i) daily meetings for consultation; (ii) unity in action; (iii) adherence to old injunctions; (iv) respect for elders; (v) respect for women who were not to be molested; (vi) reverence for places of worship within or without their territory; and (vii) protection to worthy saints (Arhats) in their territory.

Gita reflects liberal attitude of Buddhists and endorses it by repeating the stanza; striya vaisyas tatha sudras te pi yanti param gatim.[17] Thus many aspects of the Buddhist religion came to be accepted by others gradually no distinction remained. The Mahayana form of Buddhism, perhaps under the influence of non-Aryan or aboriginal popular cults in the lower strata of society, came to assume a darker and debased form of Tantrism, which was studied at the Buddhist Universities of Nalandas and Vikramasila until the end of the 12th century A.D. The beginning of the 13th century brought evil days. The monasteries of Bihar were despoiled and many of the monks fled to Nepal and Tibet, the lay Buddhists absorbed in the non-Buddhist community except a few isolated groups in Orissa, Bengal, Assam and South India, where an inscription recently discovered in Korea tells an Indian monk Dhyanabhadra visited Kancipura, where he listened to a discourse on an Avatansaka-sutra in 14th century A.D.[18]

In the latter half of the 19th century the attention of European scholars was drawn to the study of the Buddha and his religion. The story of Buddhism in India extended to Far East with its ramifications. Into different schools and sects, its literature, its education, its rulers and writers, during the fifth and seventh centuries A.D., its art, its revival and its present status in the world.

Asoka's Contribution to the Spread of Buddhism

Asoka's thirteenth rock edict stated that he tried to spread the Dhamma not only in his territory or among the people of the border lands but also in kingdoms far off, such as those of Antiochus (Antiyoko) II, King of Syria, and the kingdoms of four Antigonos (Antakini) of Macedonia, Alexander (Alikasundara) of Epirus, an ancient district of northern Greece, and Magas of Cyrenia, in North Africa Yavanas, Kambojas, Pandyas, Colas, Andhras, Pulindas, Ceylon etc. and paved the way for the Buddhist missionaries helped by kings like Kaniska to take Buddhism to Central Asia, China, Japan and Tibet in the North, and to Burma, Thailand, Cambodia and other countries in the South.

During the first and second centuries after the Nirvana, Buddhism could hardly be distinguished from other ascetic movements. It was evidently in the Maurya period that Buddhism emerged as a distinct religion with great potentialities for expansion.

Mahinda :

When the great missionary Mahinda went to Ceylon in B.C. 307, he carried with him, not only the Tripitaka but the Arthakatha which had grown up around the Tripitaka during two and a half centuries that had passed since Buddha's death. Mahinda tried to translate these commentaries from Pali into Sinhalese, the latter of which continued to exist in Ceylon for many centuries while the Pali version disappeared.

According to the traditions handed down among the Sinhalese, Pali, that is, the language used in the texts, could also be called Magadhi, not the Magadhi of the Prakrit grammarians, for latter wrote some centuries afterwards, but the one, the term of which was used in sixth century A.D. and referred to the language used by Asoka and his son Mahinda. The texts brought to Ceylon by Mahinda and his companions were not in writing, but in the memory of them. From the 11th century onwards it became a sort of fashion to write manuals in verse, or in prose and verse and the first book written in Pali in Ceylon was a chain of Pali verses.

Though Sinhalese pandits were writing in Pali, to them, of course, a dead language, they probably did their thinking in their own mother tongue. Now they had then, for many generations, so close and intimate an intercourse with their Dravidian neighbours that Dravidian habits of speech had crept into Sinhalese and its influence can be traced in the idioms and in the order of the arrangement of the matter of these Ceylon Pali books of the fifth and sixth centuries A.D. In the fifth century Mahinda's Sinhalese commentaries were retranslated by the famous Buddhaghosa.

Ancient India

Ancient India has no history of large scale religious violence where opponents were put to the sword. However, King Pusyamitra of Sunga Empire is linked in legend with the persecution of Buddhist. There is some doubt as to whether he did or did not persecute Buddhists actively.

The Divyavadana ascribes to him the razing of stupas and viharas built by Ashoka, the placing of a bounty of 100 dinaras upon the heads of Buddhist monks (bhiksus) and describes him as one who wanted to undo the work of Ashoka. This account has however been described as "exaggerated". Archaeological evidence is scarce and uncertain. However to many scholars. Sunga kings were seen as more amenable to Buddhism and as having contributed to the building of the stupa at Bharhut. With the possible exception of reign of King Pusyamitra, Buddhism and Hinduism seem to have co-existed percefully with almost all Buddhist temples, including the once at Ajanta Caves being built under the rule and patronage of Hindu kings.

Decline of Buddhims in India

The decline of Buddhism in India, the land of its birth, occurred for a variety of reasons, and happened even as it continued to flourish beyond the frontiers of India. Buddhism was established in the area of ancient Magadha and Kosala by Gautama Buddha in the 6th century BCE, in what is now modern Uttar Pradesh and Bihar. Buddhism, over the next 1500 years become the region's dominant belief system, spreading across the Indian sub-continent (see history of Buddhism).

After the death of Gautama Buddha, Buddhism saw rapid expansion in its first century, especially in northern and central India. The Mauryan Emperor Ashoka (304-232 BCE) and later monarchs encouraged the expansion of Buddhism into Asia through religious ambassadors.

Chinese scholars traveling through the region the between 5th and 8th centuries CE, such as Faxian, Xuanzang, I-ching, Hui-sheng, and Sung-Yun, began to speak of a decline of the Buddhist sangha, especially in the wake of the White

Hun invasion. A continuing decline occurred after the fall of the Pala dynasty in the 12th century CE, continuing with the later destruction of monasteries by Muslim conquerors. Buddhism was virtually extinct by the end of the 19th century. In recent times, Buddhism has seen a revival in India from the influence of Anagarika Dharmapala, Kripasaran Mahasthavir, Dr. B. R. Ambedkar and Tenzin Gyatso, the 14th Dalai Lama.

The Rise and Decline of Buddhism's Indian Social Base

The Buddha's period saw not only urbanization, but also the beginnings of centralized states. While the Brahmin Law-givers of this time were explicitly hostile to towns, there is evidence that the Buddha's message appealed especially to town-dwellers and the new social classes. Buddhism became successful by filling the moral vacuum in the new social world of commerce and city life with a universalistic social morality which was lacking in both the Brahmanical and shramana religions. In turn, the successful expansion of the Buddhist movement, with its surge of monasteries and monuments, depended on the growing economy of the time, together with increased centralized political organization capable of extracting and channeling surplus. Regardless of the religious beliefs of their kings, states usually patronized all the important sects relatively even-handedly. This consisted of building monasteries and religious monuments, donating property such as the income of villages for the support of monks, and protecting previously donated property by leaving them exempt from taxation. Donations were most often made by private persons such as wealthy merchants and female relatives of the royal family, but this was correlated periods in which the state also gave its support and protection. In the case of Buddhism, this support was particularly important because of its high level of institutional organization and the dependence of monks on donations from the laity. State patronage of Buddhism took the form of massive propertied foundations. Buddhism flourished in the strongest states, and was welcomed by rulers in India and later throughout Asia who were centralizing power in areas previously organized on the basis of clans. Although the Buddhist monks deliberately kept themselves uninvolved in affairs of state, they were useful for rulers as they promoted peaceful societies with their moral preaching and provided institutions for literate education. During the Maurya Empire, in which period Ashoka banned Vedic sacrifices as contrary to Buddhist benevolence, Buddhism began its spread outside of its Magadha homeland. The successor Shungas reinstated the sacrifices and persecuted Buddhism, but without much success.The overall trend of Buddhism's spread across India and state support by various regional regimes continued. The consolidation of monastic organization made Buddhism the center of religious and intellectual life in India. The Gupta Empire period was a time of great development of Hindu culture, but even then in the Ganges Plain half of the population supported Buddhism, and the five precepts were widely observed. The Hindu rulers and wealthy laity gave lavish material support to Buddhist monasteries. After the Guptas, the Shaivite kings of Gujarat also patronized Buddhist monasteries, building a great Center of Buddhist at learning Valabhi. The Buddhist emperor Harsha and the later Buddhist Pala dynasty were great patrons of Buddhism, but Buddhism has already begun to loss its political and social base.

The gradual expansion in the scope and authority of caste regulations shifted political and economic power to the local arena, reversing the trend of centralization. The caste system gradually expanded into secular life as a regulative code of social and economic transactions. In ancient times, the four varnas were primarily a categorization scheme; the Vedas contained no prohibitions regarding intermarriage. There were, however, large numbers of jatis, probably originally tribal lineage groups. Brahman legists organized these groups into castes. The law books of Manu and Yajnavalkya, which were attributed to legendary figures, reached their canonical forms around 200 CE. These lay out caste duties, prohibitons, and penalties for violating their regulations.

Brahmans developed a new relationship with state. It became the duty of political officials to enforce the caste regulations written by Brahmans. Caste regulations grew over a long period of time. As they did, states gradually lost control of landed revenue. A key transition was the downfall of the

Guptas. Indian social structure developed in a manner opposite to that of China or Rome, where administration of law was dominated by government officials. Instead, Brahmans became hereditary monopolists of the law in a series of weak, ephemeral states. Brahmans came to regulate more and more aspects of public life, and collected fees for the performance of their rituals. Eventually, caste laws controlled everything from guilds and interest rates to criminal penalties. Caste law, administered by Brahmans, was built up to control all local economic production and much of its distribution. The transformation of Brahman priests to linchpins of the caste system transformed the functioning property system. The political ascendancy of Hinduism and its displacement of Buddhism's political and social base came by this indirect route. The Sungas: Following the Mauryans, Pusymitra Sunga is linked in legend with the persecution of Buddhists and a resurgence of Hinduism that forced Buddhism outwards to Kashmir, Gandhara and Bactria. There is some doubt as to whether he did or did not persecute Buddhists actively.

A Buddhist tradition holds him as having taken steps to check the spread of Buddhism as "the number one enemy of the sons of the Sakyas and a most cruel persecutor of the religion." The Divyavadana ascribes to him the razing of stupas and viharas built by Ashoka, the placing of a bounty of 100 dinaras upon the heads of Buddhist monks (bhiksus) and describes him as one who wanted to undo the work of Ashoka. This account has however been described as "exaggerated". Historian Romila Thapar writes that the Asokavadana legend is, in all probability, a "Buddhist version of Pusyamitra's attack of the Mauryas", and reflects the fact that, with the declining influence of Buddhism in the Imperial court, Buddhist monuments and institutions would receive less attention.

The accuracy of the Buddhist texts that record Pusyamitra's persecution of Buddhists has been debated by historians. The first accounts appear two centuries after Pushyamitra's reign in Asokâvadâna and the Divayâvadâna. Sir John Marshall states that it is possible that the original brick stupa built by Ashoka was destroyed by Pusyamitra and then restored by his successor Agnimitra. Archaeological evidence is scarce and uncertain. Following Ashoka's sponsorship of Buddhism, it is possible that Buddhist institutions fell on harder times under the Sungas but no evidence of active persecution has been noted.

The Sungas were patrons of Hinduism and their lack of royal patronage was also a setback to Buddhism, resulting in the splintering of Buddhism into many forces. Some of them were : The Saravastivadins, Mahasargikas, Sthaviravadha, and Yogacara. This resulted in a diversity of opinions and interpretations that led to a conflict between warring schools shortly after the fall of the Mauryans.

Traditional Hinduism is said by some writers to have competed in political and spiritual realm with Buddhism in the Gangetic plains while Buddhism flourished in the realms of the Bactrian kings.

Contribution to Buddhism: However to many scholars, Sunga king were seen as more amenable to Buddhism and as having contributed to the building of the stupa at Bharhut.

An inscription at Bodh Gaya at the Mahabodhi Temple records the construction of the temple as follows : "The gift of Nagadevi the wife of King Brahmamitra." So then this further means that the Sungas were in support of Buddhism. Another inscription reads: "The gift of Kurangi, the mother of living sons and the wife of King Indragnimitra, son of Kosiki. The gift also of Srima of the royal palace shrine."

Guptas : Buddhism saw a brief revival under the Guptas. By the 4th to 5th century Buddhism was already in decline in northern India, even as it was achieving multiple successes in Central Asia and along the Silk Road as far as China. It continued to prosper in Gandhara under the Shahi kingdom.

White Huns: Central Asian and North Western Indian Buddhism weakened in the 6th century following the White Hun invasion, who followed their own religions such as Tengri, Nestorian Christianity, and Manichean. Their Saivite King, Mihirakula (who ruled from 515 CE), suppressed Buddhism as well. He did this by destroying monasteries as far away as modern-day Allahabad, before his son reversed the policy.

Harsha: In the north and west collapse of Harshavardana's kingdom gave rise to many smaller kingdoms. This led to the rise of the martial Rajputs clans across the Gangetic plains. It also marked the end of Buddhist ruling chans, along with a sharp decline in royal patronage. This carried on until a revival under the Pala Empire in the Bengal region.

Buddhism in Southern India: In the south of India while there was no over persecution of Buddhists at least two Pallava rulers Simhavarma and Trilochana are known to have destroyed Buddhist stupas and have had Hindu temples built over them. However, Bodhidharma, a patriarch of Zen Buddhism was a Brahmin prince from the Pallava dynasty.

Nagarjuna, the founder of Mahayana Buddhism, was a Brahmin from southern India, the Satavahanas were worshipers of Buddha as well as other Hindu gods such as Krishna, Shiva, Gauri, Indra, the sun and moon. Under their reign at Amaravati, the historian Durga Prasad notices that Buddha had been worshiped as a form of Vishnu. Furthermore, a vigorous Hindu revival of Vaishnavite Hinduism in the region led to a sharp decline of Buddhism.

Muhammad bin Qusim: In AD 711, Muhammad bin Qasim conquered the Sindh bringing Indian societies into contact with Islam. Nicholas Gier believes that he succeeded partly because Dahir was an unpopular Hindu king that ruled over a Buddhist majority. Gier also believes that Chach of Alor and his kin were regarded as usurpers of the earlier Buddhist Rai Dynasty. However, Chacha's brother was a Buddhist ascetic and he succeeded the kingdom from 671-679. It is believed by some scholars that Chacha himself may have been a Buddhist. Further, after Dahir took control, he allowed for a Buddhist monk to run the city of Virun in his kingdom. However, in the war with Qasim, the monk surrendered to Qasim. The forces of Muhammad bin Qasim defeated Raja Dahir in alliance with the Jats and other Buddhist governors. His campaign's success is ascribed to the support of Buddhist and the people of lower castes like Jats, Meds and Bhutto tribes.

The Chach Nama records a couple of instances of conversion of stupas to mosques such as at Nerun as well as the incorporation of the religious elite into the ruling administration such as the allocation of 3 per cent of the government revenue was allocated to the Brahmins. As a whole, the non-Muslim populations of conquered territories were treated as People of the Book and granted Hindu and Buddhist religions the freedom to practice their faith in return for payment of the poll tax (Jizya). They were then excused from military service or payment of the tax paid by Muslim subjects—Zakat. The jizya enforced was a graded tax, being heaviest on the elite and lightest on the poor.

One revealed inscription reads, 'The nephew of Dahir, his warriors, and the principal officers have been dispatched, and the infidels converted to Islam or destroyed. Instead of Idol temples, mosques and other places of worship have been built, pulpits have been erected, the Khutba is read, the call to prayers is raised, so that devotions are performed at the stated hours.'

While proselytization occurred, the social dynamics of Sind were no different from other Muslim regions such as Egypt, where conversion to Islam was slow and took centuries, and generally came from among the ranks of Buddhists.

Mahmud of Ghanzi

By the 10th century Mahmud of Ghazni defeated the Hindu-Shahis, effectively removing Hindu influence and ending Buddhist self-governance across Central Asia, as well as the Punjab region. He demolished both stupas and temples during his numerous campaigns across North-Western India, but left those within his domains and Afghanistan alone, even as al-Biruni recorded Buddha as the prophet "Burxan".

Mahmud of Ghazni is said to have been iconoclast. Hindu and Buddhist statues, shrines and temples were looted and destroyed, and many Buddhists had to take refuge in Tibet.

Palas: In the East under the Palas in Bengal, Mahayana Buddhism flourished and spread to Bhutan and Sikkim. The Palas created many temples and a distinctive school of Buddhist art. Mahayana Buddhism flourished under the Palas between the 8th and the 12th century, before it collapsed at the hands of the attacking Sena dynasty.

However, some scholars believe that they were also Shaivaite judging by the image of Shiva and His ox on their coins and the etymology of their names. Art of Shiva also exists in temples such as the Melakadambur in Bengal where Nataraja and his bull are found.

They had also dedicated to Vishnu. Figures of Vishnu were substantial in number in the Pala Era.

Other than figures of Buddha, Vishnu and Shiva were also of Sarasvati.

Muhammad of Ghor

Muhammad attacked the North-Western regions of the Indian subcontinent many times. Gujarat later fell to Muhammad of Ghor's armies in 1197. Mahammad of Ghor's armies destroyed many Buddhist structures, including the great Buddhist university of Nalanda.

In 1200 Muhammad Khilji, one of Qutb-ud-Din's generals destroyed monasteries fortified by the Sena armies, such as the one at Vikramshila. Many monuments of ancient Indian civilization were destroyed by the invading armies, including Buddhist sanctuaries near Benares. Buddhist monks who escaped the massacre fled to Nepal, Tibet and south India.

The Mongols: In 1215, Genghis Khan conquered Afghanistan and devastated the Muslim world. In 1227, after his death, his conquest was divided. Chagatai then established the Chagatai Khanate, where his son Arghun made Buddhism the state religion. At the same time, he came down harshly on Islam and demolished mosques to build many stupas. He was succeeded by his brother, and then his son Ghazan who converted to Islam and in 1295 changed the state religion. After his reign, and the splitting of the Chagatai Khanate, little mention of Buddhism or the stupas built by the Mongols can be found in Afghanistan and Central Asia.

Timur (Tamarlane): Timur was 14th century warlord of Turco-Mongol descent, conqueror of much of western and central Asia, and founder of the Timurid Empire. Timur destroyed Buddhist establishments and raided areas in which Buddhism had flourished.

Mughals: Mughal rule contributed to the decline of Buddhism. They are reported to have destroyed many Hindu temples and Buddhist shrines alike or converted many sacred Hindu places into Muslim shrines and mosques. Mughal rulers like Aurangzeb not only destroyed Buddhist temples and monasteries but also destroyed Hindu temples and replaced them with Islamic mosques.

Ideological and financial causes: The period between the 400 BCE and 1000 CE saw gains by Hinduism at the expense of Buddhism. Some Hindu rulers resorted to military means in an effort to suppress Buddhism. However, it is seen that the evolution of Hindu ideology influenced by Buddhism was more important factor for the growth of Hinduism.

Hinduism became a more "intelligible and satisfying road to faith for many ordinary worshippers" than it had been because it now included not only an appeal to a personal god, but also seen the development of an emotional facet with the composition of devotional hymns.

Xuanzang's Report: Much of what we know about the state of Buddhism the second half of the first millennium CE comes from the 7th century Chinese pilgrim Xuanzang, who traveled widely and documented his journey. Although he found many regions where Buddhism was still flourishing, he also found many where it had sharply and startlingly declined, giving way to Jainism and a Brahmanical order. Xuanzang compliments the patronage of Harshavardana. He reported that Buddhism was popular in Kanyakubja (modern day Uttar Pradesh), where he noted "an equal number of Buddhists and heretics" and the presence of 100 monasteries and 10,000 bhikshus along with 200 "Deva" (Hindu) temples. He found a similarly flourishing population in Udra (modern Orissa). He found a mixed population in Kosala, homeland of Nagarjuna, and in Andhra, and Dravida which today roughly correspond to the modern day Indian states of Andhra Pradesh and Tamil Nadu. In a region he calls Konkanapura, which may be Kolhapur in southern Maharashtra, he found great numbers of Buddhists coexisting with a similar number of non-Buddhists, and a similar situation in northern Maharashtra. In Sindh he finds a large Theravada population. He reports a fair number of Buddhists in what is now Pakistan.

In Dhanyakataka (today's Vijayawada), he found a striking decline, with Jainism and Shaivism ascendant. In Bihar, site of a number of important landmarks, he also found a striking decline and relatively few followers, with Hinduism and Jainism predominating. He also found relatively few Buddhists in Bengal, Kamarupa (modern Assam). He reported no Buddhist presence in Konyodha, few in Chulya (in the Tamil region), and few in Gujarat and Rajasthan, except in Valabhi, where he found a large Theravada population.

During the reign of the Chalukya dynasty, Xuanzang reported that numerous Buddhist stupas in regions previously ruled by Buddhist-sympathetic Andhras and Pallavas were "ruined" and "deserted". These regions came under the control of the Vaishnavite Eastern Chalukyas, who were not favourable to Buddhism and did not support the religion. Xuanzang's report also mentions that, in the 7th Century, Shashanka of the Kingdom of Gouda (Bengal), was expanding his influence in the region in the aftermath of the fall of the Gupta Empire. He is blamed by Xuanzhang and other Buddhist sources for the murder of Rajyavardhana, a Buddhist king of Thanesar, Xuanzang writes that Shashanka destroyed the Bodhi tree of enlightenment at Bodh Gaya and replaced Buddha statues with Shiva Lingams. However, it has been claimed that Xuanzhang had a Buddhist bias in favour of the Buddhist rulers such as Harshavardhana and that his account may therefore be slanted.

Philosophical convergence: Literary evidences point towards an absorption of Buddhist elements by Hindu culture over a period of centuries. Anti-Buddhist propaganda was also reaching its peak during the 8th century when Shankara modeled his monastic order after the Buddhist Sangha. An upsurge of Hinduism had taken place in North India by the early eleventh century as illustrated by the influential Sanskrit drama Prabodhacandrodaya in the Chandela court; a devotion to Vishnu and an allegory to the defeat of Buddhism and Jainism. The population of North India had become predominantly Shaiva, Vaishnava or Shakta. But in the 12th century a lay population of Buddhist hardly existed outside the monastic institutions and when it did penetrate the Indian peasant population it was hardly discernible as a distinct community. Buddhist monasteries were well-funded and life within was relatively easy. To avoid unwanted members, many monasteries became selective about whom they admitted, in some cases based on social class.

Islam: The Turkish invaders described Indian Pagans as but-parast (idol worshippers), and idol-breakers as but-shikan. The word "but" is derived from Buddhism, but the Turks used if for "Indian paganism" in general. When the Arabs arrived in Sind there were only glimpses of Buddhism nor any evidence of a provincial government in control of the Buddhists. During the seventh to thirteenth centuries when Islam arrived it replaced Buddhism as the great cosmopolitan trading religion in many places accompanied by a consolidation of the communal peasant religions of Hinduism. The Tibetan scholar of the seventeenth century Taranatha writes that during the time of the Sena king Stag-gzigs (Turks) has begun to appear on horses and that monasteries had been fortified with troops stationed in them; however, they were overrun and monks at Uddandapura were massacred, the monastery razed and replaced by a new fort and further north-east Vikramshila was destroyed as well. Hardly a contemporary evidence however exists on the destruction of Buddhist monasteries. Brief Muslim account and the one eye witness account of Dharmasmavim in wake of the conquest during the 1230s talks about abandoned viharas being used as camps by the Turukshahs. Later historical traditions such as Taranathas are mixed with legendary materials and summarized as "the Turukshah conquered the whole of Magadha and destroyed many monasteries and did much damage at Nalanda, such that many monks fled abroad" thereby bringing about a sudden demise of Buddhism with their destruction of the Viharas. Buddhism lingered longer in Iran than South Asia and was officially professed under fifty years of Mongol conquest. With the conversion of Ghazan to Islam in 1295, the backlash resulted in the destruction of many Buddhist places of worship and the further migration of monks into Kashmir.

Many places were destroyed and renamed. For example, Udantpur's monasteries were destroyed in 1197 by Mohammed-bin-Bakhtiyar and the town was renamed. Taranatha in his history of Buddhism in India (dpal dus kyi 'khor lo'i chos bskor gyi byung khungs nyer mkho) of 1608 C.E. gives an account of the last few centuries of Buddhism, mainly in Eastern India. His account suggests a considerable decline but not an extinction of Buddhism in India in his time.

Sufi and Bhakti movement : When Islam arrived in India, it sought conversion from, not assimilation to or integration with, the already present religions. Under Sufi influence, the pressures of caste, and with no political support structure left in place to resist social mores, many converted to Islam in the Bengal region.

After the Mongol invasion of Islamic lands across Central Asia, many Sufis also found themselves fleeing towards India and around the environs of Bengal. In Bengal, their influence, caste attitudes towards Buddhists, previous familiarity with converting Buddhist, a lack of Buddhist political power, Hinduism's resurgence through movements such as the Advaita and the bhakti movement, all contributed to a significant realignment of beliefs that relegated Buddhism in India to the peripheries.

Survival of Buddhism in India: At the beginning of the modern era, Buddhism was very nearly extinct in mainstream Indian society. Some tribal people living in the territory of modern India did continue to practice Buddhism.

In Bengal, the Bauls still practice a syncretic form of Hinduism that was strongly influenced by Buddhism. There is also evidence of small communities of Indian Theravada Buddhists existing continuously in Bengal in the area of Chittagong hill tracts among the indigenous Chakma people up to the present. Though they are under increasing pressure from mostly Muslim Bengali settlers. There was genocide of the

Chakma and Buddhists by Islamists in East Pakistan. The Chakma spiritual practices are a blend of Buddhism/ Vaishnavism.

Buddhist institution flourished in eastern India right until the Islamic invasion.

Buddhism still survives among the Barua (through practicing Vaishnava/Hindu elements), a community of Bengali/ Magadh descent that migrated to Chittagong region. Indian Buddhism also survives among Newars of Nepal.

Buddhism survived in Gilgit and Baltistan until 13-14th Century, perhaps slightly longer in the nearby Swat Valley. In Ladakh region, adjacent to Kashmir valley, Tibetan Buddhism survives to this day. The historic prevalence and history of Tibetan Buddhism in the above mentioned Northern regions of Jammu and Kashmir is reported in the Rajatarangini of Kalhana written sometime during 1147-1149 CE. In Tamilnadu and Kerala, Buddhism survived until 15-16th century. At Nagapattinam, in Tamil Nadu, Buddhist idols were cast and inscribed until this time and the ruins of the Chudamani Vihara stood until they were destroyed by the Jesuits in 1867. In the South in some pockets, it may have survived even longer.

Revival: On pilgrimage to Bodh Gaya in 1891, the Sri Lankan Buddhist leader Angarik Dharmapala was shocked to find the temple in the hands of a Shaivite priest, the Buddha image transformed into a Hindu icon and Buddhists barred from worship. The Buddhist revival then began in India, when he founded the Maha Bodhi Society. The organization's initial efforts were for the purpose of resuscitation of Buddhism in India and of restoring the ancient Buddhist shrines at Bodh Gaya Sarnath and Kushinara. The Buddhist renaissance inaugurated by Anagarika Dharmapala through his Mahabodhi Movement is also described as "conservative" for it held the Muslim Rule in India responsible for the decay of Buddhism in India in the then current mood of Hindu-Buddhist brotherhood. The organization's initial efforts were to restore various Buddhist shrines that had been neglected under Hindu administration, and to open to the public various Buddhist sites and temples that had been destroyed in various periods of Muslim invasion.

Later in the 1950s Bhimrao Ramji Ambedkar pioneered the Dalit Buddhist movement in India. Dr. Ambedkar saw conversion to Islam and to Christianity as a factor contributing to the "denationalisation" of India. The revival movement of Buddhism in India underwent a major change when after publishing a series of books and articles arguing that Buddhism was the only way for the untouchables to gain equality, Ambedkar publicly converted on October 14, 1956 in Nagpur and then in turn led a mass-conversion ceremony for over 380,000 dalits. Many other such mass-conversion ceremonies organized since and has become a politically charged issue. Since Ambedkar's conversion, numerous similar many more people from different castes have converted to Buddhism. Many Dalits employ the term "Ambedkar (ite) Buddhism" to designate the Buddhist movement, which started with Ambedkar's conversion.

In 1959 Tenzin Gyatso, the 14th Dalai Lama transitioned from Tibet to India and set up the government of Tibet in Exile in Dharamsala, India, which is often referred to as "little Lhasa." Tibetan exiles numbering several thousand have since settled in the town. Most of these exiles live in Upper Dharamsala, or McLeod Ganj, where they established monasteries, temples and schools. The town is sometimes known as "Little Lhasa", after the Tibetan capital city, and has become one of the centers of Buddhism in the world.

2

Globalisation and Dalits

C. D. Naik*

How globalization helped socio-cultural movements of the poor? Privatisation and marketisation process acted against emancipation project and tended to engulf entire dalit population in its anti-social impact. They promoted vilest and venomous onslaughts on dalits, minorities, reservations, subsidy, and positive discrimination with derision and vehemence. Reforms have obliterated dalit consciousness formed over centuries long struggle and fortified reactionary regimes against entire oppressed people thirsting for radical change. Privatisations aggravated present civil society's swallowing of reservations as unrightfully share of dalits and minimalist role for the state both combined with bureaucracy, and judiciary created impediments in implementation of this policy. Dalit candidate qualifying without any concession not to be placed in the reserved seat implied that the percentage representation of dalits in services or educational institutions would be more than its prescribed value, and that dalits are intrinsically an inferior specie. Privatisation hit reservation policy, the sole contributor to advancement of the dalits.

Adam Smith (1776) with Wealth of Nations was held as the father of capitalism, who advocated free trade and regulated State's role in economy of the nation. John Maynard Keynes (1930) put forth his critique of wealth of Nations in terms of full employment and capitalism. Joint efforts of the Government and financial institutions worked successfully till 1960. USA emerged as one and only such state which harnessed the State-cum-bank ideology and became global leader of capitalist order. It went along this course to the extent of dictating the erring states like Italy in 1948 and assumed the role of political leader and financial banker too during the post-war period. Then came Nixon who waged war against debts and released capital flow.

Thus, the real economy of joint efforts of state and bank coordination produced 90 percent result to productivity but speculation crept in and this joint venture declined in giving productivity. Consequently public interest benefits reduced to 10 percent in 1971-1990 and 5 percent in 1995.

The philosophy of globalization rested on neo-liberalism, rule of market, withdrawal of state, cut in public expenditure, in social services, no public good and the principle that private sector overcomes inefficiency of public sector by free market dynamics.

As the corporate sector, private economy or profit maximization replaced its dependence on other factors of production, perpetual environmental degradation, inequality and poverty ensued. International monetary fund and world bank provided stabilization programmes amidst such crises in the world. They were adopted as panic-drive and not as strategy with a vision of long-term development in India also.

Globalisation in India

As crisis-package against fall in foreign exchange reserve, rise in inflation, public and current account deficits and mounting foreign and domestic debts India, like every other world nation, accepted globalization in July 1991.

It was compelled to do so by political crisis such as rise and fall of two governments in four months from November 1990 to March 1991, deferment of representation of union budget, assassination of former Prime Minister Rajiv Gandhi, shift from majority rule, and loss of confidence among leaders in India and abroad.

Position of Dalits

Out of 13.8 million Dalits 1.1 million (08%) made use of reservation in 1991. More than 75 per cent dalit workers are connected with land, 25% being marginal and small farmers and 50 % landless labourers. In urban areas they work mainly in unorganized sector. They belong to two categories of poverty viz., (1) ultra poor and, (2) poverty line poor. As such they suffer from poverty including deprivation of food, income and employment and, being socially disadvantaged group Dalits suffer from backwardness in education, discrimination in employment, atrocities and suppression in social, cultural and religious matter.

IMF and World Bank

These two world financial institutions offered two programmes on macro-economic stabilization and socio-economic structural changes. The former included seven items as follows:

1. Devaluation of currencies for making exchange rate more realistic
2. Imports without restrictions
3. Fiscal Deficits and balance of payments to be reduced or eliminated
4. Decontrolled exchange rate and interest rate
5. All subsidies to be reduced or eliminated
6. Free entry of foreign financial institutions and introduction of financial structure reforms, and
7. Complete outonomy of central bank to pursue independent economic policy.

Structural References

Its structural reforms incorporated (1) decontrol of industries, (2) privatization of government–owned entities, (3) export-led growth structure, (4) free entry of foreign capital and technology without any let, hindrance or conditons, (5) free entry and exit of foreign firm including financial and service industries, (6) free cross border movement of capital and other funds, (7) protection of intellectual property rights by legislative safeguards and (8) creation of legal climate for enforcement of legal contracts, private property rights, and (9) free entry and exit of business and firms both industrial and financial.

Economic Crisis World Over—Status

Fall in living standard, widespread riots and socio-political unrest are the stories of other countries during reform periods. GDP growth rate fell due to reforms. Trickle can never be equal to outpour. Latin America's growth rate exceeded that of industrial countries including USA before but it suffered later during reform period. Argentina, Brazil, Chile, Mexico and Peru had per capita income level ten decade ahead in 1970 but its average real growth rates of per capita income level had gone ten decades back from 1980 to 1985. GDP growth rates fell in Columbia and were erratic in Ghana, Indonesia, Ivory Coast and other subject countries despite IMF and World Bank assertions to the contrary. Unemployment went up in Venezuela. Industrial wages declined in African and Latin American countries, Tanzania, Zambia, Bolivia, Costa Rica, Egypt and Kenya. Gross Domestic investment declined in Philippines, and social expenditure declined in West Asia. Investment in social infrastructure suffered in Sri Lanka, Turkey, Guyana and Sudan, Somalia and Tanzania, Morocco, and Ecuador by cut in spending on health, education and food subsidy.

According to UNICEF report there are 53.6% poor families (1992) in Bulgaria, 21.3% poverty in Hungary (1991), 18.2% poverty (1992) in Czech Republic, 41.4% in Poland, 51.1% in Rumania, 43.8% in Russia and 30.2% in Slovakia excluding more percentage of child poverty in those countries. Mongolia had 25% population living below 10 dollars a month poverty line. Mortality rate also increased in these countries due to decline in living standard. In east European countries unemployment also soared to 6.5 million in 1992. Inflation too hit them. Exemplary country for free market advocates–Poland had industrial cities with 16% unemployed and more in rural areas, 14% of people lived on doles and one third of total families lived below official poverty line.

Inequality in the world has been consistently growing. Low income countries' per capita income fell from 584 to 380 dollars and their share in total income fell from 5.44 % to 4.83 % but per capita income for rich countries went up from 17,080 to 23,090 dollars between 1988 and 1993. Gap between poor and rich increased by 30 % over the last decade. Reforms enriched billionaires in USA from 49 to 120, in Asia Pacific region from 40 to 86, in Europe from 36 to 91 and in West Asia and Africa from 8 to 14, according to the Forbes magazine of July 18, 1994.

As on today (10th October 2008) the front page news of the English Daily is "World on brink of recession", "Iceland (North Atlantic Island nation) called Nordic Tiger may go bankrupt", first national casualty of financial meltdown revealed from Washington and Reykjavik respectively that "The US financial crisis has gone global, putting the world on the brink of recession that can only be resolved through international cooperation, International Monetary Fund management director Dominique Strauss-Kahn said on Thursday." And "The Government of Iceland on Thursday seized control of the country's largest bank—the third Bank takeover this week—and suspended trading on the stock market, as the North Atlantic Island nation grapples with an unprecedented financial meltdown that has made it the first national casualty of the global economic crisis."[1]

Effects of Globalisation Philosophy on India

Impact on Food Security : Budgetary outlay on agriculture and irrigation, subsidy on fertilizer, devaluation of rupee by 25 per cent, diversion of land to export production of non-food primary products, corporate farming for export horticulture and floriculture, and exportable surplus of food grains and dairy products in the developed countries that craved for market, and international market for agriproducts being a monopoly of three to six giant companies, whose control over market extended to 80 to 90 per cent, and increasing level of export of foodgrains for foreign exchange earning, non-cost effective export thrust as showed, in Africa have impaired food security of people. Reforms in banking led to squeeze on agriculture lending under this philosophy.

Reduction in Food Subsidy : As a measure of ensuring food security to the large masses of Indian population, public distribution system was instituted in India in the wake of the calamity of the Great Bengal famine 1942-43 and the World War II, with 4,24,000 fair price shops, but despite the fact that Government subsidized food distributed through PDS and stored in FCI, reduction in subsidy and increase in FCI cost threatened food security for the poor.

Promising income from wheat crop resulted its substitution by coarse cereals, which too dwindled in output, and endangered food security of poor people.

Globalisation philosophy threatened food security by reducing food and raising early procurement and issue prices of rice and wheat and by passing it on to consumers. Off-take of wheat and rice came down. Export attraction of wheat led to shortage from situation of surplus met by expensive imports.

Difference between consumer-end PDS retail prices and market prices became marginal and unaffordable prices made the poor to cut their consumption that led them to starvation death under this philosophy.

Impact on Dalits : Fall of per capita net availability of cereals and pulses impacted Dalits more severely than shown by average. Malnutrition of women was more than it was for men due to male preference attitude of Indians. As many as 350 children died of malnutrition in Amravati District of Maharashtra–the most industrial and relatively progressive state in India under this philosophy.

This philosophy induced by world bank advice to further reduce food subsidy and wanting to target only BPL poor under PDS cover since not-so-poor left it for market price purchase being equal to retail PDS price it provided only 16.6 million tones or 36% of requirement against 46.5 million tones of requirement of foodgrains for even BPL poor of 1991 level. This new scheme based on the executive's reluctance to acknowledge poverty further pushed many people to starve and die.

Inflation

Reduction in budget and fiscal deficit, devaluation, privatization, elimination or reduction in subsidies and export promotion unleashed by this philosophy contributed directly to inflation which hit poor people the hardest. It also resulted in curtailment of capital expenditure and decline in capital formation. Fall in public components can lead to fall in output and with inelastic wages caused inflation. It contained budgetary deficit and furthered privatization. Increase in prices gave fillip to inflationary spiral in the economy.

Devaluation of currency contributed to inflation by raising cost of import of petroleum crude and its products as raw materials that entered into domestic production or consumption. Most of these imported products being of common use contributed to the rise of general price level also. Devaluation made imported products for home users dearer. It had multiplier effects. Price rise was effected by this philosophy through devaluation of rupee, export—led growth, import, reduction of custom and excise duties, increase in money supply and huge flow of foreign exchange elevating general price level. Cuts in food and fertilizer subsidies and free market disposition also contributed to the general price rise.

Employment

Globalisation philosophy raised jobs in private sector but not in public sector, organized or unorganized sector, non-agricultural rural or urban informal sector, central government establishment and in employment exchange as a result of contraction in public expenditure. Small scale industries also suffered under banks charging high interest rate, collapse of demand for their products and liberalization of imports of capital goods. Big industries overpowered the sick industries and cut employments.

Unemployment in agriculture and non-agriculture rural sector rose to 25 million including 10 million of those from unorganized urban and non-agricultural rural areas due to reduction of bank credit to them. Foreign investment companies earned 5,472 billion dollars sales equivalent to 27 times India's GDP producing only 25 million jobs not equivalent to even third of its sale amount in 1992. Corporate farm and contract system descended in agriculture and turned marginal and middle farmers jobless. The cropping pattern of capitalist farms tended to make unskilled agricultural workers redundant.

As exemplified by 110 weavers of Andhra Pradesh starvation deaths were caused due to unemployment catalysed by export thrust and unmindful of demand of the domestic requirements.

As is evident from Pepsi which brought in its technology to convert potatoes in chips and sell them at a price 80 times over, import of modern technology and investment with its financial and organizational superiority and imperative global competitiveness rendered millions to joblessness, deindustrialization or restructuring and downsizing of domestic companies.

Restructuring of companies under competitive pressure involved engaging foreign consultancy firms for millions of dollars threatening native consulting firms into seeking alliance with foreign firms for sheer survival. As a result of reorganizing state units under competitive pressure nationalized banks declared 4 lakh persons surplus, Railways stopped recruitments, and Department of Post and Telecommunication was to retrench 2 lakh workers. Even as the value of fixed assets of sample companies rose by 27% regular employment fell by 3.3 per cent. Share of contract and non-regular employment in total employment rose to one third in 1993.

Strategies of labour flexibilisation, individual contract, subcontracting and outsourcing, and multi-skill workers in management, informal sector, businesses and HRD led to death of trade unionism, casual labour, and hiring and firing practices, and labour exploitation.

Impact on Poverty

Poverty is owing to 50% rural farming households having less than one acre land and needing supplementary work in non-agriculture sector or sundry works related to farm. Caused by Government cut in poverty alleviation programmes despite its human face reforms in 1994-95 and 1995-96, budget increase for alarming situation and political election gain providing less than 20 days work per person a year at Rs. 21.

Cut in expenditure on disease prevention and control programmes after 1990-91 by centre withdrawing assistance to states under social sector programmes poverty prone diseases like T.B., Malaria, Fileria, leprosy and epidemics like Plague, Jaundice, Influenza, Pneumonia and Dengue emerged and reemerged during reform period further aggravated the situation.

Impact on Society

Conscious creation of world order, governing it and transforming it into moral order was defied by market reform and globalization. The social disadvantage suffered by the dalits was taken note of in the constitution of India through safeguards of social elevation, educational progress, cultural preservation and religious freedom, economic upliftment and political participation and right of livelihood or employment. Positive discrimination embodied in these safeguards are not compatible with Reform spirit, which goes against one vote one value system since market grants moneyed person more value. Dalits will aspire for change against odds of upper caste-class-reform's attitudinal resistance.

Impact on Educational Institutions

How globalization affected reservation and financial assistance in educational institutions? Globalisation freezed grants to many institutions on basis of which they admitted dalit students whose parents income is below specified level, being eligible for freeship, and scholarship and it stagnated expenditure on education. Commercialisation of education offered specialized education from capitalist social utility point of view, ignored dalit, individual justice and manipulated its product-prices with hefty dollar equivalent in alliance with many foreign universities. IIMs and IITs raised fee and other prices many fold and went beyond the reach of dalits, how much more so when they were self-financed. It polarized elites and commoners on educational job market level and development portals.

Impact on Reservation

How global liberalized privatization affected reservation? In organized private sector there is no dalit employee except for scrubbing floors and cleaning latrines in contrast to representation of dalits in proportion to their population in all the public services including government, public sector, autonomous bodies and institutions receiving grant-in-aid from government. Privatization shook the foundation of reservation, nay the economic means of livelihood, social prestige for at least 1.5 million landless labourers' sons and daughters, bureaucratic authority for at least 50,000 dalits, hope, and bond with nation and constitution.

How can there be reservation policy implementation when there is no state agency to act on it as the reform envisaged minimalist state, public sector privatized, denationalized, disinvested and endangered by reform package. Public sector undertakings and Joint Venture Companies together share 49:51 equity stake and the former turning out to be financial holding companies nullify reservation policy. Same is true about other public services released for private investment in the pretext of super imposition of utility view.

Impact on Education

Globalization divided vernacular and English schools on primary educational level. Corporatisation transformed education into an profit enterprise benchmarking its input, and product of city and town in job market against vernacular medium village student, not to speak of dalit student, who is the last even among rural backward socio-economic-cultural scenario fraught with alarming rate of school dropouts due to his supplementing his meager family income and disillusioned at education being an instrument of revolution and growing more aggressive as reforms progress.

Impact on Atrocities on Dalits and Weaker Sections

How atrocities are augmented under reform regime? There were no atrocities of the kind Dalits experienced during this saner globalization period. They are in the form of physical punishment as dalit minds are enlightened enough to thwart dominant's subjugation. They are perpetrated by rough middle castes succeeding the traditional refined upper caste for their assertion of human rights and competition on equal platforms with themselves and winning them away in some cases with the help of reservations. Thus atrocities are dependent on the factors of dependence on middle castes powered further by reform boost to caste system of inequality reinforced by reduction in jobs, deteriorating health care, expensive education and biased income distribution and so on. Has the new reform given dalits land in rural setting? It, on the contrary, acted on depeasantisation of Indian agriculture and consolidation of their holdings for their corporate farming. It has thus made collective farming ideology of Dr. Ambedkar's conception neutralized. Its ally will be the rich farmers of the village as part of the management of corporate structure making marginal, small farmers and vulnerable dalits more dependent.

Impact of Caste and Culture

Will caste go with reform? Far from striving for economic equality the reforms tend to accentuate existing inequalities. Neither caste nor feudalism can be neurtralised completely by capitalism as contradictory forces. So caste would co-exist with Reforms. Privatization and free market as components of globalization established inequality, reducation of food, Job and addition of atrocities.

Vision: Which has something to do with future. It is a hope for better and excelling life led in the past and being treaded upon now also. It is but a creative energy input in the innovation of some tool never discovered before and efficiently working fifty or hundred years ahead of its time.

From Agriculture Shift: According to the current knowledge every person of estimated 15 billion people in 50 years hence needs an average of 0.9 hectares of arable land for his needs, taking into account the conventional agricultural method. The earth altogether has a land surface of 3.2 billion hectares. The said document described that if the agriculture is to become an agrarian (food) factories, in which a farmer will act as a food-chemist in order to feed 15 billion people with good quality food in sufficient quantities the earth will need six times as much food as is produced today. Conventional agriculture cannot achieve this on its own, it will not be possible to eliminate hunger from this world. The moving from outdoor fields to the light flooded halls of modern agrarian factories has already started. Food can be produced everywhere on this earth without farmland, and it can be harvested the whole year round. At the beginning of the next century 50% of the world's food supply could already be produced synthetically. Division of agriculture into industries and analysis of the needs of these industries are to be taken into account.

Recycling of Raw Materials: Soon, there will be no more raw materials, and then there will not be any more new products, and our throw-away society will become a dying society. The only way to cope with our throw-away industrial society is to turn it into a natural cycle, as it does in nature. A tree grows, dies, decomposes and thus provides the basic material for the growth of a new tree civilization. In the same way our throw-away industrial society must recycle the whole of industry.

If the scrap products of the industrialized world are recycled then the raw materials not yet exploited are sufficient for the development of the non-industrialised countries of the earth and for the growing population. In the Federal Republic of Germany alone every year we produce 400 million cubic meters of waste (approx. 800-1,000 kg for one cubic meter). There will still be "rich" and "poor" but "poor" in this world of 15 billion people will mean a life with all technical achievements and all social possibilities.

The said IFM opined on survival, advertising, capital, and technology in the form of an advice as follows:

Make use of the experiences of the past in order to master the future. In a competitive market there is no security without continuous struggle. Advertising has to be truthful. Increasing returns can be better than reducing costs. Profit is an indispensable reward for the performance of a company. Be technically flexible and innovative.

According to David Ben Gurion, "Anyone who doesn't believe in miracle is not a realist.[2]"

Our vision gives only a tiny idea of the living conditions on our earth within a conceivable period of time.

Exceptions to the Trend of Decline

The notable exception to the above is the experience of East Asian countries—People's Republic of China, Indonesia, Korea, Malaysia, Philippines, Thailand and Indochina, where population below poverty line declined from 35% to 10% over this period, where social indicators, viz., life expectancy, infant mortality, adult literacy and population growth improved impressively due to their specific historical setting, high levels of literacy, particularly female literacy, and substantially better health standards. Better female participation in the labour force led to rapid increase in household and overall domestic saving rates. Their higher level of social consumption with relatively better distribution of incomes and wealth vastly widened the demand of those economies and facilitates more broad based development. Higher literacy and health standards were the most crucial factors in enhancing labour productivity, which in turn went to facilitate significant import substitution and export promotion[3].

Globalization, Agricultural Crises and Socio-Economic Justice from Ambedkarian Paradigm

Dr. Ambedkar viewed society as an ocean of men and women and material forces and living species including animals and various living organisms interacting and sustaining life of human and inorganic worlds in such a way as to support the entire planet in balanced and healthy growing manner.

Globalization has come to mean a free flow of labour, capital, goods and services, and technology across the world through borders of every nation-state for the profit maximization of the few corporate companies and wider deprivations of the marginal peasants and landless workers with nation-state promoting privatization to the extent of 51 per cent of resources share allocated to them against 49 per cent of that for domestic purpose, in cahoots with foreign financial institutions and banks, decontrolling and deregulation for big industries and reduction in subsidies, in public spending, in budget outlays, import duties, with export-orientation, devaluation of currency and mercerization of foodgrains and values of socio-economic life.

Food supply is related to public distribution system, subsidies for FCI for transportation, storage and supply, to cash crops in place of cereals and pulses, to export of foodgrains at the cost of indigenous people's starvation to death, to importation of dear products from foreign companies, to horticulture and floriculture dominating agriculture and to loss of jobs for many and accumulation of profit for the corporate sector of three to six companies coming together for trading across the globe.

Inflation is a part of the process of globalization, which increases supply of money in larger proportion to that of products and try to maintain deficit and foreign exchange reserve, cutting credit for agricultural share in the GDP and soaring foodgrains prices, particularly retail ones nullifying difference between the procurement price and issue price against the market price and compelling the population on ultra and marginal poverty line to consume less, live shortly and die in a large number unreported, unsung and unrepented by the concerned.

Unemployment is the corollary of cumulative effect of capitalist incentive over labour welfare and state responsibility for all round development and sustainable environmental concern.

Dr. Ambedkar was a real economist, who recognized the roles of capital, labour, land, rent and entrepreneur in any firm or industry. He was not in favour of 1776's Adam Smith's Wealth of Nations' argument favouring capitalist class interests at the cost of life of the working class. He inclined to endorse the view of 1930's John Meynard Keyne's Labour intensive employment theory for maximum production with proportional investment of capital. He also recognized the twin enemies of society, viz. caste and capital. In the current globalization imperial era scenario his dream of transforming social order into moral order would remain a distant ideal if our nation too blindly imitated the American model of false economic theories and praxis and ignored the real economist vision and voice of the poor and socially disadvantaged upheld by Dr. Ambedkar.[4]

Ambedkar's Philosophy

Dr. Ambedkar said *on Small Holdings* in India that "The evil of small holdings in India is not fundamental but is derived from the parent evil of the mal-adjustment in her social economy." (p. 472, Vol. 1)

On a *love of money* criticized by Bertrand Russell without inquiring into the purpose of it, Dr. Ambedkar set the matter right by saying that "In a healthy mind, it may be urged, there is no such thing as a love of money in the abstract. Love of money is always for something and it is the purpose embodied in that "for something" that will endow it with credit or cover it with shame.[5] (Vol. 1, p. 489)

On *deficit* Dr. Ambedkar opined that "What has disquieted

me is this, that the deficit in the budget is not due to any inclusion in it of a large policy of social advancement." (p. 4, Vol. 2)

On *Government duties* Dr. Ambedkar advised that education, public health, medical relief, and water supply are by common standards now prevailing in all modern countries, other duties which Government must undertake, I find, are unemployment benefit, sickness insurance, old-age pensions, maternity benefits and premature death benefits to dependents.[6]" (p. 14, Vol. 2)

World of Righteousness

Dr. Ambedkar's philosophy of righteous world order is summarised in his magnum opus *The Buddha and His Dhamma,* which lays a foundation of moral order from the existing social order. The world of righteousness lies on earth and is to be reached by man by righteous conduct. To remove misery each one of the people must learn to be righteous in his conduct in relation to others and thereby make the earth the democracy of righteousness (p. 283). Panch Shila, Ashtang Marga and Paramitas can make man righteous. Only righteousness can remove this inequity and the resultant misery.

Two functions are necessary to practice righteousness, (1) to know what is right and what is wrong and, (2) to follow right and not to follow wrong.

Further two things of absolute necessity for this are:

(1) Training of man's instincts and dispositions. If there is no training of the mind to turn bad dispositions into good dispositions there is no use of not committing fresh misdeeds by expiration and purge of former misdeeds as explained in Jain philosophy. A good disposition is the only permanent foundation and guarantee of permanent goodness. Training of the mind is the same as the training of a man's disposition and (2) Courage to stand by what is right even if one is alone. Referring to Sallekha-sutta of the Buddha Word he narrated that "You are to expunge by resolving that, though others may be harmful, you will be harmless. Though others

may kill, you will never kill, though others may steal, you will not. Though others may not lead the higher life, you will. Though others may lie, traduce, denounce, or prattle, you will not. Though others may be covetous, you will covet not. Though others may be malignant, you will not be malignant. Though others may be given over to wrong views, wrong aims, wrong speech, wrong actions, and wrong concentration, you must follow (the Noble Eightfold Path in) right outlook, right aims, right speech, right actions, right mode of livelihood, right effort, right mindfulness and right concentration. Though others are wrong about the truth and wrong about Deliverance, you will be right about truth and right about Deliverance. Though others may be possessed by sloth and torpor, you will free yourselves therefrom. Though others may be puffed up, you will be humble-minded. Though others may be perplexed by doubts, you will be free from them. Though others may harbour wrath, malevolence, envy, jealousy, niggardliness, avarice, hypocrisy, deceit, imperviousness, arrogance, forwardness, association with bad friends, slackness, unbelief, shamelessness, unscrupulousness, lack of instruction, inertness, bewilderment, and unwisdom, you will be the reverse of all these things. Though others may clutch at and hug the temporal or loose their hold thereon, you will clutch and hug the things that are not temporal, and will ensue Renunciation".

It is the development of the will which is so efficacious for right states of consciousness, not to speak of act and speech. And therefore, Cunda there must be developed the will to all the foregoing resolves the Buddha had detailed[8]. (pp. 285-286)

Revolution in Antique Vs Modern Society

How Dr. Ambedkar distinguished modern society from ancient and tribal society on the criterion judging ideal scheme of government through revolution is shown by the following excerpts culled from his writings and speeches volume 3 thus:

At one end of the Revolution was the antique society with its Religious ideal in which the end was society. At the other end of the Revolution is the modern society with its Religious ideal in which the end is the individual. To put the same fact in terms of the norm it can be said that the norm or the criterion, for judging right and wrong in the antique society was utility (food, clothing, shelter, education, health of the citizens in the socialist countries as the responsibility of the State) while the norm or the criterion for judging right and wrong in the modern society is justice (liberalism, neo-liberalism from 1776 Adam Smith to 1930 Keynes, corporatisation, privatisation, globalisation of the present time). The Religious revolution was not thus a revolution in the religious organisation of society resulting in the shifting of the centre—from society to the individual—it was a revolution in the norms to judge what is right and wrong in the conduct of men and was appropriate to current notion of what constitutes the moral good. Justice as a criterion became appropriate to the modern world in which individual being the end, the moral good was held to be something which does justice to the individual. If it is said that these norms are not transcendental enough; Ambedkar's reply would be that if a norm whereby one is to judge the philosophy of religion must be Godly, it must also be earthly[8]. (p. 22)

Findings

1. Globalisations has pro-rich bias. Reform programmes worsened conditions of poor people in the world unless guarded by local conditions and cultures as has happened in East Asia. Dalits in India have been the worst victims of the Bretton Wood Institutions. They have been affected doubly as socially disadvantaged and economically deprived masses of people. Indian reforms are more crises driven than strategically planned. Whether in form of common minimum programme of the later government or in that of feel good factor of the former one the economic reform of India missed the reality and momentous feature of the situation.

2. In Indian agrarian economy over 70 per cent of its population live in villages. Its heinous socio-cultural

inequality defies any statistical description and depth. It has inequalities abiding in economic and socio-cultural terms. Its capability poor amounts to 554 million (61.5 %). Its rank among 174 descending poverty countries is 135. It has income poor to the extent of 229 million as per the Human Development Report 1996.

3. India has a parallel economy in black money as is shown by the recent spate of scams. Reforms have given them boost. Whatever little surfaced is a tip of an iceberg. This black money is unofficially estimated by world bank to the tune of 100 billion dollars, Finance India (September 1995 Issue) estimated that the range of such capital outflows was between $1065 million to $ 1370 million in 1993. A sum of $ 10 billion shown in the non-resident account belongs to resident Indians. Reforms can bring in just four to five billion dollars of foreign direct investment a year but political will can give it the above scam and black money to better its destiny in multiple way[9].
4. Dr. Ambedkar's aim of transforming world social order into righteous global order was adversely affected by capitalist privatized corporate market economy neglecting human labour and its contribution for new products and new order of humanity.

Suggestions

1. India should unearth the black money treasure and instead of capital she must invest political will and power to revolutionize society both economically and socially.
2. Government should understand that its nation has its own reality and there is need of growing a widespread purchasing power for free and sustainable market reforms in economy.
3. The reform strategy should embody sustainable economic empowerment of the rural masses; investment to enhance their capability and effective measures for

accelerated development of the disadvantaged people by means of radical land reform, massive rural investment in agricultural infrastructural projects, universalisation of primary education, primary health care system, reinforced positive discrimination policy, freedom from fear of basic survival, fraternity in place of fratricidal caste system, and elimination of reframed and more vigorously effected discrimination measure after dalits have come on par with general population.

4. No radical change is possible without dalit participation.

References

1. Free Press, Indore, 10th October 2008, front page.
2. Corporate named IFM from Internet Surfing on 5th October 2008.
3. Dr. Anand Teltumbde, Globalisation and the Dalits, Internet Surfing dated October 5, 2008 Dr. Ambedkar, The Buddha and His Dhamma, Mumbai, 1957, reprint 2001.
4. C.D. Naik, Social and Political Thought of Dr. B.R. Ambedkar, New Delhi, 2007.
5. The Writings and Speeches of Dr. Babasaheb Ambedkar, Vol. I, Mumbai, Education Department, Government of Maharashtra.
6. The Writings and Speeches of Dr. Babasaheb Ambedkar, Vol. II, Mumbai, Education Department, Government of Maharashtra.
7. Dr. B.R. Ambedkar, The Buddha and His Dhamma, Peoples Education Society, Mumbai, 1957.
8. The Writings and Speeches of Dr. Babasaheb Ambedkar, Vol. III, Mumbai, Education Department, Government of Maharashtra.
9. EPW Research Foundation (1994): Three Years of Economic Reform in India, EPW Research Foundation, Bombay, pp. 6-9, *ibid.*

* Dr. C.D. Naik is Professor and Head of Dr. Ambedkar Thought and Philosophy, and Dr. Ambedkar Chair in Dr. Babasaheb Ambedkar National Institute of Social Sciences, Dr. Ambedkar Nagar, A.B. Road, (Mhow), District Indore, Madhya Pradesh-453441, India.

3

Social Message of Buddhism

C.D. Naik*

Social Message of Buddhism

The last and most popular book on social Buddhism by Dr. Ambedkar is Buddha and His Dhamma. In this book he asked whether Buddhism had any social message to humanity suffering from social ills and answered it positively with references culled from the original Tripitaka texts. Sigalovada sutta, for example, gave one of such message in which the Buddha specified how ideal family and ideal society should live and maintain themselves. Talking about social religion Dr. Ambedkar gave three yardsticks to judge the sociality of any religion, including Buddhism, namely, equality, liberty and fraternity. Adopting the Mill, Bergson, Plato, Altekar and other social scientists' measures of judging religious social values Dr. Ambedkar postulated that Buddhism and Buddhist India gave these values as revolution to counter the gospel of inequality, slavery and hatred propagated in the name of religion in the world in general and India in particular.

Buddhism also believed that parents not only transmit body to their offspring but character also unlike the thinking of the soul believers. According to Ambedkar 'social Buddhism gave three things in combination—Understanding, Equality and Love, which no other religion does. Understanding to remove superstition and supernaturalism and have correct view, Samata or equality to hold all beings equal and respectable, and Karuna or love to help any sentient being in crisis.' This is all man wants for a happy life. And this is why he liked Buddhism in comparison to other religions.

It is interesting to note that American Professor Christopher Queen admired Dr. Ambedkar as having unique vision of social transformation through Buddhist strategy and goals and compared him with Thich Nhat Hanh of Vietnam, Sulak Sivaraksha of Thailand, Dalai Lama of Tibet and other socio-spiritual leaders of the world, nay, has even designated his Dhamma as the Fourth Turning of the Wheel.

According to Ambedkar all religions are neither same nor of similar values but some are ethically more advanced and superior, of them Buddhism is the best and teaches sublimest message of social unity and mental faculty par excellence.

Democracy, Religion and Society: Meaning

In Quebec Peace Conference Dr. Ambedkar represented his view that westerners are mistaken in the conception of democracy as voting system of adult franchise and religion as belief system of god, soul, and personal purification only and society as hierarchy of caste, race, gender, nationality, colour, language and so on. But he declared that democracy is a way of life of an individual and his association; religion is not only knowing truth but also loving it, and society is free communicative educational relationship of improvement of life and its constituents from one end to the other without social barriers.

Asian World Contribution to Buddhism

As the inheritor and successor of Indian Buddhist way of life Asia, the largest continent in area and population has its world role to play in global society to bring in a new better dispensation of existing conditions through the means of their legacy of Buddhism. It may be asked whether the North Vietnamese Buddhists, figuring more than Indian Dalit Buddhists by 22,000,000 (2007) knew the social significance of Buddhism? Perhaps they did as during their national freedom struggle, Thich Quang Duc burnt himself alive on May 11, 1963 in Saigon in response to suppression of religious freedom. And now they demand social unity between China and Vietnamese.

The Buddhists of Soviet Union contribute largely to the cause of world peace, national security and the world Buddhist Congress.

Tibet with 9,90,000 Buddhists (1967) have greater significance of Buddhism for their independence and autonomy for the 1,00,000 refugee Buddhists in India and for keeping friendly relationship with China.

Thailand with more than Indian Dalit Buddhists by 41,814,742 (2007) can maintain the status of Buddhism as Vinaya practicing nation and set its example for the other Asian nations.

Taiwan with its 24,522,395 Buddhists (2007) can contribute to education of the Dhamma preachers, including both monks and nuns, highly educated and trained in Japan and American universities, and employing the most advanced modern techniques to propagate Buddhism in secular society today.

Sri Lanka (2007) with 16,050,484 Buddhists can direct the world in Higher Buddhist studies through its set up of Universities such as the University of Buddhist and Pali Studies in 1982, Dhammachakra Vidyapitha at Gotambe, Peradeniya, Sri Lanka in 1985, etc.

Singapore with its 12,65,000 Buddhists (2007) is very small and surpasses any European country in beauty and cleanliness.

Siberia (1968) with its 1,2,65,000 Buddhists can follow the USSR pattern.

Pakistan (2007) with its 1,64,742 Buddhis can preserve Buddhist civilization, art and sculpture in and around Gandhar region near Taxila and Peshawar, Lahore and Karachi.

Nepal (2007) with its 60,69,376 Buddhists can glorify itself as the birthplace of Buddha if only it would materialize, in the words of late U Thant "The word Lumbini will become a forum, where the people of the world work together to bring about peaceful co-existence and planetary well-being, aiding in the birth of a harmonious world as envisioned by the man, who was born there 2500 years ago and taught that peace in the world begins with peace within ourselves".

The Buddhist population of 28,16,644 of Mongolia (2007) had significance of social Buddhism in developing their philosophical and national consciousness from the writings and inspirations of Nagarjuna, Asanga, Dharmakirti, and Vasubandhu.[1]

Malaysian Buddhists numbering 59,70,800, signified that Muslims could be as liberal with Buddhists as any Buddhist with Muslims in Sri Lanka.

The presence of 62,61,118 Buddhists in Laos (2007) showed the preamble of the Constitution of the Royal Kingdom of Laos established in the 10th century stating that – "Buddhism is the State Religion. The king is its high protector and he shall be a devout Buddhist".

In North Korea 15,10,6,650 and South Korea 23,53,1874 Buddhists (2007) stressed social service through its educational institutions despite being divided in south and north portions with the communist effects as in Vietnam.

Japan's (2007) 122,336,154 Buddhists reposed their utmost faith in Buddhism with the resounding slogan—*Jinrui no kiki wo sukuu bukkyo* raised which meant that Buddhism resolved the crisis of mankind.

A population of 5,397,962 Buddhists in Indonesia (2007) formed the part of the world of Indian culture with its magnificent Buddhist art works.

India (2007) with 16,947,992 Buddhists and estimated more than 20,000,000 Dalit Buddhists presented their modern saviour Buddha with his social Dhamma - Dr. Ambedkar before the world.

Hongkong (2007) have 6,701,580 Buddhists but it established homes for the aged and care centres to accommodate the old people and the crippled, who have nobody to turn to and a Buddhist hospital, devoting time and energy to the work of saving life and caring for the sick etc.

China with 1,057,481,510 Buddhists in 2007 can prove itself to be elder brother caring with special favour the interests of all other younger growing brother countries and its equal and senior Brother or Bhai-India.

Compared to other Buddhist countries' population India stands spectacularly high in Buddhist population from 1951 to the present as shown in the following table.

BUDDHIST POPULATION IN ASIA (2007)

S.N.	*Year*	*Country*	*Total population*	*Buddhist population (Percentage to World Buddhist Population)*	*History of Buddhism and other Religions Practiced in the country*
1	2007 (E)	**Central Asia**	95,398,532	2,879,280 (3.018)	Buddhism under Buddhist Khans
I		Afghanistan		63,780 (0.2 approx of P.)	Buddhism from ancient time before Christ till 9th Century
II		Mangolia		2,816,644 (98)	Buddhism during the reign of Mangol Khans, Mangu
III		Tajikistan		7,076 (0.1 of P.)	Seceded from USSR after 1991
IV		Uzbekistan		55,560 (0.2 of P.)	Seceded from USSR after 1991
V		Kazakhstan		84,067 (0.55 of P.)	Seceded from USSR after 1991
VI		Kyrgyzstan		18,495 (0.35)	Seceded from USSR after 1991
VII	1968	Siberia	1,265,000	1,265,000	Hulgu Khan rule with Buddhism
VIII	1967	Tibet	1,000,000	990,000	Kuble Khan ruled and Buddhism
					Was Set up Since 625 C.E.

(Contd.)

S.N.	*Year*	*Country*	*Total population*	*Buddhist population (Percentage to World Buddhist Population)*	*History of Buddhism and other Religions Practiced in the country*
IX	1977	U.S.S.R.	241,748,000	unlisted	Buddhism till 7th century and its revival into Lamaism since 15th century
2	2007 (E)	**South Asia**	1,491,019,011	38,601,550 (2.588)	Original Buddhism in Pali texts
I		Maldives		1,661 (0.45)	Buddhism later centuries
II		Bangladesh		1,053,138 (0.7)	Buddhism since 3 C.B.C.
III		Bhutan		2,250,014 (97 approx)	Buddhism since 8 C.E.
IV		India		16,947,992 (1.5)	Buddhism since 6th C.B.C.
V		Nepal		6,069,376 (21)	Asokan pillars testify ancient Buddhism there
VI		Pakistan		1,64,742 (0.1)	Gandhar Buddhism
VII		Sri Lanka		16,050,484 (76.7)	Original Buddhism
3	2007 (E)	**Southeast Asia**	592,738,430	216,615,239 (36.544)	Buddhism borrowed from SEA

(Contd.)

(Contd.)

S.N.	*Year*	*Country*	*Total population*	*Buddhist population (Percentage to World Buddhist Population)*	*History of Buddhism and other Religions Practiced in the country*
I		Brunei		54,600 (14.4)	
II		Cambodia		13,938,460 (96.5)	Buddhism since 9th Century
III		East Timor		1,085 (0.1%)	Buddhism spread later
IV		Indonesia		5,397,962 (2.3)	Buddhism till Majopahit dynasty's fall
V		Laos		6,261,118 (96)	Buddhism as State Religion since 10th Century
VI		Malaysia		5,970,800 (22)	Buddhism till medieval period and its revival since 17th Century
VII		Myanmar		43,918,200 (90)	Buddhism since 600 C.E.
VIII		Philippines		2,276,932 (2.5)	Buddhism spread later
IX		Singapore		2,781,888 (61.1)	Buddhists of both Theravada and Mahayana traditions
X		Thailand		61,814,742 (95)	Buddhism of present form since 7 centuries ago

(Contd.)

(Contd.)

S.N.	*Year*	*Country*	*Total population*	*Buddhist population (Percentage to World Buddhist Population)*	*History of Buddhism and other Religions Practiced in the country*
XI		Vietnam (North)		42,631,178 (50)	Buddhism in 189 A.D.
XII		Vietnam (South)		74,268,750 (85)	Buddhism in 189 A.D.
4	2007 (E)	**East Asia**	1,585,083,298	1,247,740,793 (78.717)	Buddhism adopted earlier than in SEA
I		China		1,057,481,510 (80 approx.)	Buddhism since 58 C.E.
II		Hong Kong		6,701,580 (93)	Buddhism for the last 1000 years
III		Japan		122,336,154 (96)	Buddhism since 552 C.E.
IV		North Korea		15,106,650 (63.5)	Buddhism since 372 C.E.
V		South Korea		23,531,874 (48)	Buddhism since 372 C.E.
VI		Macau		11,427,436 (23.3)	Buddhism's advent later
VII		Taiwan		24,522,395 (50)	Revival of Buddhism

Source: Internet, Free Encyclopaedia 2007.

From the above table it is clearly seen that India as a part of South Asia has its estimated Buddhist population upto (16,947,992) which surpasses all its Buddhist lands including Sri Lanka. Among the East Asian seven countries it exceeds the Buddhist population of Macau, North Korea and Hong Kong. Out of the twelve countries of Southeast Asia Indian Buddhists are far more in number than those of Cambodia, East Timor, Indonesia, Laos, Malaysia, Philippines, and Singapore. The whole Central Asian Buddhist demography is more than five times less than that of Indian Dalit Buddhists.

Major Schools of Buddhism

Since European scholars found Buddhism based on the Pali canon located in Ceylon and Southeast Asia, they named it "Southern Buddhism"—in contrast to the Buddhist schools of East Asia, which at first sight appeared completely different – referred to collectively as "Northern Buddhism." – geographically agreeable terms. Both stemmed from India.

The eighteen sects of the lesser Vehicle in India, were not autonomous Buddhist organizations but tendencies of schools existing in the same monasteries.

Conservative (Theravadi) and Mahayana both held the opinion that man must work out his own salvation, and that man must tread the path by his own efforts. Monastic Order constitutes the core of Theravada – bound to historical change through the Sangha. For many centuries not a single letter in the numerous strict precepts was altered in Conservative Sangha. Also denied is the elimination or modification of archaic rules such as the prohibition of any contact with money, of speaking or travelling with women, of taking meals after noon, and so forth. The only significant variation from this teaching has been the dependence of the Pure Land Sect upon the help of the external power of Amitabha Buddha.

The definition of 'Dependent Origination' wisely accepted in conservative Buddhism, especially in the Sarvastivada, is the "inter connection according to causal laws of all the elements co-operating in the formation of individual life." The Consciousness-only school of Buddhist idealism

(Vijnaptimatrata) occasionally took it to mean "the process of the appearing of all phenomena out of the Fundamental consciousness (alayavinnana)."

In Mahayana, especially in Maddhyamika school and the Kegon (Hua-Yen) school in China and Japan, Dependent Origination meant, "inter-dependence of all phenomena in the universe throughout the past the present, and the future" or "relativity of things and ideas."

Mahayanist tendencies existed in the first century B.C., at the time the Pali canon was set down. Mahayana Buddhism recognizes countless Buddhas and Bodhisattva. Mahayana Buddhism can be designated as religion especially oriented to the laity. Mahayana is more dynamic.

Theravada and Mahayana are subject to history which brings modification, development, and accommodation to the changing times.

History of Buddhism's Growth

Buddhism as a triple gem stands for Buddha as educating human agency, Dhamma as remedy for social ills, evils and wrong understanding and Sangha as nothing but purifying collective force.

In India Kautsa and Brihaspati, a Guru of Charvaka (Lokayata) denounced Vedism and Brahmanism. The six Indian philosophical schools advocated against cruelty, caste, devas and death (says Naren Bhattacharya). Buddha developed Anatmavada[2] and Buddhism made free access in religion for the Shudras, the Untouchables in particular and all others in general, and opposed priestcraft, caste, vedic ritual, and sacrifice. Emperor Ashoka expelled 60,000 imposters lay hidden in the Buddhist order in 246 B.C. and purified the Sangha.[3]

As a result Pushyamitra Brahman General usurped the throne of the Buddhist Mauryan King, Brihdratha. In Pandu Epic, Buddhist monuments are nicknamed as "edukas" in contempt. Organized suppression of Buddhism was carried out. All Hindu books eulogize the Brahmins or priests and maintain caste attitude[4]. Madhavacharya (4th century) in his "Sankara Vijaya" loudly cries that Buddhists have ridiculed Brahma, Veda and sacrifices.[5] In 700 A.D. Kumaril Bhatta, a Bihari Brahmin and the Guru of Sankara preached against the Buddhist accusing Buddha in his book, Tatvavartika as "a disturber of hereditary occupation and caste".[6]

The Untouchables did not join renaissance of Hinduism[7]. In the 11th century the world famous Nalanda University and its colossal library as well as the Odantapuri University had been damaged by the Muslim conqueror Bakhtiar Khilji, who took lives of Buddhist monks also[8].

But in 1829 Brian Haughten Hogson discovered in Nepal, *vajrasuchi*, the diamond needle, refuting Brahmanism in the rational arguments of Ashvagosha. In 1873 a debate between Buddhist monk M. Gunanada and Christian priest David Silva influenced Olcott and Blavatsky to their conversion to Buddhism. In 1884 C. Olcott (who presented 14 Fundamental Principles of Buddhists approved by Buddhist Congress in 1891) started schools for Pariahas and in association with Dharmapala, established the Theosophical Society in Madras. In the same year C. lyodhi Dass, a native doctor and scholar, along with his companion Krishna Swamiar became Buddhist in Sri Lanka, (His noted associates being P.L. Narasu, Appadurai and Singaravelu) and established South Indian Buddhist Association, edited Tamil Weekly, wrote his famous book '*Buddharathu Adi Vedan*', converted thousands of Untouchables to Buddhism and (due to his request the Government of Madras separately held census of Buddhists in 1910) and propagated Buddhism till his death in 1914. Narasu's (d. 1934) famour book '*Essence of Buddhism*' was recommended highly by Dr. Ambedkar and Dharmapal. Appadurai was of another revivalists, who spread message of Buddhism and mission of Ambedkar in Karnataka State. His close associate was Periyar E.V. Ramaswami, who started a Tamil Daily, 'Viduthalai' and rendered great service in spreading Buddhism in South India.

Like Malas and Madigas in Telugu province, and Holeyas in Karnataka, Pariyars are the untouchables of Tamil Districts. They wear neither name of Vishnu nor ashes of Shiva. Buddhism survived in the South India is evident from the book of Mylai Seeni entitled "Bauddhamum Tamilum"[9]. Popularity of Buddhism in the south was due to the services of Buddhist monks, who ignored caste differences in dealing with all people[10].

In the North India Anagarika Dharmapala was busy in renovating Bodh Gaya temple. He founded the Mahabodhi Society, started Maha Bodhi Journal, founded many colleges and hospitals, held Vesak celebration for the first time in modern India and introduced Pali studies in the University of Calcutta with the help of Asutosh Mukherji.

Unlike Indian National Congress, Brahmo Samaj, Prarthana Samaj and Arya Samaj the Booker T. Washington of Maharashtra as Sayajiro Maharaja of Baroda called him and popularly regarded as Mahatma Phooley (11th May 1828) and his Satya Shodhak Samaj (founded in 1873 later led by Rao Bahadur S.K. Bole) dealt with social reform in Maharashtra after Namdeva, Mukunda Raj and Jnyanoba in the 13th century and Chokhamela, Nandanara and Ravidass in the 14th century.

During the second half of the 17th century Untouchables started revolts against Hinduism and, Buddhism posed challenge to Hindu religion. The outcaste and tribal people amounted to about a sixth of the total population of India, which shook the foundation of Hindu social order.

Ambedkar's Role in Buddhism

Dr. Ambedkar, the greatest crusader against caste system was born on 14th April 1891, in 1920 he started *Mook Nayak* fortnightly to awaken his masses. Sahu Maharaj of Kolhapur reposed in him the full faith as the savior of the untouchables. On his passing matriculation K.A. Keluskar presented to him *Buddha Charita. Ambedkar once said that he became a Buddhist when he was a boy of sixteen*[11]. Loknath, an Italian national, converted to Buddhism, viewed that had Dr. Ambedkar adopted Buddhism earlier, partition of Burma from India could not have taken place in 1936[12]. At Yeola Dr. Ambedkar made firm decision to adopt Indian religion that would give social and religious equality. His 21 years of quest of religion disillusioned his mind about Sikkhism, Islam and Christianity, which were all more or less coloured by Hindu social inequality. Ambedkar adopted Buddhism in 1956 along with millions of his followers and at the same time, 2500th years of Buddhism was celebrated as Buddha Jayanti throughout India. Since then revival of Buddhism began in Maharashtra and other states of India fervently among the masses. Rahul Sankrityayan said that "Ambedkar laid such a foundation of Buddhism in India that nothing can shake it". He ranks Ambedkar in the line of Vasishtha, a son of a prostitute and Vedavyas, a son of Satyavati, daughter of fisherman, who were endowed with great learning despite their birth in poor family, unlike Jaimini and Patanjali[13]. Dr. Anand Kausalyayan, a Buddhist monk, noted Hindi writer and world-renowned scholar of Buddhism, who devoted his whole life (1905-1988) to the service of Indian Buddhists and Ambedkar mission, once said - "After my death my tomb should bear only a line that the man buried under this tomb died while serving the mission of Ambedkar."[14]

Growth of Buddhist Movement

The present Dalit literature is a revolutionary trend in Indian traditions of writings, which considers man as greater than a god, a religion and a country aiming at destruction of caste system and it revolves round its hero, Dr. Ambedkar[15]. Since 1956 Buddhists from the Scheduled Caste community have made their all round development in social, economic and educational spheres. In Nagpur itself there are as many as fifteen organizations that carry out functions of Ambedkar's ideology[16]. Concentrating only on Maharashtra, we find that Mahars are 6.45%, non-Mahar SCs are 4.64% and registered Buddhists are 6.39% of total population. Nine Districts of Vidarbha and three of Marathwada only have more than average of 6.39%, Akola being highest of percentage *i.e.* 16.79%. Mumbai has first highest number (5,57,089) and Nagpur district second highest (4,93,208) number.

According to the 1961 census there were 3,2,50,227 Buddhists in India. In the census of 1981 but for SC/Buddhist social milieu the number of Buddhists should be more than 20 million. Buddhists got organized under the world fellowship of Buddhists, Buddhist councils, impact of Dr. Ambedkar, and Buddhist publication and history of 2500 years of Buddhism. In the year (1959) world's attention turned to Indo-China-Tibet political problem in relation to Buddhism, when the Dalai Lama left Tibet and took political asylum in India along with his followers. Four years later political obstacles hindered Buddhist developments as Buddhists in Vietnam were being persecuted by the communists in the year 1963. Buddhist movement got impetus by formation of Buddhist Union in Europe followed by establishment of Buddhist Viharas in Toronto, Canada in 1978 by the Srilankan and Ambedkarite Buddhists there.

Ambedkarite Buddhist Society

Ambedkarite Buddhist society was developed under the direction of Bhadant Anand Kausalyayan at Nagpur, India.

From the year 1985 to the present many developments of Ambedkar movement and Ambedkar-oriented Buddhism took place in India and abroad due to spread of Ambedkar's followers across the world, international intellectuals' interest in the studies and research on Ambedkar and growth in knowledge, information, thought and philosophy of Dr. Ambedkar.

Presently the massive Stupa of Deeksha Bhoomi, Dragon Temple at Kamptee and Nagaloka educational institutions and hostels and Buddha Bhoomi in Nagpur-Kamptee are living witnesses to the spirit of Ambedkarism in India.

Lastly but not in the least the Dr. Babasaheb Ambedkar National Institute of Social Sciences at the birth place of Ambedkar, Mhow has been functioning since 1988 for giving impetus to the thought and philosophy of Ambedkar by its research works and projects and M.Phil. and Ph.D. courses and evaluation of its impact on the masses in general.

Ambedkar and His Contributions

1. Demographic Contribution : The first and foremost contribution of Dr. Ambedkar is to establish Buddhist demography in Indian society. According to the census of 1980 the Buddhist population in India is estimated to amount to 20,000,000. At the time of Ambedkar's birth in Mhow in 1891

Buddhists in India were a few and far between. Before the conversion of Dr. Ambedkar and his followers to Buddhism in 1956 all Buddhist places of interest and history belonged to the—south-east Asian countries-to Chinese, Japanese, Sri Lankans as the Indian so believed, be it Nalanda site, statues of the Buddha or Ajanta-Ellora caves of Maharashtra—but conversion created new centres and more number of Buddhists in India.

Three and half million Untouchables in India became Buddhists since 1956, which in 1961 amounted to 3,250,227 (an increase of 1671 per cent) over the 1951 census. The conversions centered in Maharashtra, where Buddhists in 1961 registered to the strength of 2,7,89,501 and the rest in Madhya Pradesh (1,13,365 Buddhists), Uttar Pradesh (12,893 Buddhists) and Punjab (14,957 Buddhists), Mysore (8,000 increase) and Gujarat (3,000 increase). 2001 census recorded the number of Buddhists in Maharashtra alone as 60 lakh or six percent of the State's total population in contrast to .9 per cent of the Indian population.

Thus the demographic contribution of Dr. Ambedkar in creating number of Buddhist population in India is more than that of South Asian counties like Pakistan, Nepal, Bangladesh, Bhutan, and Central Asian Siberia or Southeast Asian Cambodia, Laos, and Malaysia put together or more than that of single Sri Lanka.

2. Knowledge : Social philosophy in India is classified into classes of untouchability (400 A.D.[17]) and castes[18] with religion and politics supporting this system perpetrated by a 2% of Indian society on the masses amounting to 98%[19]. Dr. Ambedkar struggled throughout his life against unjust features of Hindu society and finally forced his surroundings, including his own and collectivity to accede his way of life based on unity of all nations, equality of all castes, colours, races, sexes and fraternity among all world communities to give way to the new order of righteousness.

His first encounter with Buddhism was when he happened to read the Buddha's biography presented by his teacher Arjun Krishnaji Keluskar on passing his matriculation examination from Elphinstone High School, Mumbai in 1906.

After his graduation in Mumbai he went to America and England for his higher research studies at post-graduate level with the help of Sayajirao Gaikwad's financial assistance from 1913 to 1917 and with his self-finance from 1920 to 1924 and came back to India equipped with the degrees of M.A., M.Sc., Ph.D., D.Sc., Bar-at-Law, and later honoured with D.Litt, and L.L.D. degrees.

3. Development of Educational Institutions : Educational development of Buddhist minority started by Peoples' Education Society, (founded on 8th July 1945) Anand Bhavan, D.N. Road, Mumbai and during post-Ambedkar era is as follows:

S.N.	*Schools*	*Colleges*	*Hostels*
1.	Siddharth Night High School, Bauddha Bhavan, Mumbai	Siddhartha College of Arts, Science and Commerce, 1946 est. by PES	Siddhartha Vihara Hostel, Wadala
2.	Siddharth English Medium School, Wadala	Siddhartha College of Commerce and Economics, 1953 est. by PES	Hostel, Mumbai
3.	Marathi Medium Secondary School, New Mumbai Campus	Siddhartha College of Law, 1956 ets. by PES	Hostel, Mahad
4.	Dr. Babasaheb Ambedkar Public School, New Mumbai Campus	Dr. Ambedkar College of Commerce and Economics, Wadala 1972 est. by PES	Hostel, Dapoli
5.	Marathi Medium Primary School	Siddhartha College of Law, Wadala, 1977 est. by PES	Hostel, Aurangabad
6.	Milind Multi Purpose High School, Aurangabad, 1955	Dr. Babasaheb Ambedkar Memorial Research Centre, Rajgrih, Dadar est. by PES	Hostel, Nanded
7.	PES English Medium Primary and Pre-Primary School, Aurangabad	Siddhartha College of Mass Communication, Anand Bhavan est. by PES	
8.	Matoshri Ramabai Ambedkar High School, New Aurangabad	Siddhartha Institute of Industry and Administration, Anand Bhavan, est. by PES	
9.	Nagsen High School, Nanded	Junior College, New Mumbai Campus	

S.N.	*Schools*	*Colleges*	*Hostels*
10.	Nagsen Vidhyalay, Nanded	Junior College of Education, New Mumbai Campus	
11.	Gautam Vidyalay, Pandharpur (M.S.)	Milind Multi Faculties College, Nagsenavana, Aurangabad, 1951	
12.	Nagsen Vidyalay, Bangalore	Milind College of Science Aurangabad, 1946	
13.		Dr. Babasaheb Ambedkar College of Arts and Commerce, Aurangabad, 1960	
14.		Milind College of Arts, 1963	
15.		Dr. Ambedkar College of Law, Aurangabad, 1968	
16.		PES College of Physical Education, Aurangabad	
17.		Buddhist Centre, Aurangabad	

4. Constitution of India : The Preamble of the Constitution of India expressed the spirit of Indian nation-builders in these words; 'We, the people of India, solemnly resolve to constitute India into a sovereign secular socialist republic to secure to its citizens justice—social, economic, political; liberty of thought, expression, work, faith, and worship; equality of status and opportunity; assuring unity and integrity of nation and promoting fraternity amongst all and enact, adopt and give it to ourselves hereby on this day of 29th November 1949—this Constitution'.

5. Publishing of Volume on The Buddha and His Dhamma: This is a magnum opus of Ambedkar posthumously published in 1957. It has eight books covering 499 pages and has been translated into regional and foreign languages such as Hindi, Punjabi, Marathi, Sinhali, English and Kannad etc.

According to Ambedkar, Buddha upheld social issues of ritual, text, caste, age, uniform, women, shudras, education, authority, change, karma, soul, rebirth, enlightenment and a way of life based on prajna, samadhi and shila against lobha, dosa and moha. Dhamma and saddhamma open doors of social, educational, economic, spiritual opportunities to all and break all barriers between man and woman. Sangha is the transformed society for good, welfare and happiness of the world.

Ambedkar held that like Marxism Buddhism is also based on solid foundation of suffering, including exploitation, killing, issues of Shudras and women, mind, caste, government, society, ecology and so on. Individual is not alone and inactive through lives but has mind and association, environment to interact, influence and get influenced thereby in dynamic way in contrast to predetermined or *atmaic* way as some believed. He believed that Buddhism has more social significance and philosophy than any other creed or ideology and religious institutions must have social responsibility unlike soul-supersoul relationship. He also stressed that transmission of karma among and between sentient beings binds them with its nature of wholesome or unwholesome effects and harms them as a result of pain and suffering or gives pleasure in forms of welfare and happiness in proportion to their number and intensity of action.

Buddha word has to be both rational and responsible in that he transmits compassion to save man in crises and *prajna* to cut illusion of superstition and supernaturalism. Any religion which has weak foundation, weak principles and weak preachers is bound to fall and ruin. Sangha or association must be a body of serving monks rather than aiming at personal perfection. Laity should not make a monk a scapegoat of their inactivity or agency to carry their deficiency and bear their sin to let them indulge more in life with such character and hope that other will take care of their defects.

6. National Emblems : Ambedkar got the nation of India accepted the Buddhist Ashok Chakra laid on our country's tricolour flag and Lion Capital embossed on Indian currency as national emblems. On persuasion of Dr. Ambedkar Government of India adopted Saka Era which was started by Kanishka as national era on 22nd March 1957 corresponding to 1st Chaitra 1879.

Top of 150 ft. high central dome of Rashtrapati Bhavan (Viceroy's House) resembled Sanchi Stupa. Meditative Buddha statue stands in Durbar Hall used for ceremonies, awards and credential presentation of ambassadors by President. Hindu polity of monarchy was replaced by Buddhist Republic, Secular, Welfare State.

7. Religious Institution : Bharatiya Bauddha Mahasabha or Buddhist Society of India established by Dr. Ambedkar in 1955 was succeeded by Yashwantrao Ambedkar as President. He held 1st All India Buddhist Conference at Chaitya Bhoomi in 1968. Later Mrs. Miratai Ambedkar became its President and held 2nd All India Buddhist Conference in 1980 and 3rd All India Buddhist Delegates Conference took place in Ambedkar Bhavan, New Delhi in 1989. Its branches were opened in New Delhi, Lucknow, BSI, Baroda in Gujrat, BSI, Siddharth Niwas, Hyderabad and BSI, Buddha Vihara, Siddarth Nagar, Jallundur.

In number of Viharas established for Buddhist movement Nagpur stands first and Delhi second.

Indian Buddhist societies were formed in the following states of India:

STATE-WISE INDIAN BUDDHIST SOCIETIES

State	*Name of Buddhist Society*
West Bengal	Mahabodhi Buddhist Society
	Bharatiya Buddhist Association
	Indian Buddhist Council
Maharashtra	Bharatiya Bauddha Maha Sabha, Dadar
	Trilokya Baudha Maha Sangha Sahayaka Gana, 1979
Arunachal Pradesh	Lohit Bodhi Society
Assam	All Assam Buddhist Association
	International Brotherhood Mission
Jammu and Kashmir	Ladakh Buddhist Association
Tripura	All Tripura Rajya Buddhist Association
Punjab	Punjab Bauddha Mahasabha, Jallundur
Sikkim	Sikkim Buddhist Association
Mizoram	All Mizoram Buddhist Association
Meghalaya	Meghalaya Buddhist Association

8. Social Application of Buddhism : Buddhism is a remedial philosophy and public policy. It is inclusive of the merits of communism also. It is rational or scientific mode of thinking and living. It upholds the cause of the weakest members of society and make the stronger ones act in a responsible manner. It brings individual transformation and collective revolution in peaceful and ever rising height with worldly and spiritual concerns. It holds equality of men and women and all sentient beings as far as liberation permits and opposes *Varnashrama dharma* and mechanical caste or duties based on insignificant birth and not on merit of worth. It does not define religion as duty or rule based on blind faith printed in any text or book authority but treats it as principle of life to be tested by experience and human sense. It is thus based on morality, liberty of mind and its application in life.

Impermanence, Dissatisfaction and Unsubstantiality are sources of its origin. Buddhism as Nirvan dharma meant that all elements are unsubstantial or impersonal. As mental aspect it implied that all composite existence is transient and unsatisfactory. When a man sees them with application of mind in the form of a diamond cutter or *prajna* his illusions are dispelled and suffering is overcome. This is illustrated in Pali dhammapada stanzas as: *sabbe sankhara aniccati, sabbe sankhara dukkhati, sabbe dhamma anattati yada pannaya passati atha nibbindati dukkhe esa maggo visuddhiya.* Thus, comprehending this truth is the only way for purification of beings.

The vajracchedika sutra as interpreted by sixth Chinese patriarch, Hue Neng also stated that "If there were no sentient beings there would be no dhamma and if there were no preachers there would be no discourses."

Dr Ambedkar fully corroborated this view of Buddhism and said that "Religion is for man, not man for religion". That is to say that in the history of development of human beings man preceded his actions and institutions in this world. He further said that religion as a duty either breaks man or makes him to break itself. This is the nature of mechanical authoritative rule which has no force of natural principle of life.

What does a child inherit from his or her parents? According to the Atmavadi religions child inherit only body, and soul is his own contribution from his earlier lives or cycle of life. Karma and soul are personal properties and belong to personal self inseparably howsoever number of bodies it may undergo in its endless cycle of birth. Each sentient being is distinct in this possession.

Buddhism as non-self doctrine teaches transmission of both mind and matter (Namarupa) from parents to their progeny in family or from one social being to another social being in community or associated mode of life.

It is further enlightened that Paramita or perfection does not imply personal attainment to the utmost degree but instead it implies "to the opposite shore, *i.e.* opposite to this shore of existence and non-existence like the up and down of the billowy sea caused due to clinging to sense objects and such a state is figuratively and metaphorically called 'this shore'; while a state above existence and non-existence like smoothly running water, caused by non-attachment is called 'opposite shore'. This is why it is called Paramita[20]. Thus, the evenness of water current in the ocean is Paramita opposite to the violent ups and downs of waves identified with Sansara or the world of becoming. If so then Ambedkar preferred the serving men to perfect saints for his social transformation project in the world.

Lobha, Dosa, Moha are Kleshas (defilements) of ordinary human society opposed to the let go lobha, dosa, moha and become bright mirror free from stains, wrong view and impurity and purifying the whole social organization.

Sentient beings are better than saintly and godly beings, who are incapable of prajna owing to their one-sided development of bliss. They form the existence of all super ideology and philosophy, which are made and unmade for them alone. There are secular countries like India and democratic countries like Britain, America, and theocratic states like Malaysia, Pakistan and Buddhist nations like Thailand and Sri Lanka, Tibet and Laos, and Japan etc. Amartya Sen rightly pointed out that democracy has two aspects of deciding and voting or westernized voting, and Asian deciding and voting process. While the reasoning or deciding element is common to all societies individually and distinctively today it was not like this. Earlier in western legacy even in respect of voting Athenian and Greece excluded women and slaves. Comparatively the Indian, Iranian and African counterparts of Greece were excelling in methods of indigenous public reasoning and voting both. Asoka and Akbar were model rulers, secularists, and democrats while Rome was burning Bruno.

As for the treatment of different co-religionists it varied from country to country. In England it is not easy to make visits to the hospitals and prisons for other than the member of the Church of England. In Nepal until 1951 to 1960 it was at the cost of being boycotted and awarded corporal punishment for talking against caste. It is impossible for Muslims to convert themselves to any other religion in Islamic countries and in America only Christian members get priority of concern. This was revealed in public lecture by British born monk Sangharakshita.

9. Conversion : Dr. Ambedkar therefore was attracted by Buddhist societies and culture of utmost liberty and sharing collectivity amidst diverse communities. He therefore contributed to the social view of Buddhism. Buddha stands for knower, Dhamma for dispelling wrong views and Sangha for undertaking act of purity. As a social religion Buddhism as a boat is a means to cross the sea of world safely. Use of Buddhism for liberation of all is the proper application of it. It was a mission of each one, teach one and transform individually and collectively. It teaches unity of mankind and non-duality of matter and mind irrespective of caste, creed, gender, colour, nationality, place of birth, dress code and culture. Selfless communities will lead society to be selfless association of enlightened beings.

One of the reasons of fall of any religion or philosophy is its weak foundation. Buddhism and Communism are based on ground realities of suffering and exploitation as first truth to reckon with. The purpose of religion or philosophy is to inspire men to overcome suffering or exploitation, be it social, economic, political, cultural, or educational. Method of Buddhism to overcome problems is by love and persuasion while that of the Communism is by force and extermination of the opponents. Effect of suffering and exploitation is caused by self or private property or ownership of mental and material world by private limited greedy hands. Therefore state ownership of property or collective sharing of world is proposed as remedy for overcoming malady of existence. What stricter discipline can there be in communes of socialism or Marxism than the Buddhist Order norm of entitlement for its member of only eight things as personal belongings such as three pieces of wear, a bowl for food, a needle for sowing, a strainer for sieving, a razor for shaving and a belt to fasten clothes on the waist.

According to Ambedkar it may be possible for society to shed caste and class distinctions sometime but it is not probable for the state to wither away as the Communism predicts, for to regulate social life with either ethical dhamma without state or governing state including legislature, executive, and judiciary is inevitable for smooth functioning of life.

Dr. Ambedkar's life, mission and revolution should be made known to everyone in time so that it will inspire humanity and imprint- upon its heart the motto - Educate, Agitate and Organize and vitalize its members to awaken to the greatest path of truth (Cattari-ariya-saccani) and get disillusioned from spiritualism which today has come to mean "just words, words and more empty words"[21] before it is 'just five minutes to midnight and one must better change' to put it in Dr. Capra's phrase.

10. Philosophy : Ambedkar's philosophy was a philosophy of a religion that states that each religion has its own particular philosophy distinct from other in both content of experience and value of reasoning. Thus, we can get as many philosophies as there are religions in the world and are faced with the problem of choice of the best from among them all. So it is a matter of choosing better one as one improves upon one's existing view of religion and philosophy and settles with one that suits him best.

The test of reality is definite as defined by Dinnaga and Dharmakirti in their norm of *arthakriyakaritva i.e.* whatever is causally efficient is real. For example, fire which does not burn and does not cook is not real fire and the concept may be extended to the extent of real nirvana also. A.J. Ayer had to change his position from empiricism to logical positivism through linguistic philosophy to value judgement.

Michael Bakunin (1814-1876) preceded Ambedkar to dislike dictatorship even of the proletariats and peasants and Aquinas detected in human nature moral base that defines good as an act of individual perfection that everybody might cherish as desirable state. Bistani Bayazid's (d. 874) words 'that a mystic should be beyond good and evil' marked higher value over good aspect.

The feminist existentialist Simon De Beauvoir (1908-1989) propounded ethics of freedom. Heidegger said "Neither man nor world are separate from each other, some of the beliefs express our non-cognitive attitudes." This is to imply that we cannot evaluate religion as true or of any definite value.

According to Mahayana (about 200 B.C.) and Tantrik Buddhism 'having thought of enlightenment' and 'being enlightened' are practically two different things or stages.

Bernard Bolzanio (1781-1848) was compelled to resign from his position of professorship in Prague due to his rationalistic tendencies in theology.

Bertrand Russell's philosophy of logical atomism (1956) and E. Husserl's ideas in pure phenomenology are distinct from Buddhist infinite sublime states of mind called Brahmaviharas. Franz Brentano (1838-1917) defined mind as ability to refer to something beyond itself. Martin Buber (1878-1965) was a religious existentialist who highlighted man's two primary attitudes and relations as I-Thou and I-It; the former in the fields of psychotherapy, social philosophy and religion and the latter as in impersonal kind of relationship and secondary.

Ambedkar's reference to a philosophy of a religion is applicable equally to the realm of economics. Nikolai Bukharin I's (1888-1938) critique of marginal utility school may be studied for comparison. He did not agree with Joseph Butler

(1692-1752) who viewed that God concerned with the affairs of men.

Material Mode of Language compares right speech in reducing the public speech to performance of its right kind of role. Material object is what sensory experience can refer and by means of which people communicate with each other and that which can exist in space and time independently of any conscious being.

Materialism is an ontological view asserting the primacy of matter and putting thought or spirit in the secondary or derivative status. This view was propounded by Charvakas in India and by the earliest materialist school of atomism in the Western Europe.

Dialectical materialism explains the natural process in terms of dialectics such as unity and diversity of opposite forces, transformation of quantity into quality and the law of negation of negation i.e. shunyata of shunyata to put it in Nagarjuna's terminology.

According to the Buddhist linguistics and dynamics "the word can only express being and non-being. Buddha and Nagarjuna and Chandrakirt expressed silence, quietude, pacification or absolute truth as flying in the wind 'A flight, without any support, in the wind of empty space'[22].

Meaning is a coordination among speakers and listeners within a speech community that organizes a communication network by interlacing tokens, Acts of Interpretation, various objects, events, thinkables by complex rules of formation and their deconstructions that go for picking and doing our thought in public discourses by their rules. Kausalyayan (1905-1988) says that "Our relation to society is through speech or words only".

The arguments for the philosophy of Mayavada (Advaita or illusion) have been surreptitiously borrowed from Buddhist philosopher Nagarjuna's Negation of Negation or Madhyamika.

11. Ethics : Generally people are prone to behave as giving for giving, lying for lying, tit for tat or measure for measure. Considering this as the general standard of behaviour at least one Dhammapada *gatha* refers to higher conduct than the above as given below:

akkodhena jine kodham : Win anger by calmness

asadhum sadhuna jine : Win roughness by gentility

jine kadariyam danena : Win stinginess by liberality and
saccenalikavadena : Win falsehood by truthfulness.

Surely it may be admitted by all that the standard of higher conduct of man is expressed by the Buddhist Dhammapada aphorism as mentioned above.

Take for example other virtue such as not to hurt or kill. The historians will be one on the point that in the history of religions and religious warfare for worldly affairs Buddhism is conspicuous by the absence of bloodshed in its policy towards others in the world and philosophy of life.

In the same way relatively speaking Buddhist ethics, Buddhist logic, Buddhist philosophy, Buddhist language, literature, aesthetics, art, architecture, painting and sculpture and above all its culture and a way of life are comparatively worth more than what other philosophies, religions and cultures can offer to mankind.

The roots of all evil social deeds are three namely (1) temptation (Lobha), (2) aversion (Dosa) and (3) ignorance (Moha) to be counteracted by equally powerful wholesome social roots of same number viz. (1) Non-greed (alobha), (2) Non-hate (adosa) and (3) knowledge (amoha).

There is one universal moral order of righteousness and unrighteousness that is developed, increased and consolidated by number of additions or subtractions of moral-deeds to or from the existing changing status of morality in the world. The human deeds are responsible for making the earth worth heaven or hell by their respective dispositions. Ages of human actions and reactions gave rise to a universal moral law in life of man everywhere now as before. The mechanism of this rule is explained in Buddhist philosophy by using the same terminology as was introduced by the Buddha (563-483 B.C.) originally under the caption of *paticca-samuppada* or the law of social association. Dr. Ambedkar applied it to social sphere also. According to this law past, present and future moments of social life in particular and the whole life in general are interdependent and inter-connected.

Ignorance means misapprehension. This brings disaster in the words of Mahatma Jyotirao Phule and it brought hell, in the words of Dr. M. Iqbal, to the class of Shudras in the Hindu society. This misapprehension is not a simple thing but a compound of ingredients of social avarice and social aversion against certain sections of society and as such it causes various concomitants of social consciousnesses such as volitional, cognitional and emotional associations and that in turn bring different sense organs, different looks and different objects within its sphere and form social contact, social feeling, social belongingness together and hold society together to elevate itself and pass it on to future generation as it was to the former from the history.

Right understanding gives it vision. Right thoughts make it act accordingly. Right speech establishes communications based on truth talks avoiding falsehood, slandering, harsh words and pointless chattering. Right action leads to refrain from harming any living and human beings, from taking anything that is not given, from misusing senses of carnal pleasure and from taking drugs or drinks that tend to cloud the mind. Right living guarantees peaceful and creative life for oneself as well as for others. Right effort maintains goodness from within by striving to preserve or eliminate respectively already existing virtues or vices in itself or by striving to inculcate or shun in itself merits or demerits respectively from without. Right mindfulness (*samma sati*) is to be aware at every point of doing or undoing anything anywhere at any time. Right concentration (*samma samadhi*) cultivates its mind to the highest plane of sublimity.

Theories of Observation, Meaning and Understanding

Thoughts may be identified with and distinguished from the thought as an act of mind positing a content and as a term used for its articulation. This is distinct from theory which means anything in the form of a statement or a set of statements offering an explanation of something. Philosophers like N.R. Hanson, T. Kuhn, P. Feyerabend and K. Popper claimed that those theoretical assumptions influence the facts that are obtained in observation since they don't remain theory-neutral. The view of science philosophers about the theory laden-ness of observation called inductionist view is opposed by recent view as it held observation as selective process which cannot operate without certain theoretical assumptions regarding the law-like behaviour of the object. So observation is always theory-laden.

Theoretical terms refer to unobservable events, unobservable aspects or features of events such as electrons, atoms, gene, electro-magnetic wave which cannot be pointed to and there are no overt procedures for identifying their referents. Experimental descriptions contain only terms that refer to observable or operationally definable terms such as pressure, magnetism, red, soft etc., that are immediately intelligible independent of theories, or experimental procedure of science, whose truth and falsity is epistemologically prior to that of any theories; they can be confirmed as true or false directly by carrying out experimental operations implicitly or explicitly specified in the meanings of their component terms; and they act as verifiers of the rest of scientific enterprise.

Leibnitz formulated the doctrine of theodicy. Actually the term "Theodicy" was the French word meaning God's justice and it is loosely used for "Philosophy of Religions" also, but it addresses the problem of the evil in the main. He gave justification of existence of evil in the world created by God, the wholly Good is to promote moral values such as forbearance, courage, kindness etc.

Donald Davidson discussed the theory of meaning or understanding as leading one straight into a priori structure of language as a system of rules with internal structure presupposed to explain meaning and interpretation as rationally constituted meaning representing structure of human understanding to lay bare the common agreement conditions.

A theory of goals or ends is to be realized by human beings and other living creatures as an expression of their essential nature *i.e.* sociality and rationality as essential and not specific/ contingent/accidental characteristics such as height, colour of hair and skin, weight etc.

Teleological ethical theory holds that an action is right if it is conducive to the goal which is generally regarded as good. If the action does not produce the effect it intends *i.e.* the greatest balance of good over evil it is wrong action.

Philosophy's fate in religion as discussed by Chattopadhyaya and Sankrityayan eclipsed as that of Buddhism under counter-revolutionary forces in India's history.

For betterment of socio-economic, religious and political way of life Ambedkar's threefold prescription is liberty, equality and fraternity as principles of his philosophy; Buddha, Kabir and Phule as human preceptors to be emulated in one's daily routine; and educate, agitate and organize and self-respect, morality and knowledge, etc., as deities to be internalized in living moments.

Positive and Negative Trinity in Buddhism

Buddhism as the best method of living is based on trinity of morality, mental development and correct understanding. This positive trinity is derived from the Middle path or Noble eightfold path prescribed as remedy for the ills of avarice, aversion and ignorance, the negative trinity that is responsible for suffering of all human beings and existence of world.

If we make negative the trinity of liberty, equality and fraternity then we get bondage, inequality and fratricide that stand for alternative negative trinity of avarice (bonded-ness), aversion (fratricide) and ignorance (bondage); the positive trinity of which is giving (alobha), loving (adosa) and understanding (amoha), the antidote of negative things as referred to above.

Giving is a morality in action, loving is cultivation of mind and accumulation of all wholesome thoughts and understanding is comprehension of mechanism of suffering as it really is and correctly *i.e.* to see that *evadhe anartha eka avidhyene kele* such an devastation could be visited on humanity by this one single ignorance to cite the words of Phule.

The Buddhist perspective gleaned from the Vissuddhi Magga of Buddhaghosha was "*sile patitthaya naro sapanno cittam pannanca bhavayam atapi nipako bhikkhu so imam vijataye jatam*" that be it any person, whether a layman or recluse, whosoever is established in morality, cultivates mind in good thoughts and correct understanding with perseverance and valour, he only can disentangle this entanglement of misapprehension or ignorance.

Ambedkar's perspective was more rational and empirical in the sense that he identified the abstract mental perversities with existing social elements and conflicts of communities of people and practically prescribed for the downtrodden masses to come up with their other counterparts in every dimension of life with the help of having such philosophy as will free them from bondage by liberty of thought, from inequality by change and from fratricidal caste-class relations by loving and unifying attitude towards their fellow beings and other living things.

12. Recognizing the Democratic Spirit of Buddhism : Why the Indian Government is revitalizing the world Buddhist holiest shrine of Bodhgaya? Does it recognize Buddhism's contribution to the world culture or does it see economic gain of tourism in it? Any way one looks at the issue Buddhism's contribution to world psyche against international terrorism and world's developing nations struggle for egalitarian order and empowerment of the powerless and emancipation of the suffering population cannot be denied.

The fact that the Mahabodhi temple complex was declared a world heritage site in mid-2002 by UNESCO, and its dedication ceremony taking place among dignitaries like the Princess of Cambodia Norlam Bhopa Devi, her daughter Princess Sita Nordom Wood, 55 Buddhist spiritual leaders, 400 other Buddhist figures and a horde of monks and Government functionaries from 25 countries with the Union Minister for Tourism and Culture, Jagmohan announcing the central aid of Rs. 25 to 35 crores to improve the world heritage site, is gratifying despite the damages done to the world heritage of Bamiyan Buddha in Afghanistan and Dr. Bhandarkar Oriental

Research Institute, Poona, preceded by the Babri mosque demolition in ancient Buddhist holy city, Saket, which is now known as Ayodhya.

In India Buddhism is a patent caste annihilating philosophy and democratic popular way of life forceful for establishment of class-caste-less sovereign secular democratic republic and nation-building with dignity of man, empowerment of marginal person including child, egalitarian society, universal loving-kindness to all beings, perfect understanding for new rational ideology and ever refreshing change in every walk of life as signified by Dhamma revolution initiated by modern India's greatest builder Babasaheb Ambedkar when he adopted such indigenous Buddhalogy along with lakhs of his other brethren at ancient Naga capital Nagpur on 14th October 1956.

Buddhism as the light of Asia lit up Europe and America also. It does not endorse the practice of racial discrimination that existed between the Pro-Civil Rights Act of 1870 Blacks and pro-White Ku Klux Klan organizations that ultimately resulted in the murder of Martin Luther King Jr. by James Earl Ray, the then newly released imprisoned convict on April 4, 1968 because the former opposed the Vietnam war launched by the President Lyndon Johnson and his Congress just as Nathuram Godse shot dead Mahatma Gandhi in India on January 31, 1948 because the latter followed the Buddhist principle of non-violence during the Indian national upsurge against the British Raj.

Democratic spirit of Buddhism adopted in Vietnam or in Iran should be heartening to every public power loving nation and the superpower in particular needs to commend every successful turn of democratic governance taking place in any smaller country of the world. But this goodness of rule instead of becoming an enviable quality among member countries of the world, has been an instrument of causing heartburn and bane to greater and lesser powers respectively as expressed by the top Iranian cleric in Tehran during the US election in 2004 in a Friday prayer sermon in these words: "Each ballot cast in the Islamic Republic's Parliament (Majlis) elections would be akin to firing a bullet into the heart of Bush."

Culture of Buddhism in Contemporary Society

Science has by its interesting discovery of atomic energy proved the Buddha's law of change (*Anicca-Dukkha-Anatta*) to be reality. Psychology has already proved the existence of an unconscious mind and may well one day, through age-regression experiments or by some new means of psychoanalysis prove rebirth to be a reality. The scientific proof of rebirth would remove the last stumbling block in the way of the worldwide recognition of the teaching of the Buddha. Buddhism shows itself ready and willing to carry on the twofold dialogue with the secularized world and with other world religions.

Gautama the Buddha is the voice of Asia, and the conscience of the world. It was 600 years before the Christ. It was the period of Mahavira and the Buddha in India, of Parmenides and Empedocles in Greece, of Zarathustra in Iran and of Lao Tzu and Confucius in China. Today we are living in the age of science and technology. The world has undergone tremendous change. Tension has been created in society. Population growth is gigantic. The propagation of Buddhism was an attempt to save society from superstition, crass materialism and ethical skepticism. Buddhism has left its impact on all – culture, civilizations, religion, ethics, logic, psychology, sociology, and other disciplines. Its civilizing influences are discernible in the remains found in the stately architecture, lovely sculpture, magnificent paintings, superb embroidery and several arts and crafts.

Its cultural impact is witnessed even today in the gentle behaviour of its followers, in their deportment, dance, drama, music, and poetry, in their social customs, superb hospitality, in their work, play, festivals and celebrations and also in their traditions, household furnishings and way of thinking as expressed in their acts, their law and literature. Buddhists are found habitually cheerful in disposition, gay in their living and remarkably carefree in their lives, in pleasure dignified and in adversity remarkably serene, they accept joy with gusto and obstacles with fortitude and are ever charitable and attentive to wholesome deeds with a view to facing the future with a happy hope.

Not being riddled with caste complications, their social fabric is without appellations of high or low, all beings accepted as brothers and sisters, sharing each other's weal and woe. With the ingrained spirit of socialism born of Buddhism, they naturally share their possessions freely with the needy. Moreover, their womenfolk enjoying freedom and equality with their men-folk, are with an independent outlook, which makes them outstanding in business and social life.

The contribution of Buddhism to art and architecture throughout history is well evidenced by the impressive remains on the sacred soils of Pagan and Prome in Burma, Borobudur in Indonesia, Anuradhapura and other sites in Sri Lanka, Angkor Wat in Cambodia and Nakorn Pathom in Thailand; sweet Buddha images and other pieces of art discovered in India, China, Japan and other parts of Asia. Also in central America, and parts of Russia, they speak volumes in favour of the world wide civilizing influence exercised by Buddhism in the past.

Contribution of Buddhism to Society

The *Panchashila* is a great traditional contribution to the well being of human family. The Panchasila of the Buddha found expression in the political field as they were enunciated by Nehru in Africo-Asian conference at Bandung in Indonesia in 1955-56 as: 1. Mutual respect for each other's territorial integrity and sovereignty (panatipata veramani), 2. Mutual non-aggression (adinnadana veramani), 3. Mutual non-interference in each other's internal affairs (kamesumicchachara veramani), 4. Equality and mutual benefit (musavada veramani) and, 5. Peaceful co-existence (suramerayamajjapamadatthana veramani).

Buddhism distinguished itself in making noteworthy contributions to human well-being in the field (1) Promotion of sanitary standards. It makes people live cleanly and well. (2) Upholding of occasional continence or complete celebacy as admirable virtue. This naturally helps to check population explosion. (3) Universal literacy is a result of monastic education universally offered. (4) Anti-social elements kept down because of the practice of harmlessness. (5) Among Buddhists there is no dowry system in vogue, and (6) They have high percentage of literacy. Buddhist literary arts have surpassed in linguistic variety, geographical extent, cultural influence unlike Confucius, Hindu, Islamic and Taoist literature.

The world's oldest printed book, dated 11 May 868, is the *Vajracchedika-Sutra*, on transcendental wisdom which is now in the British museum, printed on paper, with a frontispiece, showing the Buddha preaching to the aged Apostle Subhuti who is kneeling on the ground. Buddhism gave birth to printing in India.

Breakthrough in Knowledge of Unconscious

The breakthrough of unconscious discovered by Freud, Adler, and Jung caused European thinkers to realize the import of the Eastern meditation above all of Buddhist meditation. Buddhism had developed a methodical mental discipline in regions that had largely been hidden to European science. Not only did this centuries old discipline lead to a deep knowledge of the unconscious; it also served to exercise voluntary control over the images, moods, passions, and intuitions of the unconscious mind. Thus, a novel, attempt was made to incorporate Eastern meditation into European psychotherapy.

Buddhist forms of meditation have been direct incentives to revive a long-dormant tradition of Christian meditation. Jesuit father H.M. Enomiya Lassalle built a Christian Zen centre in the mountains above Tokyo in 1970. In this and similar ways, long-lost or underdeveloped elements of the Christian tradition of prayer and piety received new inspiration from Buddhism.

Philosopher Max Scheler in his essay "Man in the age of compensation" highlighted the impact of Buddhism when he wrote "Buddhism spread all over Europe by way of a spontaneous appeal, a completely unorganised and adventitious reception".

Buddhist literature and ideas have been accepted in the West in inverse ratio to the degree of instinctive resistance with which East Asian Buddhist countries met Christian missionaries. Clement of Alexandria, the head of the Christian Catechetical school in that city (Hellenistic countries) makes one mention of the name of the Buddha. The life of Buddha is transformed in the legends of Barlaam and Joasaph by John of Damascus. Eastern Christian mysticism bears indirect Buddhist influence on asceticism. Important Buddhist teachings reappear in the guise of Christian parables, as for example, in the story of the man, pursued by a tiger, who saves himself in a well shaft. Islam regards Christians as the religion of Gog and Magog, who are to arise and threaten Christianity at the time of its last persecution.[23] The first European researchers presenting scriptural sources of Buddhism to the West were Turnour and Hodgson.

Political events among the Buddhist population of Asia, the founding of new, independent Buddhist states in Southeast Asia after World War II; the revival of Buddhism in India; the shift of worldwide political interest to Buddhist countries of central Asia hardly ever touched by global politics; the Chinese occupation of Tibet and the Chinese threat to Buddhist Nepal and Bhutan; the Vietnam war and the role of Buddhism in Vietnam, Laos, and Cambodia; and the numerous exhibits of Buddhist art - all these have done much to turn the world's eyes towards Buddhism today.

Ethics of Buddhism

The Buddha reduced things, substances and souls, to forces, movements, functions and processes, and adopted a dynamic conception of reality. Buddha dealt only with the matters of human conduct. The ethics of Buddhism stressed the universal norms (Dharmas) which are constant and apply to everyone. They should not conflict with human nature.

If a man could live a life of the right path, unvarying patience and kindness to all, not binding his hearts to worldly things that rise and, pass away — If one could still the cravings for one's petty self, and endevour only to do good for others — then for him the fountain of evil would vanish — then for him the principle of individuality, that fundamental and worst delusion of mankind, might be overcome. Only then is peace of mind possible.

Toward the natural world the monks of the early Buddhism observed the attitude of non-attachment. Devout Buddhists practice good actions spontaneously. Buddhism holds man superior to gods and demons for Gods are too happy to feel a dislike for conditioned things, and they live much too long to have any appreciation of the teaching of impermanence whereas animals, spirits, demons, and the damned lack sufficient clarity of mind to enable them to overcome their ignorance. Therefore, Buddhas appear as men, and the human state in general is more favourable than any other to the attainment of enlightenment.

Buddhism advises man to let him cultivate towards the whole world - above, below, around, a heart of love unstinted, unmixed, with the sense of differing or opposing interests, let a man maintain this mindfulness all the while he is awake, whether he be standing, walking, sitting, or lying down. This state of heart is the best in the world, (mettanca sabba lokasmin manasam bhavaye aparimanan, uddham adho ca tiriyanca asambadham averam asapattam, tittham caram nisinnova sayano va yavatassa vigatamiddhu etam satim adhitheyya brahmametam viharam idhamahu- Karaniya Metta Sutta).

If there is nothing in the world except bundles of constituent elements instantaneously appearing and perishing all the time, there is nothing which friendliness and compassion could work on — this way of meditation abolish our deep rooted egoism in our own experience.

Because one identifies oneself with more and more living things, the whole world and the individual are intimately and indissolubly linked.

Sabbe tassanti dandassa sabbe bhayabti maccuno attanam upaman katva na haneyya na ghateyya — Do as you would be done unto; neither kill nor cause to kill.[24] The cudgel and the sword he has laid aside, putting away the killings of living beings, and ashamed of roughness, and full of mercy, he dwells compassionate and kind to all creatures that have life.[25]

World Buddhist Leaders and Ambedkar

Ambedkar (1891-1956) who changed the life of six million Untouchable people and transformed Indian social order by the world's best known constitution of India is spectacular by his absence in the list of world leaders.[26] However, the world Buddhist leaders of Asian origin owned him as their own and Thich Nhat Hanh's interbeing and Vietnamese Buddhism agree with social practice of Buddhism envisioned by Ambedkar. Dalai Lama and Ambedkar belonged to the low status of social sections. Sulak Sivraksha of Thailand founded International Network of Engaged Buddhists that recognized Buddhism as social vision as Dr. Ambedkar. Friends of Western Buddhist Order founded by Sangharakshit followed the footprints of Ambedkar in their daily social schedule. In addition there are many internationally reputed scholars like Eleanor Zelliot, Barbara Joshi, Gail Omvedt, Christopher Queen, Tartakhov and so on who upheld the turning the wheel of Law by Ambedkar as the new peaceful revolution.

Dr. Suriyabongse claimed that "The Buddha was the greatest discoverer and scientist of all time." "Buddhism and science are in complete agreement, and the more science one learns, the better one will understand the Buddha Dharma."

G.P. Malalasekere maintained that the Buddha utilized scientific methods for his own purposes but the ultimate mysteries which he discovered were beyond the reach of any purely scientific approach, nevertheless, in spite of the differences in degree and emphasis, modern Buddhists have been agreed in affirming the harmony between Buddhism and Science and in making it a central element in their apologetic within the Buddhist world and in the west.

D.C. Vijayavardhane emphasized the need for the rebirth of Buddhism as a "social religion."

U Ba Swe, a prominent member of the Burmese cabinet during 1950's maintained that Buddhism and Marxism, are the same in concept'; Marxism provided a basis for a social organization which was in accord with Buddhist teaching and Buddhism completed the Marxist program.

Ledi Sayadaw, an eminent monk (1856 - 1923) encouraged meditation in the face of 'Physical wear and tear is excessive, the load on the mind is sometimes unbearable leading to mental disturbances. This is the age of the psychopath and the neurotic'.

Maha-Pandit R. Sankrityayana (1893-1958) married at the age of nine, ran away at 14, studied Sanskrit, Vedic literature, Arabic, Persian, Tibetan, Pali and Buddhism, Russian, Japanese, made visits to Sri Lanka, England and Europe, Japan, and Russia. His associates included Dharmanand Kausambi and Stcherbatsky. In later life he married an untouchable lady named Kamala. He resigned from Communist party and said 'Buddhism has more freedom of thought than it is found in Communism' (as reported by his collegue Anand Kausalyayan).

Hungarian nationalist Sandor Csoma de Koros (1784-1842), canonized as Bodhisattva cSoma-Bosatsu by Japanese Shin sect in Tokyo on February 22nd, 1933 set out on foot and reached Tibet in 1823 after 5 years of traveling.

President Ikeda showed his concern for the eradication of poverty in these words "The poor man will become happy, the sick man well, the fool wise; unhappy life will be transformed into a life of happiness".

Soka Gakkai was very social when he said "To call a life happy and pleasant, when it is without clothing or money, with sickness in the home and debt collectors at the door that is of no use".

The Zen Yamada Mumon presented his feelings at Bodhgaya temple in the form of a Waka Poem reading 'While I peer up at the lofty Stupa, towering into the red dawn, softly my tears fall'.

Chinese Buan-an (Anagarika Sthavira, Ashin Jinarakkhita Thera) was the apostle of Buddhist revival of Indonesia. He propagated Buddhism among Chinese and Indonesians.

The English Bhikkhu Sargharakshita (Lewis Lingwood) and American Buddhist Subhadra (Dallan L. Steding), call for a new kind of monk.[27]

Shosan Suzuki, Zen master taught - you should attain to Buddhahood through your work. There is no work that is not a Buddhist exercise."

Soto Disciple Shosan Suzuki criticised meditation as idle pastime.

Phrakhru Aduu, the chief architect of the Dhamma Training program sees his disciples to be “wayfarers for the help, assistance, advantage, and happiness of the people of the world.

Buddhadasa, abbot of wat Manadhatu in Chaiya, Southern Thailand has adopted expression and propagation of Buddhism in a modern mass-media communication way.

Modern Buddhist scholars honour the Buddha as the first humanist in the world.

Future Prospects and Role of Buddhism

The Zen Scholar Reiho Masunaga formulated the goal of the new Buddhist movement in these terms: “The Buddhism of the future will overcome the differences between man and woman, wise and foolish, high and low, as well as national barriers; it will be grounded, in a philosophy which includes the natural sciences, and in a humanism which liberates and cultivates human nature; and it will be open to all the world.

Ambedkar warned the Asian countries to save their youth from rolling into the communist fold as Buddhism is lasting and superseding method of bringing social and economic revolution peacefully and democratically. He wanted to reorganize the institution of Buddhist Order by reforming traditional Bhikkhu Sangha in accordance with contemporary needs of the world oriented to social service and selfless aim. He felt like preaching Dhamma as gospel of emancipation of mankind. He strived through his Buddha and His Dhamma to have only one body of texts containing essence of all Buddhist literature and truths. He was after pursuit of Buddhism as a thing for daily practice in one’s life and application of the Buddha-word for social and collective purposes.

Socio-Economic Equality Model of Ambedkar

The following pages discuss some salient points on ancient society and state of affairs in those situations and how the norms of life called Panchasheel were challenged and how these were dealt with in just and fraternal model of society put forth by the Buddha and Babasaheb.

Vedic Society

Vedic Society was a tribal society and morally weak though it was a later phase of the primitive tribal warfare stage. In Rigveda there are hymns praying to Indra for helping the supplicants to kill their enemies. For obtaining a son the Veda prescribed a certain *karmakand*, which was criticized by the opponents as false and it referred to the names of beings that suggest that the origin of the Veda came later than them and hence it lost its claim to the eternality. The characters of Yama and Yami disclosed the incestuous appeal of a sister to her brother. Drinking soma, an intoxicating stuff, was the habit of the time as is evident in case of Rama and Sita also. Madhuparka containing beef was later made a welcome drink and hospitality for the guests at the Yajman's. Sacrifices took toll of beings including human, crops, grass, and useful animal products, extorted from the peasants and poor farmers of the day, who were left with tears in their eyes while watching their wealth of crop, vegetables, grass and animals being carried by force for sacrificial purpose. Later Buddhist literature depicted such cruelties in details. Naturally there was revolt among the peasants, women, labourers and masses against such state of affairs going on in the leisuredly class.

Panchasheel

Recluse culture led by Mahavira and Buddha was especially oriented to withstand nasty developments by their strong ethical social values of Ahimsa, Asteya, Satya, Brahmacharya and Aparigraha, on the one hand and abstaining from Panatipata, Adinnadana, Kamesumicchachara, Musavada, and Suramerayamajjapamadatthana, on the other. According to Buddhism the above five precepts are called Panchasheel, which are routine rules of a lay Buddhist. When one lay person desires to observe more principles on certain special occasions of full moon day, Ashtami or new moon day then they follow other rules such as (1) Not to eat food at odd hours, (2) not to use high bed for rest, (3) not to use gold or silver ornaments to decorate one's persona, (4) not to visit dance, singing, drum-beating, or such other plays and displays for public entertainment so that one's time is used for one's own better purpose, (5) not to apply flower-garlands, scents, body lotions, beautification to keep one's body natural, simple and desirably maintained. In place of the third principle of not to indulge in illegal sexual activity one is expected to observe celibacy completely on such occasion and the rest of the rules are as above, viz., not to harm any living things, not to take anything that is not given by others or does not belong to oneself, not to speak untrue, harsh, pointless and slandering words, and not to take any drinks or drugs that tend to cloud the mind.

Eightfold Path of Buddhism

These five principles of social life laid down in Buddhism are called Sheela or morality and they form a part of the fourth noble truth called Madhyama marg or Eightfold path. The other parts of the path are Samadhi and Prajna. But the foundation of purification of mind and society is this morality and it helps to tread the other parts of the path smoothly after that. Right speech is covered under the fourth precept of panchasheel and right action is also covered under not to harm, not to steal, not to indulge in sensual pleasure and not to take intoxicants. Right livelihood means to select a career of life in which no being is put at peril as a result of one's own livelihood and it gives peace of mind and support one's life comfortably.

Right effort, right mindfulness and right concentration comprise the *Samadhi* part of the path. By right effort is meant a fourfold effort of removing and not again entertaining unwholesome thought and to entertain and cultivate wholesome thought. Right mindfulness means being aware of every phenomenon of body, sensation, mind and thought. And right concentration is one-pointedness of fivefold trance of *vitarka, Vichara*, *preeti*, *sukh* and *ekagrata*. This helps man to settle mind peacefully and apply it for higher purposes. The highest aim being to develop insight or wisdom to cut superstition, develop rationality and compassion.

Therefore the final part of the path is *Prajna* which is made of right understanding and right thought. When one recognises reality of change, suffering and unsubstantiality of existence as it is then one understands truth correctly and then aspiring for well-being, welfare and benefit of others and harbouring such wholesome thoughts in one's own mind makes man develop such insight as is useful for alltruistic mission and action.

Thus, morality, meditation and wisdom form the fourth truth called *nirvan* to be lived here and now by every aspirant according to Buddhism. The other truths are suffering and origin of suffering and cessation of suffering. Suffering is accompanied with change. So there is no fear of suffering because though it is painful it is also changing by nature and has no essence like soul or permanence. Origin of suffering is tied up with cessation of suffering. Suffering originates at the source of unsatisfactory conditions of life and suffering ceases at the source of satisfactory conditions of life. Thus, right understanding, meditation and morality create satisfactory social conditions and give rise to peaceful, creative and enlightening social constructions and end of suffering. These four truths are thus one whole truth of *nirvan* of deliverence from pain.

Dr. Ambedkar in his the *Buddha and His Dhamma* beautifully depicted this truth. According to him, he liked Buddhism because it has three things which other religions do not possess, which are equality, compassion and *Prajna*. Equality sets stage for friendship among all beings, compassion makes one man run to help other man in crisis and *prajna* cuts all superstition and brings in the dawn of enlightenment on the face of society.

In fact, inequality is like a palm with five fingers put one above the other in vertical position and Dr. Ambedkar's equality model changed this palm in horizontal position in social context. Justice is the name for trinity of the principles of liberty, equality and fraternity, which Dr. Ambedkar desired for the social, economic, and political way of life called democracy.

Conclusion

Buddhist developments in Asia since 1950 are numerous, unprecedented and effective. Dr. Ambedkar is reckoned as the modern Indian true interpreter of Buddhism, which he reflected in his own writings as well as in the legal and national document of the constitution of India. He aspired the establishment of the New World Order on the governing principle of righteousness on the foundation of challenging realities equally numerous, unprecedented and overwhelming. Humanity torn between self-effacement and worldly disorder needs to be awakened in ever widening circle with infinite compassion, joy in others' happiness, love and tolerance of the Buddha's paradigm.

Recommendations and Suggestions

1. For a Democratic world Government Buddhism in any form can help any member nation of the world to formulate its new policies so as to shape its developed status not only in matter but in mind also.
2. All governments should establish a department of Buddhist affairs and inter-faith dialogues.
3. International community may benefit from Buddhist practices and principles in its secular, political, cultural as well as spiritual life.
4. Buddha Zones may be established at the center of the world, and at the two extremes of the Eastern and Western Hemispheres.
5. With adoption of Buddhism as international communities' way of life a safer, better and happier world order may be established on this globe, where every man, woman and child may find it worth living and loving.

References

1. Baatr Dorj Bazarov, *Buddhists in the USSR*, New Delhi, 1979.
2. Stcherbatsky, *Central Conception of Buddhism.*
3. P.C. Ranasinghe, *Buddha's Explanation of the Universe,* Ceylon, 1957, p. 383.
4. E.W. Hopkins, *The Great Epic of India*, 1920: P.L. Narasu, *ibid.* Winternitz Maurice, *ibid.* Vol. I, Calcutta, 1927.

5. P. Laxmi Narasu, *A Study of Caste*, Madras, 1922, p. 15.
6. W.W. Hunter, *Indian Empire, 1983: Narasu, A Study of Caste.*
7. Walter Elliot, The Untouchables, New Delhi 1948 and the Right Hand and Left Hand Castes (Jivanayakam) Nagercoil 1913, p. 22: *The Balfour Encyclopaedia of India.* Vol. III, p. 422.
8. Hunter, *Indian Empire*, p. 202.
9. Edgar Thurston, *Castes and Tribes of Southern India*, Government Press, Madras, 1909, Vol. VI, p. 103.
10. H. Dharmaratna, *Buddhism in South India*, Ceylon, 1968, p. 6.
11. Conversation with W. Rahula, *World Buddhism*, Ceylon, 1969.
12. Loknath's letter to Babasaheb Ambedkar in 1936.
13. Article of Sankrityayan about Ambedkar in Dharmayuga.
14. Kausalyayan's speech at Morris College, Nagpur in 1984.
15. Baburao Bagul, Dalit Sahitya, Ajache Krantivijnana, Nagpur, 1981.
16. P.N. Agalave, Modernisation in the social life of Buddhist community in Nagpur city, a dissertation submitted for the M.Phil. Degree in Sociology to Nagpur University in 1984, p. 78.
17. B.R. Ambedkar, *The Untouchables*, Mumbai 1948: H.S. Olcott, *The Poor Pariah*, Madras 1893: Nagendranath Bose, *Modern Buddhism and Its Followers in Orissa.*
18. Arnold J. Toynbee, *A Study of History*, Vol. IV, Oxford 1940, p. 230.
19. Leaflet issued by All India Canara Bank, SC and ST Employees Union, Nagpur, 1986.
20. The Sutra of Hui Neng, Shanghai, November 21st, 1929, p. 30.
21. C.D. Naik, *Buddhist Developments in East and West since 1950*, New Delhi, 2005.
22. Vincente Fatone, *The Philosophy of Nagarjuna*, Delhi, 1st ed. 1981, rep. 1991, p. 151.
23. Revelation 19:20, Rev. 20:8.
24. Dhp. 129, 130.

25. DN. II, 49, Vol. L, p. 62.
26. Whitaker's *World of Facts*, New Delhi, 2007, pp. 150-151.
27. The Journal '*World Buddhism*', Colombo, November 1961; Young East, Tokyo, Summer 1962.

* Prof. Dr. C.D. Naik is Head of Dr. Ambedkar Thought and Philosophy and Dr. Ambedkar Chair in Dr. Babasaheb Ambedkar National Institute of Social Sciences, Dr. Ambedkar Nagar, A.B. Road, Mhow (District Indore), Madhya Pradesh-453441, India.

4

Sociological Aspects of Buddhism

C.D. Naik

"U.S. History, Population and Geography", includes sections on civil rights, population and diversity and geography. This collection includes our popular materials on the civil rights movement in the United States, along with sections on the rights of the disabled, women's rights, and Native Americans. Such is the diversity of the said chapter.

From region to region, diversity in the social structure is prominently seen. The north Indian social traditions and customs are markedly different and so those of the eastern India from those of other parts of the country. And here lies the tantalizing element of mystery associated with India.

The gender inequality is a phenomenon causing concern in the Indian society. One social infection is the Indian system of caste-ism adhered to by all racial groups belonging to the Hindu religion fold.

Ambedkar always thought of the role of caste system and its ultimate demise was superior to any other. And as history has shown, he was too optimistic in his predictions. However, with respect to the discourse of nationalism, the chief application of Ambedkar's political thought may be seen today to reside in his reflections on social and distributive justice. The subsequent course of Indian politics was to prove him correct; it was not the nation state but its opposite, - irreconcilable political clashes between religious communities and caste-wars that would become the order of the day.

He brings the heavy artillery of neo-classical theory of marginal utility developed by "Cournot, Gossen, Walras, Menger and Jevons" to counter Russell's position that it is all due to individual preference, and that people will give up things as soon as they have too much of anything.

Reviving Cultural Heritage

Buddha said "We shall be loving men amidst hating people". There is need of loving culture in the spirit of the Moghul prince, Dara Shikoh, who had translated the Upanishads, of Muslim Pathan rulers of Bengal, who arranged translations of the Sanskrit Mahabarata and Ramayana, and Buddhist scholars, who revived literary tastes of our traditions. There is need of being critic in the spirit of Pundit Javali, who not only not treated Rama as God, but called his actions 'foolish'. There is need of reviving cultural heritage of India after a Buddhist emperor of India, Ashoka in the third century BCE, who laid down the oldest rules for conducting debates and disputations with the opponents being 'duly honoured in every way on all occasions', continued by Mughal emperor Akbar in 1590 when the Inquisition was in full swing in Europe.

Poverty and Social Atrocities Inter-relationship

The Indian scenario seems bleak as women and downtrodden men became the victims of dominant interest. During the year 2006-2007 Bindu Devi, Ramffajju Manjhi, Bhola Chowdhary, and Sanoj Paswan in Bihar; Rakesh in Haryana; Asha, Vidhya, Hakim Jatav, and Urmila in Madhya Pradesh; Asha, Bhaiyalal, and Madhukar in Maharashtra; Bant Singh in Punjab; a 14 year old mentally challenged girl in Rajasthan; Anju, Mukesh, and Puja in Uttar Pradesh have been victims of such heinous atrocities. Notwithstanding this ogre under anti-social conditions and political safeguards.

Social atrocities caused economic degradations also. One of the most serious causes of chronic poverty in India is social discrimination between genders, ages, ethnicity, castes and races, and impairments. The composition of chronic poor in India consisted SCs and STs in agricultural and casual labour, unskilled sector, food insecurity and access to assets. Even in developed state such as Gujarat the very poor and poor in rural and urban areas were estimated at 7 and 22, and 12 and 28 percentages of its population in 1993-94. Fortunately the India's 69 most backward districts (2003) did not include those in Gujarat state. India's global position on human development is

0.619, not better than 0.743 (of Sri lanka in 2005) and gender development index is 0.600, worse than 0.525 (of Pakistan in 2005). However poverty ratio in Gujarat in 200-07 was 4, which is below advanced state's percentage of poverty *i.e.,* 9 (2004-05). During the year 2006-07 the percentage of people living below poverty line in India is 30 approximately. Poverty ratio in rural-urban combined during rediscovery of poverty regime in 2007 was 19.3 per cent. Out of 14 million Dalits only 1.1 million (8%) made use of reservation in 1991. Under globalization privatization hit reservation policy, the sole contributor to advancement of the Dalits.

Dalits Literacy Scenario

Dalits have long way to go in literacy and education in comparison to the general literacy in terms of percentage as shown in the following table:

Decade	*Literacy percentage gap between Dalit SC/ST Males and General Males*	*Literacy percentage gap between Dalit Females and General Females*	*Literacy percentage gap between SC STs and Non-SC-STs*
1951-61	12.66	9.66	16.48
1961-71	14.78	12.28	17.09
1971-81	18.24	16.85	12.83
1981-91	18.78	15.53	02.25
1991-01	18.53	NA	NA

This is to be observed that on gender line literacy gap is more than on caste line.

A century earlier the report of the Board of Education of the Bombay Presidency for the year 1850-51 quoted the most liberal and large-hearted administrator, Mr. Elphinstone's observations, that "The missionaries find the lowest classes as the best pupils... they are not only the most despised, but among the least numerous of the great division of society and if your system of education first took root among them, we might find ourselves at the head of a new class superior to the rest in useful knowledge, but hated and despised by the castes to whom their new attainments would always induce to prefer them."

Ambedkar's Gujarat Experience and Struggle

Gujarat is related to the life events of Dr. Ambedkar also. He wrote pentalinguistic dictionary of Pali in Gujrati also alongside Marathi, Hindi, and English. Pali worlds are similar to Gujrati.

A 87 year old Gujrati from Visnagari town in Gujarat namely Babaldas B. Chavda (94389 60548) narrated his life story in the national seminar at our Institute in Mhow on last October 2008 that his surname was Chava but he changed it to Chavda to hide his identity of caste and confuse Indians to wonder whether he belonged to higher Rajput caste or SC to escape contempt of casteist people in India today.

But even 97 years ago the event in Dr. Ambedkar's life was testimony to such occurrence in Indian society. When the graduate Ambedkar was appointed as a Deputy Collector at Visnagar on 17th January 1913 by the Maharaja of Baroda State Sayajirao Gaikawad the local orthodox Hindu of Visnagar boycotted him, knowing that Dr. Ambedkar belonged to the Untouchable or downtrodden caste. He immediately left for Baroda on the same day. He discussed the matter with Maharaja, the latter then appointed him as an Lieutenant of Baroda State. No sooner the fifteen days elapsed than he was compelled to resign his such high official post. The incident is well known. He was looking for rented accommodation and no one let him in the entire city because of his untouchability. So he too showed him off as Parsi to accommodate him in Parsi dharmashala in Vadodara but notwithstanding his disguise he was detected who he was and maltreated by the so-called advanced Parsi community members of the time so much so that seated under the shade of a Banyan tree tears rolled on his cheeks as he was not spared a single day to look for another shelter. This took place in about 1917. How to expect change in society when social consciousness is not prepared to change and religion and philosophy preached *vasudaiva kutumbakam* on paper and acted contrary in practice. All is Brahma in speech but no one at par with Brahman in reality. There was cruel perversion in ethics and philosophy that denied manhood to Indian man and woman.

Pioneers of Buddhist Thinking

In the light of Buddha and Kabeer, Phule and Ranade, the whole India and world are bound to reconsider Ambedkar's slogan for Education, Agitation and Organization of new world order with great men as characters of sincerity courage and intellect.

Indian culture also includes famous names of Buddhist thinkers such as Nagarjuna, Vasubandhu, Dignag, Dharmakirti, Prajnakaragupta and Jnanashri who developed Nyaya philosophy of the Brahmin Pundits Akshapada, Satsyayan, Vachaspati, Udayanacharya, and Gangeshopadhyaya. Parallel to Panini was Chandragomin and to Katyayana and Patanjali were Jayaditya and Jinendrabuddhi and Purushottamadasa and alike hailing from Buddhist tradition during the Nalanda Age.

Lexicographer Amarsinha (Buddhist), Ayurvedic chemistry master Nagarjuna were wellknown. Buddhist Kalidas and Dandi were Ashvaghosha, and Chandragomin and Harsha. The pioneers in Apabhramsha poetry impacting nirguna poetical trend were the 84 siddhas. Places of sculptures such as Sanchi, Bharhut, Gandhar, Mathura and Amravati (Dhanyakataka) are world known; of painting Ajanta, Bagh, Alchi and Sumra are unforgettable; and of architecture Ajanta, Ellora, Karla and Bhaja are on the tongues of indigenous and foreign admirers. Needless to stress that Ambedkar's philosophy had roots in Buddhism and mission to make the Indians realize that the social philosophy affirming a life of liberty, equality, and fraternity cannot be found elsewhere but in Buddha's Bharat alone.

Education as an Unequalizer

According to S.N. Chaudhary the, Professor of Rajiv Gandhi Chair, Barkatullah University, Bhopal "Both the concepts of education and the concept of social justice are time specific and therefore dynamic. Both the Bhagavadita and the

Laws of Manu emphasized that it is better to perform one's own duties poorly, even to die doing so, than to perform another's well. And the proper discharge of the duties of one's station will be rewarded in the next life. This practice was accepted and encouraged by the existing value system and the dominant public opinion. It is said that village was a self sufficient republic and collectiveness was the main binding force which united and sustained self sufficiency of Indian society. Education was an inequalizer and those who possessed it has higher social status and those who could not do so, had lower social status. Eklavya during the Mahabharat and Shambuk during Ramayana period were perceived as violators of normative structure of Vasudaiva kutumbakama. Education during those days was not only informal, privately managed but also directed to isolation and exclusion for vast majority of Indian population especially women, poor and all those who are today termed as marginalized population. During this modern period also education could not include the excluded population. British education created and contributed to the formation of India within Bharat. Education could not contribute to social justice. Seed of inequality was sown by Varna system and its doctrine became big tree".

Education and Perception of industry as the temples of modern India proved to be poles apart. If one organ of society will go downward and the other in the opposite direction the result will be chaos called "cultural lag" by Ogburn. Beteille (1965) presented case of Shripuram village in which the Brahmins (first recipient of modern education) did not even recognize those of other castes in their count of the village's population, and non-Brahmin caste Hindus likewise did not count untouchables (p. 25). This situation is a routined affair in Indian society.

Modern education eroded tribal culture who knew about Mahatma Gandhi but not about their own social reformers from their own locality. They know about modern cough syrup but they did not know about herbs and medicinal plants meant for removal of cough available in their own locality. Education made them unfit to compete for education-based-new occupation. Hence they are neither local nor global. Their bride-price system was replaced by dowry system for educated tribal youth. There is positive correlation between education and dowry.

The new Education system eroded the feeling of collectivity. Their leadership is from upper castes and existence of poverty, illiteracy, hunger deaths, crime against women, poor quality education in rural schools, casteism, regionalism, and corruption are rife in their locality. New change agents are also suffering from the trauma of "deresponsibilization" as their predecessors suffered.

Modernization in India contributed to economic development without social change. Y.B. Damle in one of his articles rightly said that modern education is an effective instrument of occupational and social mobility in individual's life. It is not an effective instrument of social change in Indian society. Technical education is global minus local. Its result in increase of middle class in size and national economy created bottlenecks between regions and communities. Students from marginalized group entering more technical education suffered from cultural conflict and unable to adjust they committed suicides as a Mumbai IIT Dalit student is an example.

Because of coming of globalization gap between state and society is further accelerated. In the past there was collective voice of protest against state led oppression but increasing individualism coupled with lust in favour of consumer culture and modern life style have damaged the voice of collective protest. Hence the situation compels to debate the thought and philosophy of Ambedkar as an argumentative Indian to borrow the phraseology of Professor Amartya Sen and instill hope among the hopeless during this crisis.

5

Buddhist Tantra

C.D. Naik

Buddhist tantrism is a philosophy of cataphatic presentation of Buddhist universal and sublimest spirit underlying the aim of realizing ultimate truth of Buddhahood. It is a developed system of texts woven round the actual meditational experiences of adepts on the ladder of spiritual advancement from ephemeral to ultimate nature of shunyata. Out of a variety of philosophical and literal flavours of bookish and monkish conservatism only Mantryana embraces larger humanity. Sahajayana and Kalachakra systems of Buddhism, despite their occultism, survive even today as the living testimonies of embodiments of true dhamma transcending apophatic expression, mechanical ritualism and conventional modalities. Hermeneutics of tantric literature and culture warrant reinterpretation of lurking suspicions cast on the completeness of Buddhahood hidden in shocking but therapeutic treatments of the world ordinaire for the attainment of tathata extraordinaire by tantric Buddhism. It is to be noted that there is a lot of stuff and stamina within bounds of tanrtic school to elevate all beings including the despised and neglected masses of humanity to dignity and bring the diversified world systems under one integrated unity.

However, there is a detectable and irreconcilable difference within and without the circle of Buddhist schools as to similarities, contradictions and paradoxes in letter and spirit and, aims and objectives.

What is *shakti* in relation to *prajna*, incarnation in relation to emanation, god and atheism, self and *anatta* and sexuality and sexless spirituality and such other enigmatic terms in spiritual and philosophical domain will be the object of highlight and detailed discussion of this study.

PHILOSOPHY OF BUDDHIST TANTRA

Symposium in Memory of Csoma de Koros – March 2009

Let me pay my homage to Alexander Csoma de Koros who was declared as a Bodhisattva in Japan in 1933, who opened the Heart of the West for the teachings of the Buddha. A Hungarian memorial tablet placed on a monument erected by the Asiatic Society of Bengal read: A poor lonely Hungarian, without applause or money but inspired with enthusiasm sought the Hungarian native country but in the end broke down under the burden. Died in Darjeeling in 1842 his first authoritative Tibetan Grammar and Tibetan—English Dictionary was published in 1834. He was born on the 4th April, 1784 in Koros village in Haromszek, in Transylvania, the part of Hungary in poor family, he could get into secondary school when he was 15 years old. His two Tibetan lama-masters were: Sans-rgyas Phun-chogs and Kun-dga-chos-legs. After his is named the International Institute for Buddhology (Budapest), established in 1956 by the Arya-Maitreya-Mandala, as well as the Vietnamese Institute of Buddhology (Vung-tau) which works since 1969. In the same year in Tehran a memorial tablet was placed by the European Centre of the Arya-Maitreya-Mandal to the wall of the "British Institute of Persian Studies" telling Alexander Csoma de Koros (Korosi Csoma Sandor-Hungarian, Phyi-glin-gi-grwa-pa-the foreign pupil: Csoma Bosatsu-Japanese; Bo-tat Csoma-Vietnamese-Bodhisattva Csoma) scholar of Tibetology resided in Tehran from October 14th 1820 to March 1st 1821.

Dr. Ernest Hetenyi in his (Alexander Csoma de Koros, the Hungarian Bodhisattva) narrated, "The opening up of Tibetan studies to Western scholars was largely due to the pioneering works of Alexander Csoma de koros. Starting from his native land on foot in search of the original homes of the Magyars, thought to be somewhere in Central Asia, this remarkable Hungarian eventually reached the western borderlands of Tibet and devoted the rest of his life to the study of Tibetan language and literature.[1]

It is high time that in memory of such a towering genius we have had this 6th International Czoma de Koros Symposium on Hermeneutics of Tantrik Literature and Culture under the Asiatic Society, Kolkata and Department of Indo-Tibetan Studies, Visva-Bharati, Shantiniketan organized by Andrea Loseries, Head of the Department and Convenor, Indo-Tibetan Studies, Visva-Bharati at the Vidyasagar Hall, The Asiatic Society, 1, Park Street, Kolkata-700 016 during 13-15 March 2009.

Disappearance of Buddhist Schools

E. Lamotte in *History of Indian Buddhism*[2] observed the geographical locations of early and later history of Buddhism as under:

In the first two centuries C.E. many sects mingled and coexisted peacefully in the same establishments such as Dharmottariyas and Chaitikas in Junnar, Bhadrayaniyas and Caitikas at Karle; Sarvastivadins and Sammatiyas at Sravasti; Mahasanghikas, Bahusrutiyas, Aparasailas, Mahisasakas and Tamrapaniyas in Nagarjunakonda. In the seventh century C.E. the canopy of the Buddhism all over India was shared by four sects: Sthaviravadi, Mahasanghikas, Sarvastivadins and Sammatiyas. All of them disappeared together with the decline of Buddhism in India after Muslim invasion in the twelveth century C.E.

Philosophy of Tantra

Notwithstanding Schumann's observation that the Tantrayana (2nd C. AD.) has added little to Buddhism philosophically, there is a problem within and without Buddhist schools of thought as to how the Absolute is connected with ordinary.

Mantrayana

Popular *mantrayana* like Tantrayanic schools based on Mahayana monism interprets the essential identity of all beings with the absolute as cosmical interrelatedness. Nothing happens without some effect on everything else. Sadhakas (adepts) can unlock in himself the door to the absolute and thus to liberation by Mantras (syllables or sentences without meaning).

Vajrayana applies the word vajra to enlightenment (insight into emptiness or Buddha nature) and to absolute emptiness itself, which is unshakable, indivisible, impenetrable, incombustible and indestructible.

Liberation method of Vajrayana proceeds from conviction that for each human being the world of phenomena unfolds anew and individually from the absolute as its seed (bija) as he, through his ignorance, imagines two things, namely phenomenal world and deliverance, wherein reality there is only one, namely absolute. Supramundane figures of Vajrayana are subjective apparitions of the Absolute (emptiness, vajra, liberation). Bodhisattva embodies absolute more purely than human teacher who is affected by sansaric accidents.

Andrea Loseries Leick in her *Tibetan Mahayoga Tantra* an ethno-historical study of skulls, bones and relics[3], discussed Tantrik Buddhism as esoteric system of Sadhna, promulgated by a large number of siddhas from about 7th century onward in eastern India where Tantrik teachers gave importance to rituals (kriya), mystical diagrams (mandalas), magical spells (mantras), vows (vratas) and austerities (niyamas) and established identity of phenomenal world (sansara) with highest truth or absolute, a new system that fascinated the popular mind and had tremendous effect on the social and cultural life of that time. Tantrik Buddhism in Tibet has assimilated and integrated successfully many aspects of regional popular beliefs. Tantric teachers, living on cremation grounds, taking outcaste women as their tantric consorts, and using skulls as drinking vessels, expressed with their behaviour their transcendence of conventional action, and reactions against the unreasonable aspects of the caste discrimination of Brahmanism at that time.

Crown of bone (skull) is worn by yogin for the adoration of one's Guru and master and chosen divinity (Hevajra). Errings are worn to indicate one's deafness to evil words spoken against one's guru and vajradhara. The necklace suggests the mantra intoned, the bracelets one's renunciation of harming living beings, the girdle one's service of the Mudra (tantric consort). The body should always be signed with these signs of the Five

Buddhas[4]. The Lord Vajrasattva, the one unity of all that is, explained to Nairatmya (The selfless Lady, name of the consort of Hevajra) the different means used in the reciting of mantras. For petrifying one uses beads of crystal, for subduing one uses red sandalwood, for bewitching one uses wood of the soap-berry-tree, for causing hatred one uses human bone. For driving away one uses bone from a horse, for conjuring forth one uses the bone of a Brahman, for causing rain one uses bone from an elephant, for slaying the bone of a buffalo.

Kapalapa (the man with the skull), listed among the line of 84 siddhas[5] was a man of low caste in the country of Rajapuri, was initiated into the Mandala of Hevajra by Krishnacari after death of his wife and five sons, practiced developing stage (utpannakrama by visualizations, gradual generations of deities and production of mandalas) and perfecting stage (samopannakrama) by recitation of mantra, breath control, manipulation of energies etc., and made six sets of ornaments from the bones of his wife. This skull was the developing stage, the fact that it was empty inside showed him the perfecting stage. In nine years, he achieved the total integration, and attained *siddhi* and spoke to his trainees: I am the Yogin of the skull. The nature of all existing things, I know to be like this skull. So I behave according to my inner power. He became famous as Guru Kapalapa and worked for the benefit of living beings for five hundred years. Then with a circle of six hundred, he went to the realm of the *dakas* (p. 23)[6].

Meditation

Truly such logic as is impotent to make realization of Absolute as emptiness is useless. This is also a demarcating line between the Hindu self and Buddhist non-self as Stcherbatsky and Maurya expressed in the following sentences: Aise tark se kya labh hai jo nirpeksha ka jnana nahi kara sakta[7]. According to A.S. Maurya they do not admit change in consciousness, as Yogacara believed which is an unbridgeable gulf between Buddhism and Vedanta (p. 11). In Vedanta *maya* is developing on Brahman but *avidya* in Vijnanavada is not depending on any eternal substratum (p. 12).

A text on meditation written in Sri Lanka[8] probably about 18th century showed how meditation at the time had degenerated into a ritual of reciting formulas, burning candles, etc. In psychology of Buddhist Meditation W. Rahula (1980: 273) refers to *gata-paccagata-vatta-on* observance of going and returning. According to this, the meditator took a vow never to take a step without being mindful of his kammatthana-topic of meditation. If he walked a few steps without being mindful, then he returned to the point where he forgot his topic of meditation and walked forward again with mindfulness. It is almost as if he went back to pick up his topic of meditation dropped on the ground at that point. This is more of a ritual than a meditation.

Satipatthanasutta-sutta[9] itself at the end without using the term bhikkhu, simply says: "Whosoever (yo hi ko ci) should thus cultivate (practice) these four applications of mindfulness—" One of the two fruits (*phala*) is to be expected of him in this very life: either perfect gnosis (anna, *i.e.* arahantaship) or, failing that, the state of non-returner (anagamita, the third stage among the four supramundane attainments). The commentary (MAI, p. 269) further elaborates that this *yo hi ko ci* (whosoever) means any monk, nun, layman or laywoman.

Ashvaghosha, a contemporary of Kanishka (78-101 A.D) composed *Mahayana Shrodatapadashastra* (Sangraha) tr. in Chinese in 534 and later in 710 A.D. also gave first introduction of Mahayana or Sunyavada. His Vajrasuchi (diamond needle) vajrachedika or vajrasuchikopanishada was translated by B.H. Hudson and edited later by L. Wilkinson in 1839 generalised common human nature of both high and low castes in the following stanza meaning truth, austerity, control and compassion are characteristics of a Brahman and devoid of them one is a low person as Chandal: *satyam Brahma tapo brahma cendriyanigrahah. Sarvabhute daya brahma etad brahmanalakshanam. Satyam nasti tapo nasti nasti cendriyanigraha, sarvabhute daya nasti etaccaṅdala laksanam*[10].

Mandala Unification

As described below in Fig. 1 an adept crosses path of

deliverance from circumference to the centre step by step. Identity with Absolute becomes part of Sadhaka's vital consciousness. In Vajrayana art Absolute and world of phenomena are as male and female figures. Salvation seeker first crosses fire circle (17) of purification then vajra circle (16) of initiation. Lotus circle (15) symbolizes his spiritual rebirth. Seeker now steps in the arched gate (12) where he accounts for his synthesized conduct of life to a Guardian (11) Bodisattva (6-9) take burden off him if remnant of his impending karman blocks his entering. Then the Transcending Buddhas (2-5) welcome him into their paradises. Here he matures to enlightenment, wisdom and realization of Absolute while being undisturbed by wordly influences. Through the unionmystica with Primeval Buddha (1) he finally attains Nirvana (p. 162).

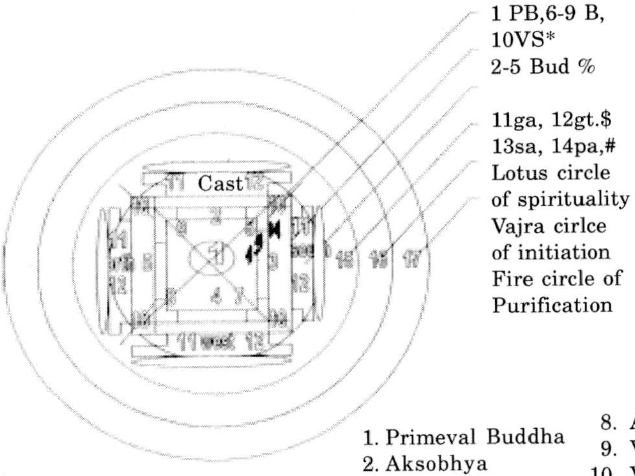

Fig. 1

1. Primeval Buddha
2. Aksobhya
3. Ratnasambhava
4. Amitabha
5. Amoghasiddhi
6. Vagrapani
7. Ratnapani
8. Avalokitesvara
9. Visvapani
10. Vajrabattra, earthly Buddha
11. Guardians
12. Archedgate
13. Sanctum
14. Palace

In Tantrayana cause begins from Primeval Buddha to the circle of fire of purificiation and deliverance starts at the circumference and ends in the centre. Dharmakaya equates Primeval Buddha or Vajrasattva (10), Paradises are located in colours—white, yellow, red and green corresponding to four directions—east, south, west and north presided over by the

Buddhas—Aksobhya (2), Ratnasambhava (3), Amitabha (4) and Amoghasiddhi(5) with Biodhisattvas-Vajrapani (6), Ratnapani (7), Avalokitesvara (8) and Visvapani (9). Earthly Buddhas are represented by (10) while guardians by (11), archgate by (12) and sanctum by (13) and palace by (14), lotus circle of spiritual rebirth by (15), vajra circle of initiation by (16) and fire circle of purification by (17). For deliverance the reverse of this order is represented.

Buddhism in Tibet : History

Tibet had indigenous Phon beliefs. In the 11th C. in the days of Atisha, Buddhism became national religion of Tibet, the first great monarch of which was Sron-btsan-Sgam-Po (born in 617 A.D.), a contemporary of Muhammad, the founder of Islam, Emperor Harsha of Kanauj and Yuan Chwang of China.

Sron-btsan's fifth successor, Khri-Sron-Ide-btsan (755-797 A.D.), inspite of Phon officials' opposition invited Shantarakshita of Nalanda University, but his Paramita and Pratityasamutpada teaching did not work there among the people steeped in primitive sorcery and charlatanism. Padmasambhava, apostle of Tantrism from Urgyen went to Swat valley, Tibetans called him Guru Rimpoche, who defeated Chinese armies as inscribed in Potala, founded Bsam-yas monastery on the model of Udyantapuri in Bihar. Santaraksita translated Buddhist works in Ldandkar palace after his return to Tibet where he died towards the end of 8th C.A.D. After him Chinese monks propagated nihilistic traditions of Buddhist philosophy, then the King invited Kamalasila from Nalanda to defeat that nihilism and in turn was murdered by partisan of Chinese philosopher.

Impressed by Sron-btsan's military prowess Bhrukuti, daughter of Nepali King Amsuvarman and Wen-Ch'eng, daughter of Chinese King Taitsung married Tibetan King Tho-tho-ri's prince, who got from his wives gifts of images of Akshobhya, Maitreya and Sakyamuni.

Ral-pa-chen (816-838), younger son of Khri-Sron-Ide-btsan extended boundaries of his kingdom and the first history of Tibet came to be written under his patronage. His elder brother Glan-dar-ma forced monks to return to the life of laymen on pain of banishment from the country after usurping throne from his younger brother. Monk killed him by dart (841 A.D.).

West Tibet ruler invited Atisa alias Dipankar Srijnana of Vikramasila monastery in Bihar, who set Buddhism of Tibetan there. Direct descendents of first historical ruler of Lhasa (Sron-btsan-sgampo) still live in Ladakh. Atisa (Chandragarbha) was born in Sahor in eastern India in 982 AD near Vikrama-vihara in Bhagalpur. Buddhism came to Tibet at a time when India was entering the age of Tantrism under Jnanapragha. In 1051 AD Atisa wrote commentary on Kalacakra.

Tantra school (secret teaching of Yoga) was founded by Shubhakara who introduced it in China in 720 AD. It absorbed prajna school and four Madhyamika treatises school also in it. It is known as Shingon (Tantrik Buddhism) in Japan founded by Kukai (Kobo Daishi) and built Koya-san monastery. It is based on Mahavairocana-sutra and not degenerated as in India and Tibet. Shingon means sacred formula and its recitation can obtain enlightenment.

Vikramsila was a centre of Tantric learning which gradually spread to Bengal, Assam and Orissa. The first European Sir John Woodroffe under pseudonym Arthur Avalon rehabilitated Hindu Tantras of Kundalini-yoga. Medieval siddhas were propagators of tantric teachings of vajrayana. Tantric Buddhism influenced Hinduism. Philological derivations and iconographical comparisons, valuable though they may be in other respects, are not adequate.

Prajna and Shakti

Bhattacharya in his *Introduction to Buddhist Esoterism* (p. 47) said, "The Buddhist Tantras in outward appearance resemble the Hindu tantras to a marked degree but in reality there is very little similarity between them, either in subject matter or in philosophical doctrines inculcated in them, or in religious principles since the aims and objects of them are widely different from each other.

Buddhist Tantrism is not Shaktism in a creative female aspect of highest God (Shiva) or his emanations. Concept of power forms focus of interest in Hindu tantras against the central idea of prajna (knowledge, wisdom) in Tantric Buddhism. Shakti is maya to the Buddhist, it is the very power that creates illusion, from which only prajna can liberate us—can make us perceive those powers, which have kept us going in the rounds of life and death under their dominion and Buddhist transforms them in fire of knowledge and let them become forces of enlightenment which instead of creating further differentiation, flow in the opposite direction, towards union, towards wholeness, towards completeness.

Hindu tantra Kulacudamani asserted that "United with the sakti be full of power". "From the union of Siva and Shakti the world is created. Buddhist does not want creation and unfoldment of the world, but coming back to the "Uncreated, unformed" state of sunyata from which all creation proceeds, or which is prior to and beyond all creations (if one may put the inexpressible into human language).

In Buddhist tantrayana female represents all embracing passive principle *prajna* or *sunyata* and male represents dynamic active universal means or principle of love and compassion, if both are united then Perfect Buddhahood is attained. Where highest love and deepest knowledge unite completeness is reestablished, and perfect enlightenment is attained. Intellect without feeling, knowledge without love, reason without compassion, female without male lead to pure negation, to rigidity, to spiritual death, to mere vacuity, while feeling without reason, love without knowledge (blind love), compassion without understanding, male without female, lead to confusion and dissolution; but where both are united, where great synthesis of heart and head, feeling and intellect, highest love and deepest knowledge, male and female principles have taken place, completeness is attained unlike sakti as active principle and Siva, as the passive principle, resting in its nature, a pure state of divine consciousness or being in Hindu Tantra (p. 319).

Active element, Upaya and passive prajna in Buddhism are in contrast to active Sakti and passive Siva. Active knower (Buddha) becomes one with passive knowledge (prajna) and result in Mahasukha (highest indescribable happiness). Dyani Buddhas and Bodhisattvas as embodiments of active urge, all embracing love and compassion (upaya) are represented by common and universal symbol (male, sexless) in the embrace of their respective prajna, symbolized by female deity (sexless), embodiment of highest knowledge.

Concept of Sakti has no place in Buddhism. Just as Theravadin would be shocked if the term *anatta* were turned into *atman* to show that Buddhism was only a variation of Brahmanism, even so Tibetan Buddhist would be shocked if the term *prajna* were rendered into *shakti*. One cannot arbitrarily transplant the termini of a theistic system into a non-theistic system.

Concept of Absolute

Early Buddhism regarded Absolute unnecessary. Mahayana saw Absolute in the emptiness of phenomenal entittes; identical in their cores with the Absolute which projected historical Buddha Gautama, unlike a natural man regarded by Theravada.

For Mahayana Nirvana is becoming conscious of one's own absoluteness (liberation) and is a stale of mental aloofness from, but within, the world, Hinayana creates Nirvana, Mahayana is in it (Buddhahood). Hinayana surmounts world Mahayana helps it, the former thinks in terms of natural categories, the latter relinguishes it to experience supernatural. One has rational and the other meta-rational attitude.

Theravadi assumes a moral natural law which rules the process of karman and rebirth neither created by a deity nor is supervised by him and phenomenal world is without substance and in a constant flux and individual existence is sorrowful while the Mahayana considered person as a complex of soulless factors and his sorrowful personality is therefore extinguishable. Theravada deals with the Absolute as essence of all Buddhas and beings.

The immaterial absolute is immanent in the everything including earthly Buddhas (Mahasanghikas), heavenly Buddhas (Sarvastivadins), and Human Buddhas (Theravadins) ranking below dharma-principle or immaterial Absolute common to all Buddhas. Absolute is dharmakaya indestructible, timeless, one essence in and behind all that was is and will be and bearer and object of enlightenment (Buddhahood). It is called dharmata (reality, dharmadhatu (core of reality), tathata (thusness). Bhutatathata (thusness of existence), svabhavakaya (essential-body), sunyata (emptiness) and alayavijnana (base consciousness), Buddhata (Buddhaness), Buddhasvabhava (Buddha nature) and tathagatagarbha (matrix of perfect ones)}. There is only one dharmakaya. There is contrast between Buddhas and phenomenal world. Absolute reality is dharmakaya, besides which there is no other reality.

Absolute qualities are possessed by emptiness - non-originated, independent of conditions, immutable, imperishable and all-comprising, neither ineffective non-being nor destructible being, neither obtainable nor abandonable, but empirical by emptiness of wisdom of all things, a reason for their impermanence unlike transitoriless and sufferingless paradise-emptiness is a sole reality in all appearances, is common to both conditioned and non-conditioned dharmas.

Absolute feeling is evoked by prajnaparamita sutras which affirm in relation to empirical existent and negate in comparison with absolute and convey liberating knowledge of illusory and absolute. Non-conditioned (asamskrita) dharmas too have no self and are essentially empty. So are conditioned dharmas, this illusoriness differentiated sansara from nirvana but not in essence. Absolute is cognized by Bodhisattva in Abhimukhi stage as he realizes emptiness of all beings and things. Wordly beings and Buddhas, are opposites only superficially but in essence are one with Absolute. Liberated one returns home to the motionless ideal centre of the rotating wheel of sansara. Nirvana is permanent (absolute) bliss, freedom and purity.

Hinayana and Mahayana Nirvana

Hinayana Nirvana is pre-mortal and post-mortal, while Mahayana nirvana is active and static. A liberated one in active nirvana is free from karmic bonds, from greed, hatred and delusion and acts without getting reinvolved in sansara by his action. Natural laws no longer bind him; he can appear at will in any place and in any conceivable form.

In static (*pratishthita*) or post-mortal nirvana, the liberated one loses all individuality at the moment of death and so becomes untraceable in pure absolute ineffable. Emptiness is absolute according to Madhyamaka system and Prajnaparamita texts. Dharmas are neither isolated from each other nor in their relation to absolute. For since they are all empty and undifferentiated, and their emptiness is the absolute, there is no difference in essence between dharma phenomena and absolute (nirvana). As the absolute, as being in itself and immutable, it (base consciousness) is often compared with ocean. People who seek nirvana because they are worried by the fear of suffering which arises from the discrimination that sansara is distinct from the absolute, do not know that samsara and nirvana are identical. Attainment of liberation, has as its cause the perception of the absolute (base-consciousness), which is immediate knowledge.

Though the other Buddhist authors like Har Dayal and Dr. Medhankar upheld continuity of Buddhism from Theravada to Mahayana Mr. G.C. Pande suggested discontinuity between Theravada and Mahayana connection. He said, "Mahayana grew up neither as a simple continuation of original Buddhism, nor as a separate sect, nor even as a simple critique or development of Hinayanic ideas; it grew up as a new understanding of tradition with a new spiritual idealism"[11]. This is as if pratityasamutpada doctrine is explained in terms of evolution of Buddhist schools and philosophies across centuries.

However, it is to be noted that Abhidhamma literature is formally included in the Tripitaka though it had been a later incorporation into the canon and its contents vary for each of the schools, and most of its texts were completed during a period of compilation of Pali Canon at Alu-Vihara Council, Ceylon between 250 BCE and 101-77 BCE[12]. From this it may be surmised that what Akira held as continuity of Theravada and Mahayana Buddhism is most likely.

Mahayana Sutras appeared over several centuries, from the first century BCE, to the middle of the first millennium of the common era[13]. Some 600 Mahayana sutras have survived to the present day, either in Sanskrit or in Tibetan and Chinese translation in Nepal, Tibet and Kashmir. To mention a few of them those are 1. Saddharmapundarika (lotus of true law), 2. Avatansaka sutra (flower ornament), 3. Maharatnakuta sutra (treasury of Mahayana Gem). 4. Mahaprajnaparamita sutra (large sutra on perfect wisdom). 5. Astasaharika prajnaparamita (perfect wisdom in eight thousand slokas). 6. Heart sutra. 7.

Lankavatara sutra. 8. Vimalakirtinirdesh (teaching of Vimalakirti), 9. Surangamasamadhisutra, 10. Amitabhavyuha sutra. 11. Sukhavati vyuha sutra (Pure land), and 12. Sutras of Vaipulya corpus (collection of nine sutras).

In Mahayana Bodhisattva doctrine is the cornerstone of philosophical edifice, and is the main model of religious life. Transcendental Bodhisattvas are Avalokiteshvara, Manjusri, Kshitigabha, Mahasthamaprapta and Samantabhadra as most important[14].

Schools of Mahayana Buddhism like Yogacara or Vijnanavada school, Prasangika school, Zen school and Tantric School experienced a profound influence of prajnaparamita teachings[15].

Paramitas

Hirakawa Akira asserted that Kumarajiva, one of the most important early translator of Indian texts into Chinese, interpreted paramita as crossing over to the other shore of enlightenment or nirvana from this shore of births and deaths as is popular in China, Japan, Tibet, Taiwan, Korea and Vietnam[16].

Number of earliest Paramitas of Mahayana was four: *dana, sila, virya,* and *prajna* as per the Sarvastivadins sources found in Kashmir. A list of five Paramitas is mentioned in the Tibetan literature as well as in the sadhammapundarika, a list of seven preferred with seven bhumis but a list of six evolved through selection by addition of kshanti (patience) and dhyana (meditation).

Researches of E. Lamotte showed that on the ancient sculptures at Bharahut stupa (second-first century BCE) identified upto forty Jatakas in which the Bodhisattva in human or animal form, incarnated sometimes as male or female to perform virtuous deeds of sila, kshanti, vigour (virya) and dana.

The number of Paramitas increased from six to ten in relation to ten bhumis instead of seven because of the third or fourth century CF invention of the decimal system of computation in the science of arithmetic. Sangharakshita named four supplementary paramitas as upaya-kausalya, pranidhana, bala and jnana (knowledge)[17].

Bodhisattva in Sudurjaya (unconquerable) and Abhimukhi (face to face) stages pays attention to practice of perfection of meditation and stands face to face with reality of relational aspect of all elements of existence: This being, that becomes: this not becoming, that does not become: from the arising of this, that arises; from the ceasing of this, that ceases[18]. Dharmamegha (clouds of doctrine) fulfills Bodhisattva vows[19].

To fulfil these perfections a Bodhisattva requires a lot more span of time, for example, taking one asankheyya (incalculable) as unit of time he may take four asankheyyas-kalpas, which equal one mahakalpa or hundred thousand great aeons.

Patimokkha sutta was the oldest part of Pali Pitaka and two complete Sanskrit versions of this text have been discovered and published[20]. Number of patimokkha rules (227-311) shown in the texts of various schools is different Chinese Vinaya-Pilaka contained two sections, one devoted to Mahayana and one to Hinayana works. The latter comprises five recensions of whole Vinaya of Sarvastivadins, Mulasarvastivadins, Dharmaguptas, Mahisasakas and Mahasanghikas.

Bhumi (period required for the exercise of a paramita) referred to later development (188 CE) than establishment of six paramitas (100 BCE-100 CE). Were a Bodhisattva to shed one single drop of blood in a thousand births, he would shed more blood than there is water in a thousand oceans in the space of one paramita-bhumi. Were he, in the same number of births, to give a portion of his flesh only the size of the Undu flower, he would, in one bhumi, give more flesh than there is earth in a thousand worlds like our own[22]. Thus one paramitabhumi is incalculable period of time.

There is difference in sequence and number of paramitas. According to Ulrich Pagel the practice of Bodhisattva path proceeds on bodhicitta through benevolence (maitri), karuna, mudita, upeksha, sangrahavastu (means of conversion), dana, friendly speech (priyavadita), benevolent conduct (arthacarya), and pursuit of common aim (samanarthata). But according to Har Dayal practice of 37 bodhipaksya dharmas (4 fields of mindfulness-smritiupasthanam, 4 right efforts-samyaka prahana, 4 bases or wonder-working powers-riddhipads, 5 chief categories (indriyas), 5 powers-balam, 7 factors of enlightenment-bodhyangam and 8 noble eightfold path) is included into the Bodhisattva path.

Vimalkirtinirdesh Sutra and Vimaladattaparipriccha Sutra conjured up eight years old princess named Pure Giving possessing eloquence by cultivating Samadhi of emptiness, realization of non-arising of dharmas. Even operational space of Bodhisattva is expansive to cover dwelling in emancipation beyond comprehension employing their skill in expedient means to teach and convert living beings by appearing in the guise of devil kings (Vimalakirti 81). Upayakausalyaparivarta or the paramita of ingenuity or skill in means sutra spoke of sometimes practice of giving is performed to reinforce all the six perfections. By ingenuity, to master all paramitas by mastering one paramita because things are not different in nature, while practicing Giving, one suppresses stinginess, develops strong sense of renunciation and generosity; donor keeps precepts (morality), gives with impartiality, kindness, compassion, without hate or anger (patience), with full of vigour (virya), his mind becomes tranquil (dhyana), not tied to notion of self, recipient and gift (wisdom). Only the Bodhisattvas who have attained the realization of non-arising of dharmas can be ready to give their throne, wife and children, head, eyes and limbs[23].

Realization or certainty of non-arising of dharmas (*anutpadikadhammakshanti*): according to Madhyamika. means Bodhisattva does not see that the least dharma arises and ceases because that which is unarisen (anutpanna) is unceasing (aniruddha), indestructible (aksaya), unstained (viraja), undifferentiated (abhinna), abodeless (anayatana): calm (santa), free from desire (vitaraga); inactive (anabhisamskrita): wishless (apranihita); homeless (aniketa); that which is homeless does not leave and does not arrive (Surangamasamadhisutra).

Hermeneuties

It is a science of resolving paradoxes and intriguing esoterism to meaningful messages and practices in accordance with philosophies of all schools of Buddhist tradition, whether sautrantik, vaibhashika yogachara or madhyamika. One of the hermeneutical tests laid in the Vinaya of Theravadi tradition spoke about democratic way of settling dispute or controversy by way of jnapti, anusravana and dharana, *i.e.* holding reading of the bill presented in the assembly three times and confirming the same by acceptance of the present members by remaining in silence.

Dr. Ambedkar (1891-1956) revived Buddhism among the despised masses of the society, drafted constitution of India enforced since 1950, formulated on the foundation of Buddhist Vinaya, and suggested two yardsticks of determining Buddha Word. He said that the Buddha's statement ought to be rational and logical in the first place, and Buddha's word is aimed at man's welfare. So any other words and logic and philosophies not serving these two tests cannot be held as Buddha vacana, asserted Dr. Ambedkar in his last treatise[24].

Six methodologies of hermeneutics (1) Yogacara, (2) Sakara (3) Nirakara, (4) Madhyamika, (5) Sautrantic and (6) Prasangika. Any interpretation must belong to, or be in conformity with one of these. They are not teaching the same thing found in the Hindu texts.

Independent origination itself is unproduced (anutpada). Dharmakaya is emptiness. Rupakaya (sambhogakaya and nirmanakaya) is independent origination. Nirmanakayas are infinite emanated personalities (not incarnated) from causes and conditions due to innate capacity (sambhogakaya) of Dharmakaya. Enlightenment means realizing all the three kayas.

DzogChen or Mahamudra is free from not only attachment or aversion but also from the choice-less state. Sakya Pandit of Sakya lineage declared indifferent or choiceless state of awareness is a sure way to be reborn as an animal. Nyingma and Kargyu schools, based in the vaste lineage (vaipulya) of Asanga interpreted tathagatagarbha as being present in full form and recommended practice to gradually unveil its covering veil. Sakyapas of profound tradition of Nagarjuna interpreted it only in seed form and recommended practice to develop it into its full form.

Hindu unconditioned is atman, but DzogChan of Nyingma, Mahamudra of Kargyu, Lamdre of Sakya, and unconditioned of profound and vast tradition is anatma, tathagatagarbha, Samantabhadra, emptiness, nisvabhavata. Conditioning is conceptual (klesh) and emotional (jneya). Ignorance is cognitive, miscognition and more conditioning. Sugatagarbha exists epistemologically. Brahman exists ontologically (kutastha). Buddhanature is mode of abiding, is not-abindingness (asthita). Brahman is abiding (sthita).

Sunyata is phenomenon. Brahman is separate entity from phenomenon. Sunyata is not a thing Brahman is something. Sunyata is existing interdependently Brahman is existing independently. Brahman is inherent (svabhavasiddha), Sunyata is non-inherent (nisvabhavata). Brahman is svalaksana siddha, sunyata is laksanata. Brahman is ultimate existence (parmartha) sunyata is unfindability of such parmartha satt anywhere.

Ilevajra Tantra recommended study of Vaibhasika, Sautrantika, Yogacara and Madhyamika for initiation. Theravada, Mahayana and Vajrayana held meditation progresses from wisdom gained through hearing to wisdom gained through contemplation, to wisdom gained through meditation (srutamayi, cintanamayi, bhavanamayi).

Valid lineage masters teach according to historically accepted Buddhist hermeneutics and do not give their own personal self-contradictory interpretations. Asanga, Vasubandhu, Nagarjuna, Chandrakirti, Shantidev, and Atisha believed that it is necessary to acquire correct philosophies to be able to truly practice Buddhist meditation properly.

According to Nathan Katz there are text-based hermeneutics and adept-based hermeneutics. Jaques Derrida, the most influential of nouvelles critiques, developed an understanding of languages as laden with precritical ontological commitments which lead the reader into the philosophic traps of seeking an intentionality, an author, and a systematic coherence which becloud rather than elucidate the reading of the text.

In the Lankavatara the Buddha says (135-136) that there are yanas only so long as the mind (citta) remains moving (pravartaka) in sansara, but, when it comes to know itself, all thought of a yana ceases. Steinkellner (453) discussed the Guhyasamaja's discerning of four types of meaning in texts: the literal (aksarartha), common (samastanga), hidden or pregnant (garbhi) and ultimate meaning (kolika).

Omnicient Buddha is less a master of philosophy than a physician for universal suffering; he imparted to each the teaching that he needed- Lamotte. Hermeneutics of adept rather than the text is understood the basis for the entire lam rim genre of Tibetan literature Prof. Wayman. Wisdom in Tantric Buddhism is often symbolized by mother and method by father — Tsong Kha Pa.

The dharmakaya promulgates that which is ineffable, the sambhogakaya, the self-existing letters (Om Mani Padme Hum); and the nirmanakaya, the innumerable sutras and tantras- Prof. Guenther. According to Tantric Exegesis a fourth kaya Svabhavikaya indicates not a fourth but the interpenetration of the three. Vajrayana is understood as simply a short way to doing what takes aeons according to the paramitayana traditions.

Joining method and wisdom non-dualistically is the chief meaning of method and wisdom set forth in Mantra vehicle. Hermeneutic was rather characteristic of later Buddhism. Tsong Kha Pa. Current interest in hemeneutics is focused primarily on more modern theories of interpretation, a tradition beginning with the work of Friedrich Schleiermacher and continuing into the twentieth century with Bultmann, Heidegger, Gadamer, and Ricoeur. Prof. David Tracy was a leading formulator of modern hermeneutical theory.

Nettiprakarana and Petkopadesa formed the two most explicit treatises on textual interpretation for Theravada. Prajnaparamita literature and Madhyamika school held that one could change worldly merits into supramundane enlightenment because all things, including karma and its effect, are empty of their own being. Yogacarins follow Sandhinirmocana, and asset 1st and 2nd wheels of teaching as interpretable (neyartha) and 3rd wheel definitive (nitartha). Svatantrikas held Ist wheel interpretable and 2nd and 3rd wheels both interpretable and definitive. Prasangikas find first and third wheels interpretable and 2nd wheel definitive. Yogacarins and Svatatrika hermeneutic stood behind text to establish intention of Buddha in terms of his audience. Prasangikas held more universal and disinterested approach in judgement of time, place, audience, and mode of expression of a text.

Buddhist tradition did not lack in hermeneutical sophistication – Luis O.G'omez. In the Mahaparinirvana sutra the Buddha described the Tathagata as a permanent, blissful self, very pure, and without marks, thereby converting many Thairthikas to the dharma, but says later that in reality there is no self, thereby employing the principle of middle way to eschew both eternalist and nihilist views. Teaching of Tathagatagarbha is definitive because it refers in the end to sunyata.

Role of philosophy in Buddhist thought is essentially hermeneutical-Tsong Kha Pa. Hermeneutics has the double function of reconciling apparent contradictions between the Buddha's diverse statements while keeping alive the methodologies of interpretation by which one can extract the practical essence of each particular statement, Guhyasamaja tradition is deeply involved in hermeneutical strategies-Vajra Nagarjuaua and Vajra Chandrakirti. King of Tantras-Guhyasamaja is a jewel casket of all sutras, has its meaning sealed within by means of seven ornaments, which themselves are subdivided into twenty eight principles. Tantric refinement of Buddhist hermeneutics comletes the tradition in such a way as to make comparison with modern disciplines of hermencutics possible and fruitful- Prof. Thurman.

In general Chinese hermeneutical structure there is a progression from naive cataphasis to radical apophasis to perfected cataphasis. Tantra briefly passed through China and was established as Shingon school in Japan. Kukai's Shingon theory analyses language on three levels: cosmic, micro-cosmic and macrocosmic, the last is evaluated according to how well it leads the listener to an awareness of cosmic and microcosmic-Prof. Kasulis.

Three types of hermeneutics in Buddhist thought are (1) classifying system (2) principles and strategies and (3) theory of understanding- Prof. Alan Sponberg. Hermeneutieal enterprise plays an important role in soteriology in the sense that hermeneutics, as a theory of understanding, provides a technique for divesting oneself of illusion.

Corresponding to the four alternative of being, non-being, both, and neither, the Hinayana sutras teach being, the early Mahayanika teaches non-being, the Tathagatagarbha teaches both, and Lotus sutra (perfect teaching) teaches neither. Buddhalogy can look forward to the discovery of resources that will contribute to the hermeneutical enterprise as a whole- Prof. Tracy.

The whole universe in all its dimensions is entailed in every moment of metaphysics. The Tiantai position insisted that some evil and ignorance existed even in Buddha nature after Mencius and later discovery found that non-Confucian thinkers unanimously embraced Mencius' view of the original goodness of human nature[25].

Creator God

Even the concept and symbol of Adibuddha in later Buddhist tantra has nothing to do with god creator. Adibuddha represents universality, timelessness and completeness of enlightened mind. It is the unfolding of man's true nature.

Adibuddha as universe or man is inadequate verbalization of an all-comprehensive experience. Adibuddha is assuredly not a god who plays dice with the world in order to pass away his time, nor monotheism superimposed on atheist Buddhism. Such notions are errors of professional semanticists. Buddhism has no taste for theorization. It attempts to delve into the secret depths of our inmost being and to make the hidden light shine forth brilliantly.

Paradoxes

Confusion of Buddhist tantrism with shaktism prevented clear understanding of Vajrayana and its symbolism, iconography as well as in literature, especially that of the siddhas who clothed the highest in the form of the lowest, the most sacred in the form of the most ordinary, the transcendent in the form of the most earthly, and deepest knowledge in the form of the most grotesque paradoxes - a shock therapy necessary on account of over-intellectualisation of religious and philosophical life of those times.

Just as Buddha rebelled against narrow dogmatism of a privileged priestly class, so did the siddhas rebel against self-complacency of a sheltered monastic existence that had lost contact with the realities of life. Their language was as unconventional as their lives, and those who look their words literally were either misled into striving after magic powers and worldly happiness or were repelled by what appeared to them to be blasphemy as crude erotic cults of popular tantrism. From these degenerated forms inferences about spiritual attitude of Buddhist tantras cannot be correctly drawn.

Practices

Buddhist tantras cannot be fathomed theoretically, *i.e.*, through comparisons or the study of ancient literature, but only through practical experiences or actual contact with the still existing tantric traditions and their contemplative methods, as practiced in Tibet and Mangolia, as well as in certain schools of Japan, like the Shingon and the Tendai.

In degenerated form of tantrism the female Bodhisattvas figuring in the mandalas, like prajnaparamita and cundi, are sexless beings from whom, quite in accordance with ancient tradition, association of a sexual nature are strictly excluded.

Bengal, Nepal and Tibet schools emphasize polarity of male and female principles[26] as an idea of world-creating eroticism of shaktism and represented sexless female symbols prajna (wisdom), vidya (knowledge), or mudra (spiritual attitude of unification, realization of shunyata). They represented sexless female symbols.

Popularity of male and female principles recognized in Vajrayana Tantra also is raised upon a plane which is as far away from sphere of mere sexuality as mathematical juxtaposition of positive and negative signs valid in both realms of irrational values and rational or concrete concepts.

Male and female dhyani Buddhas and Bodhisattvas' yuganaddha (union) are indissolubly associated with highest spiritual reality in the process of enlightenment completely ignoring realm of physical sexuality.

Figural representations of these symbols are not looked upon as portraying human beings, but as embodying experiences and visions of meditation in which there is only super-individual polarity ruling all mental and physical activities transcended only in ultimate state of integration, in realization of shunyata (Mahamudra)—the great attitude or great symbol—one, the most important systems of meditation in Tibet.

Advayavajra called Mahamudra the eternal female principle, she is not nihsvabhava, she is free from vails covering cognizable object, she shines forth like serene sky at noon during autumn, is support of all success, is identity of sansara and nirvana, her body is compassion unrestricted, is unique in Great Bliss (Mahasukhaikarupa)[27].

Anangavajra said that all women should be enjoyed by the sadhaka in order to experience the Mahamudra meant higher form of love cannot be restricted to a single object and see all female qualities as prajna-paramita or transcendental wisdom or divine mother[28].

Sadhaka who has sexual intercourse with his mother, his sister, his daughter, and his sister's daughter, will easily succeed in his striving for ultimate goal (tatva-yoga). This is a very paradoxical statement found in Anangavajra, Prajnopaya-vinischaya siddhi, and also in Guhya Samaja Tantra, which means prajna symbolized by female principle in association with active love of male (sadhaka) principle can become as complete as ultimate goal[29].

Similarly in Dhammapada Verse nos. 294 and 295 we find mataram pitaram hantva rajano dveca khattiye rattham sanucaram hantva anigho yati brahmano and mataram pitaram hantva rajano dveca sotthiye veyyagghapancamam hantva anigho yati brahmano[30]. In this context it may be remembered that mother stands for craving (tanha), father for ego (asmimana), twin warrior kings for twin erroneous views of eternalism (sassata) and annihilationism (uccheda), kingdom (rattha) for five grasping groups of existence, and inhabitants (anucara) for attachment, and Brahman for a liberated monk or a bhikkhu, anigho for sinlessness, tiger (veyyaggha) for five veils—lust (kamachanda), anger (vyapada), restlessness (uddhacca-kukkuccha), laziness (thinamiddha) and wrong view (miccha ditthi).

Kingdom also stands for twelve spheres of consciousness (dvadasaayatanani)-eye-form, ear-sound, nose-odour, tongue-taste: body-tactile; and mind-thought.

Thus, having pondered over the heart of Buddhist philosophy it can easily be surmised that Ideals of sense-control and renunciation cannot teach incest and licentiousness of tantrism, nor matricide and patricide of Theravada. Yoga terminology condoned that.

In Anangavajra paradox "All women in the world" signifies all the elements representing the world including both female and male principles. Four of the female principles form a special group, representing the vital forces (Prana) of the Great elements (Mahabhuta) earth, water, fire, air and their corresponding psychic centres (cakra) or planes of consciousness within human body. In each one of them union of male and female principles must take place, before the fifth and highest stage is reached.

Intercourse with mother (earth), sister (water), fire (daughter) and sister's daughter (air) means fundamental qualities of Mahabhutas. Seek union within oneself, said Tilopa in his famous six Doctrines on which is based Kargyudpa school method of yoga, which was practiced by Milarepa also.

The vital force of the five aggregates (skandha) in its real nature, pertaineth to the masculine aspect of the nerve (ida-nadi). The vital force of the five elements (dhatu) in its real nature, pertaineth to the feminine aspect of the Buddha principle manifesting through the right psychic nerve (pingala-nadi). As the vital force with these two aspects of it in union, descended into the median nerve (sushumna) gradually there cometh the realization and one attains the transcendental boon of the great symbol (mahamudra)—the union of male and female principles (as upaya and prajna) in the highest state of Buddhahood[31].

See the relationship of body and mind, of physical and spiritual interaction in universal perspective, overcoming "I" and "mine" and whole structure of egocentric feelings, opinions, and prejudices which produce illusion of our separate individuality and rise into the sphere of Buddhahood.

Thus, legitimate heirs of Vijnanavadins and Yogacarins (Asanga) and logical and ultimate consequence of law of dependent origination are Buddhist tantras. In four noble truths and eightfold path there is nothing exclusively Buddhistic, they are generalizations of framework of Buddha's teachings. Fact of suffering and overcoming it by extinction of desire based on egoism was common ground in Indian religious thought and in other religions as well.

Goal and Way Out

As far as goal and way out of suffering is concerned Buddhism as pointed out by Hans Wolfgang Schumann[32] is as shown in the table below:

S.N.	*Goal*	*Way out*	*Details of School / Branch / founder and place of origin*
1.	Nibbana	Removal of cause	Arhatayana: {A} Original, India 563-483 BC: Pali
			Arhatayana; {B} Theravada, India 4CBC Ceylon, Burma, Thailand, Laos, Cambodia, Vietnam, Pali
			Arhatayana: {C} Mahasanghika, India 4CBC, separate schools
			Arhatayana: {D} Puggalavada, India 3CBC,
			Arhatayana: {E} Sarvastivada, India 2 CBC, Vasubandhu 5th CBC
2.	"	Realization of emptiness of persons and things by wisdom	Mahayana: {A} Wisdom School, India, 1st CBC
			Mahayana: {B} Madhyamika, India, 2nd CAD, Nagarjuna

S.N.	*Goal*	*Way out*	*Details of School/Branch/ founder and place of origin*
		Relief from unwholesome karma through Bodhisattva	Mahayana: {C} Bodhisattva School, India, 1st CAD
		Obtain rebirth in paradise through Amitabha Buddha	Mahayana: {D} Faith, Japan, Honen-Shonin, 1133-1212, Shinran Shonin, 1173-1265
		Mind only	Mahayana: {E} Yogacara, India, 3/4th CAD, Maitreyanatha; 4/5th CAD Asanga, Vasubandhu, India, Tibet, Nepal, Sikkim, Bhutan, China, Japan
		Mind only	Mahayana: {F} Zen, 6CAD, Bodhidharma, China, Vietnam, Korea, Japan
3.	,,	Mantra and Mudra enabling to identify individual consciousness with base consciousness	Tantrayana: {A} Mantrayana, India, Tibet, Sikkim, Bhutan, Mongolia, China, Korea and Japan
		Identifying oneself with Bodhisattva	Tantrayana: {B} Vajrayana, 8th CAD, India, Tibet, Sikkim, Bhutan, Mongolia, China, Korea
		Twinning of sansara and nirvana	Tantrayana: {C} Vajrayana, 3rd CAD, India, Tibet, Sikkim, Bhutan, Mongolia
		Union with Kalacakra Buddha	Tantrayana: {D} Kalacakrayana, 10th CAD. India, Tibet, Sikkim, Bhutan, Mongolia.

Although goal is common to all branches of Buddhist schools their methods vary from (1) removal of cause through emptiness to (2) identity based on the philosophy of consciousness only. Suffering was viewed during pre-Buddha period as caused, uncaused through eternal or non-eternal principles. Buddha assumed suffering and its cause with dynamic nature. Post-Buddha development conceived and continued this changing suffering for one and all through philosophies of Monism and

Absolute consciousness. From sixth century B.C. to 10th century A.D. almost for 16 centuries sixteen schools of Buddhism originating from India became recognized even outside.

Uniqueness of Buddhism

In what Buddhism distinguishes itself from all other religions, in what its uniqueness consists, is dependent origination (pratitya samutpada). It is more than a number of rigidly fixed sequences of causes and effects, it is the idea that nothing exists in itself or by itself as a separate unit, either in time or in space, but is dependent on a variety of conditions and related to everything else in the world. So there is no independent existence, non-existence, being or not-being in life.

Sanyutta-nikaya, II, 17 is addressed to Kaccana by Buddha declared addiction of dualism in the world, it is and it is not-which are dependent constructions of their opposites-anatman. Ashwajit summed up Buddha's teaching in a single sentence in its most fundamental aspect *pratityasamutpada.* When the wheel of law was set again by Nagarjuna his Mulamadhyamika-karika declared:

> *Anirodham anutpadam anucchedam ashasvatam, anekartham ananartham anagamam anirgamam, yah partitya samutpadam prapancopashamam shivam, deshyamasa sambuddhastani vande vadatam varam i.e.* without destruction and without origination, without being cut off and without being eternal, neither being one thing, nor different thing, neither coming nor going, he who can thus teach the dependent origination, the blissful coming to rest of all illusory unfoldment, before Him, the Enlightened One, the best of all teachers, I reverently bow down.

Prapanca (illusory unfoldment or differentiation or conceptually differentiated reality) is maya or illusion caused by blind world-creating-power (shakti)-leading deeper and deeper into realms of becoming, of birth and death, of matter and differentiation, unless countered or reversed by prajna or wisdom born of profound insights into the nature of world, ourselves and realization of enlightenment within our own mind. Inner and outer worlds are same, threads of all forces and events, of all forms of consciousness and all objects are woven into one.

Tantra means weaving, interwovenness of things and actions, interdependence of all that exists, continuity in interaction of cause and effect, in traditional development, which like a thread weaves its way through the fabric of history and of individual lives. Tantra means tradition, spiritual continuity or succession. Yantra, mantra and mudra; visible, audible and touchable unite the powers of mind (citta), speech (vak) and body (kaya) in order to realize the final state of completeness and enlightenment. Principles precede literature. So Hindu tantra connoting literature on tantra follows tantra principles represented by Buddhist tantra works.

Guru Gampopa applied the word tantra to represent a philosophy comprehensive enough to embrace the whole of knowledge, a system of meditation which will produce the power of concentrating the mind upon anything whatsoever, and an art of living which will enable one to utilize each activity of body, speech, and mind as an aid on the path of liberation[33].

Cittamatra is different from alayavijnana which is like flowing water, a constantly changing stream of consciousness.

Soteriologically pudgala-nairatmya (non-existence of self) and dharma-nairatma (non-existence of things of the world) are realized through removal of passion (kleshavarana) and removal of veil that covers true knowledge (jneyavarana) respectively for attainment of emancipation.

Parikalpita (illusory), paratantra (empirical) and parinispanna (absolute) are three degrees of knowledge. Illusion is false attribution of imaginary idea to an object, it exists only in one's imagination and not outside. Empirical knowledge is about an object, this is relative knowledge and it serves practical purposes of life. Absolute knowledge is highest truth (tathata). Illusory and empirical degrees of knowledge correspond to relative truth (samvritti-satya) of the Madhyamika system; which has two varieties of knowledge.

Yogacara (Asanga) attributed qualities to reality-pure consciousness (vijnanamatra. Vasubandhu 4th C.A.D.) while Madhyamika believed in shunyata.

Contemporary Value of Buddhism

Despite all the knowledge which we possess and can master only with the help of machines, we cannot cope with ageing, death and transitoriness. Our knowledge and actions move in the realm of the finite. We cannot afford to disregard the infinite as - it can be divined in the Teaching of a compassionate sage.

The wheel of the Dharma continues to turn, somewhat creakingly, under the burden of our extrovert industrial civilization and the impact of materialist doctrines, but it turns, will it come to a standstill?

Future

The style of our life has changed in the last decades, but the hearts of men have remained the same. No less strong than the urge for prosperity, joy and progress, is the longing for a glance beyond into the realm of the timeless. The heavier the present weighs on man, the more he listens to the voice of silence. And hence there will always be at least a few who hear and understand the word of the Buddha: about the way towards the termination of suffering.

References

1. Internet surfing dated 9th March 2009.
2. E. Lamotte in *History of Indian Buddhism: From the Origin to the Shakya* Era. tr. Sara Webb-Boin, 1988:347.
3. Andrea Loseries Leick, *Tibetan Mahayoga Tantra an ethno-historical study of skulls, bones and relics*, B.R. Publishing Corporation Delhi 2008: 20.33.158.
4. Snellgrove 1959:II, ch X: 118.
5. Robinson 1979:222ff.
6. Nagarjuna, Uhapoha. Shantibhikshushastri. Lucknow 1955:55.
7. Dr. Ram Kumar Ram tr. F.T. Scherbatsky, *Boudhha Nyaya*, Varanasi, 1969 p. 647.
8. Yogavacara's Manual ed. T.W.W. Rhys Davids, London 1896.
9. D II. p. 314; MI, p. 62/Rahul p. 279.
10. Vajrasuchi, Shloka 22-27.
11. G.C. Pande, *Studies in Mahayana, India*, Central Institute of Higher Tibetan Studies, Sarnath, Varanasi, 1933:24.

12. Hirakawa Akira, *A History of Indian Buddhism, From Sakyamuni to Early Mahayana, tr. Paul Groner*, rep. Delhi, Motilal Banarasidass, 1998:28.
13. Andrew Skilton, *A Concise History of Buddhism*, Windhorse Publication, Birmingham 1994:99.
14. *Shambala Dictionary of Buddhism and Zen*: 24-25.
15. Edward Conze, *Prajnaparamita Literature*, Delhi 2000: 13.
16. William Edward Soothill and Lewis Hodous, *A Dictionary of Chinese Buddhist Terms*, D.T. Suzuki, Studies in the Lankavatara Sutra, Taipei 1991:366; Thich Nhat Hanh, The Heart of the Buddha's Teaching, N.Y. 1988: 192.
17. Sangharakshita, *A Survey of Buddhism*, Pune 1996: 486-87.
18. Nanamoli and Bodhi, M. 655, Mass, 1995.
19. Avatamsaka sutra (the flower ornament scripture). Maharatnakuta sutra (treasury of Mahayana sutra) Garma CC Chang.
20. P.V. Bapat, 2500 *Years of Buddhism*, 1997:144.
21. Pachow W., *Comparative Study of Pratimoksha*, Delhi, 2000: 11-13.
22. R. Spence Hardy, R. A. *Manual of Buddhism in its Modern Development*, New Delhi. Aryan Book International, 1996: 103.
23. Garma C.C. Chang, tr. On the Paramita of ingenuity, *A Treasury of Mahayana, Sutra*, Delhi 2002:428-9: 265.
24. Dr. B.R. Ambedkar, *The Buddha and His Dhamma*, Peoples' Education Society, Mumbai, 1957, rep. 1997, pp. 350-351.
25. H.V. Guenther, Yuganadha. *The Tantrik View of Life*, Chaukhamba Sanskrit Series, Benaras 1952: 187.
26. H.V. Glasenapp, Die Entstehung des Vajrayana, Zeitschr.d.deutch morgenland. Gesellschaft, Vol. 90, 560, Leipzig, 1936.
27. Advayavajra caturmudra, yuganaddha, p. 34.
28. In prajnopaya-vinischaya-siddhi in two Vajrayana works, Gaikwad Oriental Series, No. XLIV, p. 22.
29. Anangavajra, Prajnopaya-vinischaya siddhi, v. 25, Yuganaddha, p. 106 and also in Guhya Samaja Tantra.
30. Bhadant Anand Kausalyayan, Dhammapada. Pakinnavaggo canto 21, Verses nos. 294 and 295, Nagpur 1938:70-71.

31. W.V. Evans-Wentz, Tibetan Yoga and Secret Doctrines, p. 200ff.
32. Hans Wolfgang Schumann, *Buddhism, An Outline of its Teachings and Schools.* USA 1973:179.
33. Guru Gampopa, The Twelve Indispensable Things, cf. Evans-Wentz, *Tibetan Yoga and Secret Doctrines*, p. 79.

Other Sources :

1. Lusthaus, Dan (1998), Buddhist Philosophy, Chinese, in E. Craig ed. Routledge *Encyclopaedia of Philosophy*, London, Routledge, retrieved May 25, 2005, from http://www.rep.routledge.com/article
2. Buddhist hermeneutics: A Conference report Donald S. Lopez, Jr., Philosophy, East and West, Vol. 37, no. 1 (Jan 1987) pp. 71-83, copyright by University of Hawaii Press.
3. Prasanga and Deconstruction: Tibetan hermeneutics and the Yana controversy, by Nathan Katz, Philosophy East and West, Volume 34, no. 2, April 1984, p. 185-204, © by the University of Hawai Press.

6

Buddhist Marriage and Method

C.D. Naik

Laws of Manu

For marriage you hear people fuss about keeping 7 or 8 gotras on the sides of both bride and bridegroom. This very custom seems to have been adopted from Hindus and is traced back to as old a source as the book of Laws of Manu. The Laws of Manu, chapter iii, page 75, an English version by Buhler state as:–

A damsel who is not a Saphind on the mother's side, nor belongs to the same family on the father's side, is recommended to twice born men for wedlock and conjugal union. Gotra means blood-relationship between the families of bride and bridegroom and is traceable. But these Gotras are different, for different castes. In the case of Brahmanas, intermarriages between families descended from the same Rishi and in the case of other Aryans, between families bearing the same name, and thus inter-marriages with the daughter of a paternal aunt or with the paternal grandfather's sister's descendents, are forbidden.

Manusmriti further forbids as follows:–

A prudent man should not marry a maiden who has no brother,–nor one whose father is not known, through fear lest in the former case she be made an appointed daughter and in the latter lest he should commit sin.

Twice-born men are forbidden to marry a low caste woman. For Shudras only Asura marriage rite is sanctioned. The son of twice born by a Shudra wife receives no inheritance.

He who weds a Shudra woman becomes an outcaste. On marrying a man of a higher caste a Kshatriya bride must take hold of an arrow, a Vaishya bride of a goad, and a Shudra female of the hem of the bridegroom's garment.

A Brahmana who takes a Shudra wife will sink into hell; if he begets a child by her, he will lose a rank of a Brahman.

Out of the eight marriage rites, viz., (1) the rite of Brahma, (2) that of Daiva, (3) of Rishis, (4) that of Prajapati (5) that of the Asuras, (6) of the Gandharvas, (7) of the Rakshasas, and (8) that of the Pishachas, the first six are lawful for a Brahmana, the four last of Kshatriya. Asura marriage is approved for a Vaishya and a Shudra.

It is declared that a Shudra woman alone can be the wife of a Shudra, she and one of his own caste the wives of a Vaishya, those two and one of the over caste the wives of a Kshatriya and those three and one of his own caste the wives of a Brahmana.

The gift of a daughter, after decking her with costly garments and honoring her by presents of jewels to a man learned in the Veda and of good conduct, is called the *Brahma* rite.

The gift of a daughter who has been decked with ornaments, to a priest who duly officiates at a sacrifice, during the course of its performance they call the *Daiva* rite.

When the father gives away his daughter according to the rule after receiving from the bridegroom, for the fulfillment of the sacred law, a cow and bull, or two pairs, that is named the Rishi or *Arsha* rite.

The gift of a daughter by her father after he has addressed the couple with the text, 'May both of you perform together your duties, and has shown honour to the bridegroom, is called in the Smriti the *Prajapatya* rite.

When the bridegroom receives the maiden, after having given as much wealth as he can afford, the kinsmen and to the bride herself, according to his own will, that is called the *Asura* rite.

The voluntary union of a maiden and her lover one must know to be a *Gandharva* rite, which springs from desire and has sexual intercourse for its purpose. The forcible abduction of a maiden from her home, while she cries out and weeps, after her kinsmen have been slain or wounded and their houses broken open is called the *Rakshasa* rite.

When a man by stealth seduces a girl who is sleeping, intoxicated or disordered in intellect, that is the eight, the most base and sinful rite of the Pishachas.

For the maiden to choose her husband there is no restriction whatsoever but for man to pick up his choice of girl the following ten families are avoidable. One which (1) neglects the sacred rites, or in which (2) no male children are born, one in which (3) the Veda is not studied, or the members of which have (4) thick hair on the body, those which are (5) subject to hemorrhoids, (6) phthisis, (7) weakness of digestion, (8) epilepsy, or (9) white or black (10) leprosy.

Let him not marry a maiden with reddish hair, nor one who has a redundant member nor one who is sickly, nor one either with no hair or too much, nor one who is garrulous or has red eyes, nor one named after a constellation, a tree or a river, nor one bearing the name of a low caste, or of a mountain, nor one named after a bird, a snake, or a slave, nor one whose name inspires terror.

Let him marry a female free from bodily defects, who has an agreeable name, the graceful gait of a Hansa or of an elephant, a moderate quantity of hair on the body and on the head, small teeth and soft limbs. No father must take even the smallest gratuity for his daughter; for a man who through avarice, takes a gratuity, is a seller of his offspring.

Manu also warns the couple for their conjugal union as thus:–

Sixteen days and nights in each month, including four days which differ from the rest and are censured by the virtuous, are called the natural season of women. But among these the first four, the eleventh and the thirteenth are declared to be forbidden: the remaining nights are recommended.

On the even nights sons are conceived and daughters on the uneven ones; hence a man whose desires to have sons should approach his wife in due season on the even nights.

A male child is produced by a greater quality of male seed, a female child by the prevalence of the female; if both are equal, a hermaphrodite or a boy and a girl; if both are weak or deficient in quantity, a failure of conception results.

He who avoids women on the six forbidden nights and on eight others, is equal in chastity to a student, in whichever order he may live.

Finally, a little bit of magical power is also put in the female curse by the Manu in his statements.

The houses on which female relations, not being duly honoured, pronounce a curse, perish completely, as if destroyed by magic.

The Buddhist Marriage Rite

Legally, any marriage is a custom of the couple being registered at the office or by court. But such bond of mere legality might ignore the better ties of moral, religious and social aspects of wedlock. It is therefore, a need of whatsoever society to get the engaged couple wed through the solemnity of their adopted way of custom and tradition, or a ceremony which can make a wedding socially acceptable and certainly complete.

The Principles of Marriage

According to the Buddhist tradition marriage is based on following principles.

1. A Buddhist marriage is not supposed to have to indulge in the sensuous temporary pleasures and make unhealthy children;
2. But it is to live a moral life till the attainment of the highest goal for the perfect happiness and purity.

We must understand this as the aim of the marriage and accordingly the marriage parties may choose for the bride and the bridegroom their life partner, suitable according to each other's choice.

Besides other economical and personal causes for society to bind itself to the fold of marriage, a person seeks love of morally bound wedlock for the personal best and benefit.

As a family man or woman, too, a lay person can rise from lower to the higher level of life and culture by efforts and convictions. So through marriage too, as a means of mutual love and understanding a married member unlike the unmarried one can bring growth to the life of peace and perfection.

Introduction of Bride and Bridegroom

Now we shall see what should be known by a person to conducts this ceremony. Apart from the Buddhist monks, for this, in some special cases, any person of principles, both male and female are entitled to officiate the worldly marriage rite.

First of all, on the part of a person in charge of the affair the introduction of the bride, bridegroom, their parents and other close relations must be given to the people present at the occasion. This may be introduced like this:–

The marriage of so and so, son of Mr. So and So with, such and such is being duly carried out before all of you present here at this certain place on the auspicious hour of this day.

For various reasons a marriage ceremony is held in the hall in any premises, but an ideal place is the Buddhist monastery. In the Buddhist society different countries have their different ways of conducting the wedding ceremony, but most of the Buddhists will still agree with a few central and commonly related things of the ceremony, such as the taking of the precepts and the recitation of the Mangala Sutra. Particularly, in South-East Asian Buddhist countries the wedding ceremony is not officiated by any of their spiritual monks, but they can bless the couple at the Buddha Vihara when the latter visit before or after their marriage.

In India things are changing since the Buddhist revival movement has changed there from place to place and time to time under different circumstances.

From the mass conversion ceremony of the Buddhist leader of India, Dr Babasaheb Ambedkar at the hands of the most venerable Mahathero of Burma, Chandramani Jee, at the head of the other multinational Buddhist monks at the Deeksha ground, Nagpur, in India on 14th October 1956 up till now the Buddhist devotees in the state of India prefer the Buddhist monks, as and when available at their humble respectful invitation to officiate the domestic ceremonies of mainly, birth, marriage and death; and this custom has since been popular among Indian Buddhists that need our sympathetic concern and consideration.

To cope with the need of these demands Bhikkhus in India are limited to obtain on such occasions even from distant places. Therefore there is no other option for the marriage parties but to depend on themselves to officiate the ceremony and conduct its performance according to a guide to the Buddhist rite such as this available at hand. This being a small attempt towards that direction.

Ills of the Marriage Ritual

Marriage should not at all be a business or man made ritual consuming enormous time, money and labour expenditure. It should at its best be made to look more natural than mechanical institution. Too much priesthood and ritual might make it unnatural and still give no good impressions about the marriage and ceremony. At the same time bad habits of lavishly spending to drink and let drink beer or wine and the unfair conduct of such improper things on the part of the marriage parties will even worsen the whole of the ceremony being simple and pure.

In the Indian society, mostly among Punjabi people of the labour class, who have adopted the Buddhist faith, abandoning their old one, Hinduism, certain wrong views about the marriage have got transferred into Buddhist ways.

For instance, they prefer pink or rosy colour suits for the couple to other clothes at the marriage occasion. At this time they also sing vulgar selfmade merry songs which are called Sera. Some dance is also done to amuse them. One of their superstitions about not using the white suit for the marriage couple is that the corpses are wrapped with white cloth and naturally they take it as a bad omen if white clothes are worn.

Now let us turn our attention to the ills of the marriage custom still prevalent in the modern Indian society compared to other countries.

Not only in India, but in some other countries also people have funny notions and equally funny practices are prevalent among them. One of them is the offering of the bride by the parents of the daughter either to the bridegroom or to the parents of the groom as if she is being given as a charity like the giving of a cow to a Brahmana priest, a member of the privileged class of the Hindu Society. Such a marriage cannot surely be called a legitimate Buddhist marriage. In certain cases some parents of both the bride and the groom waste a lot of money on parties and even have to borrow on such occasions. Such expenditure beyond one's means also cannot be commended in a Buddhist ceremony.

In a lot of cases dowry is expected and given either to the bridegroom or the parents of the bridegroom by the parents of the bride. In quite a number of cases, certain girls remain unmarried for a long time and if they get married the result is their whole family gets bankrupt because of this ill. Such practices also, therefore, must be denounced by Buddhists. In some cases either from the point of views of the age of the bride and the bride groom, or their size and the economic status of their families unsuitable marriages also cannot be considered as the ideal Buddhist marriage.

Considerations of castes, sub-caste—and colors while arranging a marriage are meaningless in the Buddhist wedding.

If a marriage is free from such elements then it should be accepted as a marriage worth getting blessings from everyone.

THE BUDDHIST CONVERSATION BY TAKING THE 22 VOWS

To make sure that the marriage is going to be just and proper between the Buddhists, both the bride and the bridegroom along with their parents and relations must undertake to get initiated to the Buddhist faith by going as a refuge to the Triple Gem and by uttering the 22 vows given them by the great Buddhist leader Babasaheb Dr. Ambedkar at the time of his conversions to Buddhism. The taking of these vows by the bride and the bridegroom will convince them of their disconnections with their rejected fold of caste Hindus religion and of the adoption of Buddhism.

These vows are particularly known as the 22 vows but as a matter of fact they are the essence of the Truth required by a lay practitioner. These vows originally are in Marathi, the provincial tongue of the state of Maharashtra, but their English translation with a little verbal adjustment is given here as under:–

THE TWENTY TWO VOWS

1. I shall not consider Brahma, Vishnu and Mahesh as gods, and nor shall I honour them.
2. I shall not consider Rama and Krishna as gods, and nor shall I honour them.
3. I shall not believe in any gods and goddesses like Gauri, Ganapati, etc. and nor shall I honour them.
4. I shall not believe in the god to have ever reborn as incarnation.
5. I shall not agree with this belief that Lord Buddha were an incarnation of Vishnu.
6. I shal not make oblation for deceased (Shradha), and nor shall I perform the manes for Brahmanas (Pinda Dana).
7. I shall not do anything which is opposite to the Buddhist Law.
8. I shall not get Brahman to officiate at ceremonies.
9. I shall put my trust in this truth that all human beings are equal.
10. I shall put my efforts in the establishment of equality.
11. I shall put my efforts to follow the Buddha's eight fold path completely.
12. I shall fully put myself to adopt ten perfections explained by Lord Buddha.
13. I shall have compassion on beings and shall keep them with care.
14. I shall not take what is not given.
15. I shall not speak wrong words.
16. I shall not misuse the senses.
17. I shall not take anything that cause dullness to body and cloud the mind.

18. I shall make efforts to mould my life according to three Buddhist principles which are as wisdom, discipline and compassion.
19. I do completely renounce my old Hindu fold which is harmful to progress between the human beings; and accept the Dhamma of Lord Buddha.
20. I am fully convinced that the Dhamma of the Lord Buddha alone is Sat Dhamma.
21. I believe that I am now reborn.
22. I hereby undertake this pledge so that hereafter I shall train myself according to the discipline of the Buddhist Teaching.

CEREMONIAL EXERCISE

Whether marriage is inter-caste, inter-race, inter-class, or an international marriage, it is not a point of quarrel for Buddhists. But customarily, before the performance of the wedding rite the five precepts or Panchashil are given to the bride and the bridegroom. At the same time people attending the ceremony can also repeat them along with the couple. While the couple or the other people utter it with conviction they are automatically initiated to Buddhism. And now as such having been converted to the Buddhist faith they now become entitled to undergo the following exercise according to the instructions given by the leader of ceremony as follows.

First of all the couple should bow down to the statue or portrait of Bhagawan Buddha and/or Babasaheb Dr. Ambedkar, which will be kept available in front of them. They should also honor the venerable monks present at the occasion by bending down reverentially before them. This action may be repeated three times. Then the bride and the bridegroom may stand to follow the verbal repetition of the verses of the offerings to the Buddha. One can also sit down if it is more convenient. The offering of the fresh flowers be made to the Buddha form, incense be burnt and the candles lighted and following verses of the reverence of the Lord Buddha must be repeated.

Homage to One, the Blessed, Exalted and the perfectly Awakened.

Twice, Homage to One, the Blessed, the Exalted and the perfectly Awakened.

Thrice, Homage to One, the Blessed, the Exalted and the perfectly Awakened.

I go to the Buddha as my Teacher.

I go to the Truth as my Teacher.

I go to the Brotherhood as my Teacher.

Twice, I go to the Buddha as my Teacher.

Twice, I go to the Truth as my Teacher.

Twice, I go to the Brotherhood as my Teacher.

Thrice, I go to the Buddha as my Teacher.

Thrice, I go to the Truth as my Teacher.

Thrice, I go to the Brotherhood as my Teacher.

I shall train to refrain from harming any living things.

I shall train to refrain from taking what is not given.

I shall train to refrain from misusing the senses.

I shall train to refrain from using any wrong words.

I shall train to refrain from clouding the mind by taking drugs and drinks.

I offer the mass of flowers

That are fresh and hued,

Odorous and choice

To the Noble Sage

At his sacred lotus-feet.

I adore the Buddha with diverse flowers and aspire release through this merit. Even as these flowers must fall and fade, So do I think will my body pass away.

I offer incense, perfumed and fragrant, and adore the Lord with Infinite excellence.

I revere Tathagata, the

Worthy of reverence

And offer substance compound and odorous.

I offer lights to the Enlightened One.

Who dispel the darkness of ignorance.

That light up the three worlds. That abolish the gloom brightly shining.

After this salutation the bride and the bridegroom will sit down at their appointed seats either on chair if provided, or on the floor prepared. Usually the bride takes her seat at the left side of the bridegroom. She should also be without purda or veil over her face because Buddhist women will never use it where it is not required. Let her make up and adorn herself with cosmetics naturally. The bridegroom also should be seated by his bride with decorum and in pleasing manners to look at.

Now the members of both the marriage parties of bride and the bridegroom give rings, and the garlands for bride and the bridegroom, and may provide necklace or other marriage items also to the rite leader, who will perhaps have to conduct the further wedding part with them as it will be explained below.

It will be helpful if the things spoken to instruct the couple will be simultaneously explained. For its better understanding a few more words of notes on certain Pali words will be naturally desirable.

The word "Sadhu" for instance, is traditionally used to mean very well or excellent. It is therefore frequently applied in Pali recitation and usage for the same. Similarly when this word–Sadhu—is said at the end of the Pali verses even at wedding performance it is just a positive yes sense to what is being spoken or done. It must then always be understood that it is never a personal name of anybody indeed.

So when the item of garlanding of bride and bridegroom comes to be performed we may then use "sadhu."

At this time the officiating priest or person will chant a particular Pali verse three times. Each time the word sadhu will be repeated at its end. These verses can be chosen according to the relevance of the event by the officiating person.

While chanting the verses one of the wedding garlands should be given to the bride. Then at the first sadhu after the verse, the bride should put her garland around the bridegroom's neck. Having done this she may show her respects towards him as is proper. In Indian custom, in such case the bride seems to have her forehead put on the bridegrooms feet but this kind of deep reverence is out of thought in the West countries.

Then when the bridegroom gets ready with the other garland held in his hand the second sadhu will follow after the verse and then he will garland the bride as a token of his acceptance to take her as the wife.

Now the garlanded bride and the bridegroom should be made to stand up so that they are faced to each other. And then people should be holding the paper colour flowers into their hands and will be ready to shower those on both of them as soon as the third sadhu with the last verse of the item is uttered. After this moment all present may also clap in unison to mark the wedding moment as a gesture of giving your congratulations to the wedded persons.

After this the wedded couple should be made to sit down at their respective seats. A sanctified cotton thread by the chanting be given one and each to both of them. Who will then tie it for each other on the right wrist of their right hands.

Similarly, the bridegroom can also give his necklace to the bride after this.

Then at this special moment the wedded couple can even present their gifts of love to each other and if they still have to exchange the wedding rings they can now do that, too.

According to some foreign Buddhist tradition, particularly in that of Burma the water is poured or sprinkled by the leafy branch of a tree on their joined—together palms put one on the top of the other. The jar of water and a tree branch are specially provided on the altar of the stage for that purpose.

In addition to this, the apparatus of the ceremony will also include a roll of cotton white table cloth, Buddha images, offerings, flowers, garlands, incense, candles and so many other things as will be suggested by the concerned member.

Now on reaching of this stage the couple may ask for the advice from the Buddhist monks for they will give a short sermon on their demand for their benefit, knowledge and guidance in connection with their life as householder.

Nevertheless, the relevant sermons given by the Buddha to lay people at such occasion may be related for the couple to be benefited. Then the officiating person should explain to the couple their functions and duties.

Buddhist girls in particular may, therefore, take more interest in knowing the informative tales on certain ideal characters found in the Buddhist history. These stories through the blameless married life of the Buddhist girls reveal what we call the essential meaning of the Buddhist teaching for a lay person.

The Lord Buddha had given sermons in plenty of such occasions for the ordinary people. Most of those sermons are chanted as Pali-sutras by the Buddhist monks at special occasions. One of such more popular sutras is known as "the Sigalovada Sutra" which ever so beautifully explained the family person and gave most useful advice on proper relationship between wife and husband, teacher and pupil, preceptor and disciple and so on in contrast with ten quarters. Another important sutra from lay point of view is called the Mahamangala Sutra."

Other Sutras like Jayamangal Atthagatha, etc, may also be recited to produce good effects.

The following verses may be changed at the time of uttering "Sadhu" while the bride and the bridegroom adorn each other with the garlands.

May what you wish and desire soon be successful. May all your aspirations be fulfilled like the full moon day.

This gatha or verse should be repeated each time before the use of the three "sadhus."

After this the *duties* of the bride and the bridegroom must be made clearly known to them and they are given here as these.

The bride will say:

Towards my husband I undertake to perform my household duties efficiently, be hospitable to my in-laws and friends of my husband, be faithful, protect and invest our earnings, discharge my responsibilities lovingly and conscientiously.

The bridegroom will say:

Towards my wife I undertake to love and respect her, be kind and considerate, be faithful, delegate my domestic management, please her with gifts and ornaments.

Now the Mahamangala Sutra chanting should be carefully heard by the wedded couple and by all thee seated peacefully. This is given here in English translation thus.

DISCOURSE ON THE BEATITUDES

Thus have I heard. The Exalted One was once sojourning hard by Savatthi in Jeta's grove in the monastery of Anatha Pindika. Now one night a certain Deva, illumining the whole Jetavana with his radiance, came where the Exalted One was, and bowed down in salutation to Him, and stood on one side. And so standing, the Deva addressed the exalted One in the following stanza:

Many Devas and men

Have held various things to be blessing

When they were longing for happiness;

1. Do thou declare unto us the highest good.
   The Exalted One answers:
2. Not to associate with the foolish,
   But to serve the wise,
   To honour those worthy of honour,
   This is the greatest blessing.
3. To dwell in a pleasant land,
   To have done good works in a former birth (stage & life),
   To cherish right desires in the heart,
   This is the greatest blessing.
4. Much clarity and much learning,
   And mastery over one's self,
   And a pleasant manner of speech,
   This is the greatest blessing.

5. To support father and mother,
   To cherish wife and child,
   To follow a peaceful calling,
   This is the greatest blessing.
6. To give alms and to live uprightly,
   To give help to one's kindred
   And to act without reproach,
   This is the greatest blessing
7. To abhor and cease from sin,
   To abstain from strong drink,
   To weary not in well doing,
   These are the greatest blessings.
8. Reverence and lowliness,
   Contentment and gratitude,
   The hearing of the Doctrine at due seasons,
   These are the greatest blessings.
9. To be patient and gentle to foregather with lovers of peace, to speak in reason of spiritual things,
   These are the greatest blessings.
10. Self-restraint and purity,
    The knowledge of the Noble Truths,
    The realization of Nirvana
    These are the greatest blessings.
11. The mind that is not shaken
    Amid all the leaps of life,
    That yields not to grief or passion,
    This is the greatest blessing.
12. They are scatheless on every side,
    Who set their feet in these ways,
    Their steps are attended by safety,
    And this is the greatest blessing.

THE WEDDING OF VISAKHA

There are some edifying examples of wedded Buddhist women in the Buddhist literature. So it will be beneficial to gain some knowledge of the character of Visakha, from this story.

One of the ideal and the chief among the lay women disciples of the Buddha was Visakha. She was declared by him to be foremost devotee to the order [dayikanam agga]. She was the daughter of Dhananjaya and Sumana born in the city of Bhaddiya in Anga country. When she was seven years old, the Buddha visited the city of Bhaddiyas with a large company of monks at the Brahmina Sela's concern. Her grandfather Medaka gave Visakha companions, slaves and chariots, five hundred each, to visit the Buddha and getting out of the chariot walked on foot to salute him. Then she sat on one side. And the Buddha preached her. After hearing the Buddha's speech she became a Dhamma stream enterer, Shrotapanna. For the next fortnight Medaka, Visakha's grandfather invited the Buddha with his large company of monks daily to his house for food.

Later, Visakha accompanied her parents to live in Saket, in Kosala Kingdom as Bimbisara bad him so at Prasentjit's request.

One day the Migara of Savatthi sent a messenger to find a suitable bride for his son Punyavardhana. Visakha was on her way to the bathing lake on that feast day. At that moment there came a great shower of rain. Visakha's companions ran for shelter, but Visakha herself, walking at her usual pace, came to the place where messengers were awaiting her arrival. They saw her and were greatly impressed by her manner. Then when they asked her why she did not run to shelter to protect her clothes like her other companions, she answered that she had plenty of clothes in the house, but that if she ran she might damage a limb which would be a great loss.

"Unmarried girls, she said, are like goods awaiting sale that they must not be disfigured."

A bouquet of flowers was offered to her and her father was consulted for the marriage proposal. It was confirmed by an exchange of letters between both the parties.

Dhananajaya gave his daughter to Punyavardhna along with a lavish dowry of five hundred carts full of money, five hundred vessels of gold, five hundred each of silver, copper, various silks, ghee, rice husked and winnowed; also ploughs, ploughshares, and other farm implements, five hundred carts with three slave women in each, everything being provided for them. The cattle given by him filled an enclosure three quarters of a league in length and eight rods across, standing shoulder to shoulder and in addition to these sixty thousand bulls and sixty thousand milch cows escaped from their stalls and joined the herd already gifted to her.

All this abundance of gifts beyond one's imaginations must be understood only as a token of the deepest love of Dhananjaya towards his daughter, Visakha.

On the following day Dhananjaya appointed eight house-holders to be sponsors to his daughter and to enquire into any charges which might be brought against her. He allowed any inhabitants of his fourteen tributary villages to accompany her, but Migara, fearing that he should have to feed them, drove most of them back.

When the time came for Visakha to leave, Dhananjaya gave her ten admonitions, which Migara overheard from the next room. These were:

INTERPRETATIONS OF TEN ADMONITIONS TO VISAKHA

(*i*) "The indoor fire is not to be carried outside."

"Pray how could we live without giving fire to the neighbours who live on both sides of us? Migara said the meaning of all of them is explained thus by Visakha."

"Dear daughter, if you see any fault in your father-in-law or in your husband, say nothing about it when you go to this house or to the other house, for there is no fire that may be compared to this fire.

(*ii*) The outdoor fire is not to be carried inside

"If either women or men in your neighbours' houses speak ill of your father-in-law or of your husband, you must not bring home what you have heard them say and repeat it, saying, "so-and-so said this or that unkind thing about you." For there is no fire comparable to this fire."

(*iii*) *Give only to him that gives* means that one should give only to those that return borrowed articles.

(*iv*) *Give not to him that gives not* means that one should not give to those who do not return borrowed articles.

(*v*) *Give both to him that gives and to him that gives not* means that when poor kinsfolk and friends seek assistance, one should give to them, whether or not they are able to repay.

(*vi) Sit happily* means that when a wife sees her mother-in-law or her father-in-law or her husband, she should stand and not remain sitting.

(*vii*) *Eat happily* means that a wife should not eat before her mother-in-law and her father-in-law and her husband have eaten. She should serve them first and when she is sure that they have all they care for, then and not until then may she herself eat.

(*viii*) *Sleep happily* means that a wife should not go to bed before her mother-in-law and her father-in-law and her husband. She should first perform the major and minor duties which she owes them, and when she has so done, then she may herself lie down to sleep.

(*ix*) *Tend the fire means that* a wife should regard her mother-in-law and her father-in-law and her husband as a flame of fire or as a Serpent-King.

(*x*) *Honour the household divinities* means that a wife should look upon her mother-in-law and her father-in-law and her husband as her divinities.

Visakha entered Savatthis standing in her chariot, so that all might see her glory. The citizens showered gifts on her, but these she distributed among the people.

Migara was a follower of the Niganthas, and soon after Visakhas arrival in his house, he sent for them and told her to minister to them. But Visakha, repulsed by their nudity, refused to pay them homage. The Nighanthas urged that she should be sent away. But Migara bides his time. One day, as Migara was eating, while Visakha stood fanning him, a monk was seen standing outside his house. Visakha stood aside, that Migara might see him, but Migara continued to eat without noticing the monk, she said to the latter, "Pass on, sir, My father-in-law eats stale fare." Migara was angry and threatened to send her away, but at her request the matter was referred to her sponsors. They enquired into the several charges brought against her and adjudged her not guilty. Visakha then gave orders that preparations should be made for her return to her parents. But Migara begged her forgiveness which she granted, on condition that he would invite to the house the Buddha and his monks. This he did, but owing to the influence of the Niganthas, he left Visakha to entertain them, and only consented to hear the Buddha's sermon at the end of the meal from behind a curtain. At the conclusion of this sermon, however, he became a *sotapanna,* the stream-enterer. His gratitude towards Visakha was boundless, henceforth she was to be considered as his mother and to receive all the honour due to a mother; from this time onwards she was called Migaramata. In the *Dhammapada,* the most famous Buddhist book of the Buddhas, words in verses, commentary it is told that in order to conform this declaration, Migara sucked the breast of Visakha. She had also a son named Migara, which as Anguttara commentary says was her eldest son. For Visakha Migara got made an ornament cost one hundred thousand. On the day of the presentation of this ornament, he held for her a special festival in her honour and made her to bathe in sixteen pots of perfumed water."

Visakha had ten sons and ten daughters, each of whom had a similar number of children, and so on down to the fourth generation. Before her death, at the age of one hundred and twenty, she had eighty-four thousand and twenty direct lineal descendants all living. She was in great grief when her grand daughter Datta died. Visakha herself kept, all her life, the appearance of a girl of sixteen. She had the strength of five elephants, and once she took the trunk of an elephant which was sent to test her, between her two fingers and forced him on his haunches.

Visakha owned a great reputation. She was always invited by the people of Savatthi to their houses on festivals and holidays for their good fortune. Visakha fed five hundred [two thousand according to another account] monks daily at her house. Later she appointed her grand-daughter Datta to officiate for her. In the afternoon she visited the Buddha, and, after listening to his sermon, would go round the monastery, inquiring into the needs of the monks and runs.

Eight Boons to Visakha by Buddha

Visakha begged for, and was granted eight boons by the Buddha. They are that as long as he lived she be allowed to give–

1. robes to the members of the order for the rainy season.
2. food for monks coming into Savatthi.
3. food for those going out.
4. food for the sick.
5. food for those who wait on the sick.
6. medicine for the sick.
7. a constant supply of rice gruel for any needing it.
8. and bathing robes to the runs.

In the Vinaya Pitaka the Buddha is told to have accepted a face-towel as a special gift from Visakha but would not accept an earthenware foot scrubber.

She built the monastery called Migaramatupasada in the Pubbarama and at the opening ceremony of its festival she walked round the monastery accompanied by her children, her grand children, rejoicing and entirely filled with highest bliss. It must now be understand by reader that any exaggeration in this description is sumply to show the character as lifted and greatly highlighted. Fairly I agree that all these words of euphemism probably contained little wordly truth.

THE DISCIPLINE FOR GIRLS

At the same time it is the responsibility of parents to give their children good education and right direction for their moral life. They should bother to train the girls in this discipline.

There are occasions when householders consulted Bhagawana Buddha to seek moral advice from him on discipline for girls who are grown up for marriage. These rules for girls enunciated by Lord Buddha on one such occasion when he was invited by his devotee, Uggaha are also recorded here for the general benefit. I hope you will find it worthwhile if you will go through it.

Once the Exalted One dwelt near Bhaddiya in Jetiya wood and there, Uggaha, Mendaka's grandson visited the Buddha. After his salutation to the Blessed One Uggaha invited him for a meal at his house. The Buddha then remaining silent accepted his invitation.

Next day Buddha went to Uggaha's house and took his meal there served by Uggaha. When the Lord finished his meal he withdrew his hand from the bowl. Then Uggaha sat down on one side and said to the lord. "Lord, these girls of mine will be going to their husband's families; Lord, let the Exalted One counsel them for their good and happiness for many a day!"

Then the Blessed One spoke to them and said "Wherefore, girls, train yourselves in this way; "To whatsoever husband our parents shall give us—wishing our weal, seeking our happiness, compassionate because of compassion for him we will rise up early, be the last to retire, be willing workers, order all things sweetly and be gentle voiced. Train yourselves thus girls.

"And in this way also, girls; 'we will honour revere, esteem and respect all who are our husband's relatives, whether mother or father, recluse or godly man, and on their arrival will offer them a seat and water. Train yourselves thus girls.

"We will be deft and nimble at our husband's home-crafts whether they will be of wool or cotton, making it our business to understand the work so as to do and get it done. Train yourselves thus, girls.

"Messengers and workfolk we will know the work of each according to his share."

"The money, corn, silver and gold that our husband brings home, we will keep safe, watch and ward over it and act as no robber, thief, carouser, wastrel therein. Train yourselves thus, girls."

On hearing this advice, the daughters of Uggaha felt exceedingly happy and were grateful to the Lord.

If girls were born in India and they lived there for a sufficient time they would find the above advice accurately fit in the Indian environments.

In Europe vast differences are found in its specific culture and civilization sometimes anti-climatic if compared to the Indian for that matter Asian ethnic differences.

Despite these differences we can pick up very many things of this advice to learn in any circumstances.

The Blessing

Now at the end of a Buddhist ceremony blessing is invoked for devotees. Similarly for bride and the bridegroom this should be invoked for protection by the power of the Triple Gem, the Buddha, the Dhamma, and the Sangha. For this the following stanzas of supreme blessing are recommended.

May all blessing be to you.

May all protect you.

By the power of all the

the Buddhas

may happiness all be yours!

By the power of the protection

may no misfortune result.

May your troubles come to nought.

May there be rain in due time!

May there be a rich

harvest!

May the world be contented!

May the government be righteous

By the power of all mighty

Buddhas, and all Arhatas

I secure your protection

every way.

The Buddhist Attitude towards Marriage

In the Christian tradition, marriage is usually termed a "sacrament". In some branches of Christianity it is treated as an indissoluble bond, though usually there are a few loopholes. Other branches of Christianity permit divorce in certain rather narrowly defined circumstances, and in some countries the state permits divorce and the remarriage of divorced persons, with or without the approval of the Church.

In Buddhism, marriage is not a "sacrament", as such a concept does not exist. Be it holy wedlock or deadlock, an idea is fanciful. In the Buddhist tradition it is often the custom for Bhikkus to give their blessing after the civil wedding ceremony has been performed. This choice of blessing even is entirely theirs. Bhikkhus have no authority to enforce or dissolve or in any way interfere the marriage. Today, Japan may be exception for this.

Divorce is also a civil affair.

The practice of using contraception is entirely their business. The Sangha have got no say or objection on that. It is a private thing. It is no part of Bhikkhus, advice.

As far as Buddhist Vinaya is concerned, illicit sexual matters and abortion might reasonably come to fall under a purview of spiritual advice. Unless it is a fatal risk the latter will not be condoned without involving the evil points. Because it intervenes the very first Buddhist precept of no killing.

In marriage the responsibility of the wedded couple towards each other and towards children is greatly involved. Obviously any kind of irresponsibility in such circumstances will clearly be offensive, if not fearful.

Where we call ourselves Buddhists or anything else if we carefully remember and follow the five Buddhist precepts the chances of marriage being successful are bright.

Excessive drinking is also a breach of the precept and so it is one of the potent causes of unhappiness in marriages.

The other reasons for marriages breakdown are blames of a partner. A partner can be impotent, ill, irresponsible, jealous, drunken, a compulsive gambler, deranged, promiscuous, miserly, unemployable, or several of these things. Both partners may be charming people and yet they can be utterly unsuited to each other. In these cases the marriages are held together because of their children.

For Buddhists, monogamous marriage should be ideal marriage. And it is really the same in all other Buddhist countries.

Buddhist should make use of all their opportunities—only to develop mindfulness at all times. In this way they can overcome their problems of any complications.

If a wife loves a husband for her own pleasures and the latter loves a wife for his own satisfaction then selfishness will become a sole standard of the earning of their happiness. But human experience is a real guide to person and it is clearly evident from this that the more you are self-centered the greater you get discontentment. More the craving, greater the suffering.

So at all levels Buddhists must reflect and even meditate on the following two statements quoted from a certain newspaper.

"I am in Love" means

"I want me to be happy";

"I love" means

"I want to make you happy".

Golden Rule : Never Let Passion Override Compassion
May all being be Well and Happy

7

Buddhist Marriage and Succession Act 2007

Dr. Nitin Raut*

Concept and Evolution of Buddhist Law

The name Buddhism comes from the word "Buddi", which means "To wake up" and thus Buddhism can be said to be the philosophy of awakening. This Philosophy has its origin in the experience of the man 'Siddharth Gautam' known as 'Buddha'. Who was himself enlightened at the age of 35 in circa 6th century B.C.

Lord Buddha Preached the Dhamma in the form of sermons.

(1) The Buddha claimed no place for himself in his own Dhamma.

(2) The Buddha did not promise to give salvation. He said he was 'Marga-Data' (Way finder/path finder) and not 'Moksh-Data' (Giver of Salvation).

(3) The Buddha did not claim any divinity for himself nor for His Dhamma. The Dhamma was discovered by the man for man to man relationship. It was not a revelation.

(4) The Buddha exhorted His followers not to take his teachings by blind faith but to accept them only after close investigation and inquiry as to whether the teachings are really acceptable according to one's own intelligence and experience. He did not want them to accept it without clarity of mind and complete understanding.

(5) The Buddha advocated that Man must know the truth and real truth. To Him, freedom of expression of thought was the most essential thing and He was sure

that freedom of expression and thought was the only way to the discovery of truth.

(6) Buddhism teaches a man to live in peace and harmony.

Who is a Buddhist?

Any individual who has taken refuge in the three gems, *i.e.* Buddha, Dhamma and Sangha, and tries to conduct his life according to teachings of the blessed one, is termed a Buddhist. A person who is born out of wedlock of Buddhist person. A person who has embraced and converted to Buddhism earlier to 1956 and thereafter. A worshiper of Buddha, one adheres to the system of Buddhism (Webster dictionary).

How is a Buddhist Separate and Distinct from a Hindu?

Some consider Buddhism as a reformed part of Hinduism. But the fact is that it is totally a rejection of Hinduism.

Buddhism rejects the Brahminical supremacy and dominance of priestly castes and treats all individuals as equals. It rejects tenets of caste system, existence of Gods, Avtars, Soul and concept of heaven and hell, authority of Vedas and also other Hindu teachings but strongly believes in the innate power of an individual. It teaches "Atta Deepo Bhav" meaning thereby 'be thy own light' to attain Nirvana *i.e.* enlightenment.

Dr. Ambedkar's Initiation into Buddhism

Young Ambedkar passed his matriculation in the year 1909. He was felicitated in his chawl. He was the first matriculate in the whole society. On this occasion, his teacher Arjunrao Keluskar presented him a book titled *Buddha Charitra*. Young boy up-till-now was confused with *Ramayana* and *Mahabharata*. After reading Buddha Charitra his way of thinking underwent total change and his mind was attracted towards Buddha and his teachings.

In *Yeola,* (Dist. Nasik) conference on 13th Oct. 1935 Dr. Babasaheb Ambedkar thundered "Unfortunately for me I was born a Hindu Untouchable. It was beyond my power to prevent that, but I declare that it is within my power to refuse to live under ignoble and humiliating conditions. I solemnly assure you that I will not die a Hindu". He had fulfilled his vow.

The Diksha

On 14th Oct 1956 Dr. Babasaheb Ambedkar embraced and converted lakhs of People to Buddhism by giving Diksha to his Dalit followers. On this occasion, Dr. Ambedkar commissioned his followers the *22 pledges* which emphasise that *"I will not regard Bramha, Vishnu and Mahesh" as Gods, nor will I worship them. I embrace today the Dhamma of the Buddha, discarding the Hindu religion, which is detrimental to the emancipation of human being and which believes in equality.*

Why do Dalits Embrace Buddhism?

To escape from the centuries - old caste system that puts them at the bottom of the social order.

Sources of Buddhist Law

The sources of Buddhist Law are Lord Buddha's sermons. Buddhism was founded in 6th century B.C. by Lord Buddha in India. Buddhism discards authority of Vedas and also caste system. Buddha advocated eight-fold path and five precepts which all Buddha's devotees strive to observe.

The Noble Eight-fold path is

(1) Right Understanding

(2) Right Thought

(3) Right Livelihood

(4) Right Effort

(5) Right Speech

(6) Right Action

(7) Right Mindfulness

(8) Right Contemplation

The Five Precepts are

(1) To abstain from killing

(2) To abstain from stealing

(3) To abstain from adultery

(4) To abstain from lying and loose speech

(5) To abstain from intoxicants and drugs.

When those Precepts were enunciated by the Buddha, he had in mind the unsettled conditions of society prevailing twenty five centuries ago in India. Those conditions were caused by human feelings such as: anger which leads to killing; greed which leads to stealing; undue sexual impulses that lead to adultery; egoistic feelings that lead to telling false-hood and absence of self control leads to undue consumption of intoxicants or drugs.

That every follower of Buddhism is requested to repeat these precepts again and again in daily life.

Tripitaka

The sacred book of Buddhism is called the Tripitaka. It is written in an ancient Indian language called Pali, which is very close to the language that the Buddha himself spoke. Tri means three and Pitaka means basket.

The Buddhist scriptures consist of three sections. The first section called the Sutta Pitaka, contains Buddha's all discourses. The type of material in the Sutta Pitaka is very diverse which allows it to communicate the truth, that the Lord Buddha taught. Sutta Pitaka has five nikayas; Digha, Majjhima, Sanyutta, Anyuttara and Khuddaka. The last has 15 books including Dhammapada.

(ii) Dhammapada

Dhammapada presents the Buddha's teaching through the poetry. The Dhammapada could be translated as *"The way of truth"* or *"Verses of truth"* some profound, others of considerable beauty, all spoken by the Lord Buddha. The Dhammpada is most popular component of Buddhist literature and recognized as one of the masterpieces of world religious literature.

(iii) Vinaya-pitaka

This contains the rules and procedures for monks and nuns, advice on monastic administration and procedure and early history of the monastic order. These are called the sacred epic and constitute the sources of Buddhist law.

(iv) Moral and Ethical Conduct of a Buddhist

In Buddhism there can be no real morality without the

knowledge, no real knowledge without morality, and thus both are bound up together like heat and light in a flame.

Buddhist morality is based on individual freedom *i.e.* on individual development. It is therefore relative.

> "The Buddha's doctrine of love and goodwill between man and man is set forth in domestic and social ethics with more comprehensiveness".

The most important elements of Buddhism, reform have always been in social and moral code. The moral code taken by itself is one of the most perfect the world has ever known.

The Lord Buddha was interested in the happiness of mankind. To him happiness was not possible without leading a pure virtuous life based on morality.

(v) Philo sophical part of Tripitaka is called Abhidhamma containing various volumes.

What is Dhamma?

1. Dhamma is a teaching of the Lord Buddha.
2. It's essence is to lead a Righteous life.
3. To maintain cordial relations between man and man.
4. It places man at the center of all things and believes in his potential to attain his spiritual liberation.
5. It professes Panchashila and Eight-fold path for virtuous living.
6. It teaches man to be kind and gentle, emphasizes love and peace and universal compassion.

Distinction between Dharma (Religion) and Dhamma

Dharma (Religion): Recognition on the part of man of a controlling superhuman power entitled to obedience, reverence, and worship, the feeling or the spiritual attitude of those recognizing such a controlling power, with the manifestation of such feeling in conduct or life, the practice of sacrifice or observances of a particular system of faith in and worship of a super being or god or gods.

Dhamma: Lord Buddha's saying is that this path which is his Dhamma had nothing to do with God and soul. His Dhamma had nothing to do with life after death. Nor his

Dhamma has any concern with ritual and ceremonies. The centre of his Dhamma is man and the relation of man to man in his life on earth. The recognition of the existence of suffering and the way to remove suffering is the foundation and basis of his Dhamma.

Which is a Holy Book of Dhamma?

The Buddhist Cannons are: *(I) Tripitaka, (II) Commentaries* and (*III*) Sub-commentaries on original policanon and (*IV*) part canonical literature.

1. The *Tripitika* consists of (I) *Vinay Pitika,* (II) *Sutta Pitika,* (III) *Abidhamma Pitika.* These include various discourses of the Buddha.
2. It is the richest treasure of spiritual knowledge and practical wisdom.
3. 'Dhammapada' as the 15th book of khuddakanikaya of Sutta-Pitaka is the sacred and holy Book for all the Buddhists throughout the world. It contains sound logic, superior teachings and practical philosophy of the Buddha.

In the present time, the book which is accepted by the Buddhists in general and religious historians and philosophers as an essence of Pali canon and past canonical literature is *"The Buddha and his Dhamma"* written by Dr. Babasaheb Ambedkar which is a sacred book for Indian Buddhist.

(vi) Ethics and Social Relationship

The guidelines given by Lord Buddha should be honored and respected by all who treasure and value our happy and ethical family relationship, of course some of these injunction are given since such a long time ago.

(i) Parents' duties towards their children

Restrain him from vice, exhort him to virtue, train him to a profession, contract a suitable marriage for him and, in due course of time, his inheritance.

(ii) The Teacher and Student

The teacher should train him well; cause him to learn well thoroughly, instruct him in the lore of every art, speak well of him among friends and companions and provide for his safety in every quarter.

(iii) Student and his Teacher

The students should give respect to his teachers. By rising (from his seat in salutation) waiting upon them with eagerness to learn, personal service and by attention when receiving their teachings.

(iv) The Husband and Wife

The husband should respect his wife 'By respect, courtesy, faithfulness, handing over authority to her in the home, and providing her with ornaments.

(v) The wife towards husband

She should perform her duties, show hospitality to her own kin, her husband. She is faithful, watches over the goods he brings and shows skill and artistry in discharging all her business.

(vi) Friend Towards Friend

Protect one, when one is off one's guard and on such occasions guard one's prosperity, they become a refuge in danger, do not forsake one in times of trouble and show consideration for one's family.

(vii) Master towards his servants

He should assign work according to their strength by supplying them with food and wages, attending them in sickness, sharing unusual delicacies with them, and granting them leave at all appropriate times.

(viii) Wisdom

True wisdom is to directly see and understand ourselves. Wisdom is to keep a open mind rather than being closed minded. Always be ready to change our belief when facts that contradict are presented to us that is wisdom. The Buddhist Path requires courage, patience, flexibility and intelligence.

(vii) Lord Buddha's Concept of Marriage

According to Lord Buddha: Marriage plays a very important part in this strong web of relationship of giving support and protection. A good marriage should grow and develop gradually from understanding and not impulse, from true loyalty and not just sheer indulgence. The institution of marriage provides a fine basis for the development of culture, a delightful association of two individuals to be nurtured and to be free from loneliness, deprivation and fear. Urge in living beings in this regard is called sex urge. To channelize the sex urge, the concept of marriage is developed in the society of human beings.

It involves certain rights and duties between the parties entering into wedlock, because Buddhist marriage is a sacrament and not a contract.

In a broad sense marriage means a legally and socially sanctioned union of man and woman that accords social status to them as husband and wife and legitimacy to their offsprings.

According to Lord Buddha, a society relationship is mutually inter-twined and interdependent. Every relationship is a whole-hearted commitment to support and to protect others in a group or community. Marriage plays a very important part in this strong marital relationship of giving support and protection.

The institution of marriage provides a fine basis for the development of culture, a delightful association of two individuals to be nurtured and to be free from loneliness, deprivation and fear. In marriage, each partner develops a complimentary role, giving strength and moral courage to one another. There must be no thought of either man or woman being superior. Each is complimentary to the other, as a partnership of equality.

(viii) Statement of Object and Reasons

Hon'ble J.J. Bhau Wahane in the criminal case No. 246/89 of *Suresh Rathi* Vs *State of Mah.* has observed as under:

Stressing the need of marriage for a healthy social life, the learned Judge says – "Marriage, whether considered as a contract or sacrament, confers a status of husband and wife on the parties to the marriage, of legitimacy on the children of the marriage and gives rise to certain mutual rights and obligations of spouses. All over the world, marriage began as a sacrament. Marriage as a sacramental, necessarily implied a permanent and indissoluble union. It was considered as an eternal union. It was a holy and sacramental tie and not a contractual union.

It is also further observed by him that, - A man is incomplete without his wife and it is wife who completes him. She is called as Ardhangini (half of him). The wife is verily the half of the husband. Those who have wives can fulfill their due obligations in this world, can be happy and can lead a full life, wife is not just a *patni* but *Dharmapatni* – (partner in the performances of spiritual as well as secular duties). Thus, society conceived of their marriage a sacramental union – a sacrosanct, permanent, indissoluble and eternal union. The marriage is not a contract, but it is a tie which once tied cannot be untied. Undoubtedly, marriage as a social institution is regarded solemn all over the civilized world. Thus, marriage came to be regarded as a Sacrament and an indissoluble union.

As a social institution, there is a Social Interest in preservation and protection of the institution of marriage. Thus, it is also hedged with many legal protections. Therefore, not only in the interest of the couple, but in the interest of the society, the marriage tie should not be broken, on the contrary it is to be seen that every couple must live happily and enjoy the marital life.

As marriage is said to be security, it is irrevocable. It is sacramental as well. The religious rites performed at the marriage alter clearly indicates that man accepts the woman as his better-half, by assuring her the protection as guardian, ensuring food and necessities of life as the provider, giving companionship as the mate and by resolving that the pleasure and sorrows in the pursuit of life shall be shared with her and Dhamma shall be observed. Marriage being social, it is the duty of not only the couple, but everyone in the country, whether an individual or an organization to maintain social metabolism.

The court has the obligation within reasonable limit and justifying bounds to provide food for thought which may help to generate the proper social order and hold the community in an even form. Marriage is the very foundation of civil society and no part of the laws and institutions of a country can be of more vital importance to its subjects than those which regulate the manner and conditions of forming and of dissolving the marriage contract."

In order that the rites and ceremonies of marriage could be regarded as customary, they must stand the test of time and force of law without discontinuance at any point of time. It is true that persons belonging to Buddhist community were converted to the Buddhist faith from the Scheduled Caste community sometime in the year 1956; but the Court can take a judicial notice that during the last fifty years a different form of marriage has been devised and adopted by these Buddhists or those who were converted from the Scheduled Caste to Buddhist faith at least in this part of the country especially in Maharashtra state.

The different form of marriage is not only adopted but has been recognized as a valid marriage amongst these people. Thousands of marriages are solemnized in this new form and according to these customary, rites and ceremonies of marriage. The refusal to recognize the solemnization of such ceremonies of marriage as a valid and legal marriage will lead these people with untold miseries of grave social consequences.

(i) Judgement of the Supreme Court (Full Bench) P.B. Gajendragadkar, C.J., K.N. Wanchoo, H. Hidayatullah Rajhubar Dayal and J.R. Mudholkar Punjabrao-V/s- Dr. D.P. Meshram AIR 1965, 1179 delivered by Hon'ble J.R. Mudholkar

If a public declaration is made by a person that he has ceased to belong to his old religion and had accepted another religion he will be taken as professing the other religion irrespective of whether the conversion to another religion was efficacious.

The word "Profess" in the presidential order appears to have been used in a sense of an open declaration or practice by a person of the Hindu (or the Sikh) religion. Where, therefore, a person says on the contrary, that he has ceased to be Hindu.

Judgment of the Bombay High Court of Judicature at Bombay bench at Nagpur in *Smt. Shakuntala – V/s- Nilkanth and Others* in Criminal Appeal No. 29 of 1970 decided on 25-10-1972 (Justice Masodkar)

Facts and Details

Shakuntala the bride was married to bridegroom Nilkanth in a village Sakoli, Dist. Bhandara of Maharashtra State. After some years of married life. Smt. Shakuntala, wife was deserted by her husband, Nilkanth who solemnized second marriage with another woman. Smt. Shakuntala's maintenances allowance petition against her husband was dismissed by the Judicial Magistrate First Class Sakoli, Dist. Bhandara and Smt. Shakuntala preferred criminal Appeal No. 29 of 1970 in the High Court, Nagpur Bench, which was also dismissed.

This Judgment is reported on page No. 310 of Maharashtra Law Journal 1973 as below:-

(a) Hindu Marriage Act (25 of 1955) S.S. 2.5 and 7 requirement of valid marriage—

Parties, Hindus at the time of marriage but marrying according to Buddhist rites—fact that such marriages are taking place for last 10 to 15 years is not enough to establish custom—Marriage not valid.

(iv)In another criminal Appeal No. 815 of 1979. The Bombay High Court Judicature at Bombay Hon'ble Justice R.S. Bhonsale J. decided and delivered the Judgment on 28/29.1.1981 same is reported in Maharashtra Law Journal page No. 815 of 1981. in *Babi W/o. Jayant Jagtap – V/s.- Jayant Mahadeo Jagtap (R.S. Bhonsale J.)*

(*v*) VALIDITY OF MARRIAGE BY CONVERTS TO BUDDHISM IN ABSENCE OF SAPTAPADI AND LAJJAHOMA.

Hindu Marriage Act (25 of 1955) S.7 and Penal codes. 494

Persons converted to Buddhism from Scheduled Caste entering into marriage ceremony comprising of worship and garlanding of photographs of Lord Buddha and Dr. Ambedkar and thereafter reciting before those photographs "बुद्ध सरणं गच्छामि, धम्मं सरणं गच्छामि, संघं सरणं गच्छामि" Garlanding each other and taking oath that as wife and husband they would henceforth conduct towards each other – Marriage so performed is legal. Husband after such marriage marrying for the second time commits offence under Sec. 494.

In the same Judgment in Para 13

A copy of this Judgment is directed to the Government of Maharashtra Law and Judiciary Department for consideration. The Government of Maharashtra should persuade the Government of India to introduce necessary amendments to the Hindu Marriage Act 1955, as suggested by the Government of Maharashtra State Law Commission in its Ninth report on "Some aspect of the Hindu Marriage Act" since the issues effecting millions of people involving legitimacy of their children are involved.

(vi) II 1985 Divorce and Matrimonial Cases

Criminal Revision No. 5 of 1984

Decided on 18-9-1984 present Hon'ble Dhabe J. *Rekha – V/s.- Ashok and others*

(1) Code of Criminal procedure 1973 section 125 wife's application for maintenance against alleged husband parties found as Mahar Hindu by caste – Marriage of parties performed according to Buddhist rites. No proof of conversion of Parties to Buddhism. Marriage not legal and applicant held as not entitled to maintenance under section 125 Cr. P.C.

The Supreme Court of India quoted in 1965 page No. 1181 in *Punjabrao –V/s.- Dr. D.P. Meshram*

The main object of Dr. Ambedkar was to secure for the members of the Scheduled Castes an honourable place in society and he felt that the various disabilities placed upon members of these castes were due to the fact that in Hindu religion, to which they belonged, they had been accorded the lowest rank in society with the result that they had come to be regarded as untouchables. He found that Buddhism is the only path of peace and social equality.

Buddhist Marriage: Need for Codification:

Under inspiration of Dr. Babasaheb Ambedkar on Oct. 14 1956, lakhs of people in Maharashtra embraced Buddhism. Since then a large number of Marriages have been solemnized according to the Buddhist ceremony. This ceremony is recognized by the people in the Maharashtra.

The Judgment delivered by the various courts and specially by the Bombay High Court Judicature at Bombay and Nagpur Bench in

(1) Shakuntala V/s. Nilkanth and others, 1972

(2) Babi W/o. Jagtap V/s.- Jayant Mahadeo Jagtap, 1981

(3) Rekha V/s. Ashok and others, 1985

above judgments created the doubt in the minds of the people. Whether such marriages are valid or invalid? and created a confusion in the minds of the people whether the marriages which have been solemnized according to the Buddhist Ceremony are valid.

The lakhs of Buddhist marriages have been held invalid in Maharashtra because of the Bombay High Court Judgment in the above three cases.

People are facing prosecutions lakhs of Buddhist women's legal rights are infringed and women are helpless and being exploited due to non-availability of Buddhist Marriage Act.

In Babi – V/s.- Jagtap 1981 Hon'ble Court delivered the same judgment in Para 13.

A copy of the judgment is directed to be forwarded to the Government of Maharashtra Law and Judiciary Department for consideration. The Government of Maharashtra should persuade the Government of India to introduce necessary amendments to the Hindu Marriage Act 1955, as suggested by the Government of Maharashtra State Law Commission in its Ninth report on "Some aspect of the Hindu Marriage Act" since the issues effecting millions of people involving legitimacy of their children are involved.

It is unfortunate to mention that Bombay High Court had given direction to the State of Maharashtra to take up the matter with the Govt. of India for making suitable amendment in the Hindu Marriage Act 1955. Such direction is given in the case of *Babi* V/s. *State of Maharashtra* 1981 but till date Govt. of Maharashtra has not taken any steps to carry out such judgment. Therefore, there is no other alternative than to enact a Buddhist Marriage and Succession Act.

A stage has been reached when codification at least of the law of Marriage and Succession had become virtually indispensable for fundamental changes, which had become inevitable to furnish fair and equitable solution to some of the most controversial question relating to the law of marriage and succession of Buddhist.

It has been generally recognized for a long time that the rules of marriage should be according to the Buddhist rites and ceremonies recognized under a body of law.

Buddhist Marriage and Succession Act, 2007

PART ONE

(1) Short Title

This Act shall be known as "Buddhist Marriage and Succession Act-2007."

(2) Extent

This Act shall be applicable to all the Buddhist Citizens throughout the State and is retrospective in its operation.

(3) Definitions

(1) Marriage means "Buddhist Marriage"

(2) "**BHANTE**" "**BHIKKHU**" "**MENDICANT**' means a Buddhist Monk who is authorized to solemnize Buddhist Marriage.

(3) "**UPASAKA**" means a competent citizen, a follower of "**Buddha Dhamma**" and essence of the Dhamma, is authorized to solemnize Buddhist Marriage.

(4) "**Bouddha Vihara**" means a place where people offer their obeisance (Prayer) to Lord Buddha. Such place where Buddhist marriage is solemnized.

(5) Customs and Ceremonies

Since 14th Oct 1956 conversion to Buddhism by Scheduled Caste, the Buddhists represented a simple and solemn ceremony of marriage is adopted by the Buddhist from the year 1956 onwards is said to be the customary form of valid marriage and recognized amongst Buddhists.

(a) Customs

The custom is defined as under.

There are five ingredients included in it

1. It has been continuously and uniformly observed for a long time.
2. It has obtained the force of Law
3. It is certain
4. It is not unreasonable or opposed to public policy
5. In case of a rule applicable only to a family, it has not been discontinued by the family.

As per the *Oxford Dictionary* custom means "The usual way of behaving or acting the particular established way of behaving."

The custom in general is a practice that has become habitual. In English Law, a custom is an ancient rule of law for a particular locality, differing from the common law of the country. Traditionally, much of the common law was based on what had become customary in the country at large and in this sense custom is indeed the mother of all institutions.

The parents or the family heads of both prospective bride and bridegroom exchange their wishes to tie them in wedlock having given their consent. They agree to enhance cordial relations between two families and perform a ceremony called Engagement (Saksha Gandha) before a select gathering of near and dear ones of the two families and family friends.

(b) Ceremonies

The marriage ceremony is performed even by the *Upasaka* who is a common man devoted to the duties of *Upasaka*. There is no such condition that the marriage should be performed by the *Bhikkhu* or *Monk* only.

(a) At the time of marriage bride must be 18 yrs. and bridegroom of 21 yrs age.

(b) At the time of marriage ceremony the bride and bridegroom should wear simple white dress/clothes.

(c) Bride and Bridegroom worship the photographs of Lord Buddha and Dr. Babasaheb Ambedkar, lit the candles before photographs and garland the photographs.

(d) With folded hands before the above Photographs and recital of Trisharan/Panchasheel, Buddha Vandana, Dhamma Vandana, Sangha Vandana, Mahamangal Sutta, Mahamangal Gatha and "Sadhu"-"Sadhu"-"Sadhu" are recited.

(e) After this the bride and bridegroom garland each other and the persons who witness the marriage ceremony shower flowers on them.

(f) Later on the bride and bridegroom take the oath in the presence of the assembled guests and invitees.

(g) Rubbing Ashtagandha by bridegroom to the forehead of bride.

(h) The bridegroom ties the *Mangal-Sutra* to the bride.

(i) No dowry is offered by either side.

(5) Conditions for A Buddhist Marriage

A marriage is solemnized between two major persons, *i.e.,* man and woman irrespective of their faith if the following conditions are fulfilled:

(1) Neither party has a spouse living at the time of the marriage.

At the time of the marriage neither party

(a) Is incapable of giving a valid consent to it in consequence of unsoundness of mind or

(b) Though capable of giving a valid consent has been suffering from mental disorder of such a kind or to such an extent as to be unfit for marriage and procreation of children.

(c) Has been subject to recurrent attacks of insanity.

(2) The bridegroom has completed the age of (twenty one years) and the bride the age of (eighteen years) at the time of the marriage.

The parties are not within a degrees of prohibited relationship.

(6) Rites and Rituals

Person eligible to solemnize Buddhist Marriage.

(1) BHANTE, BHIKKHU, MENDICANT, *i.e.,* a Buddhist Monk is authorized to solemnize marriage according to Buddhist Marriage Ceremony.

(2) Any Buddhist Upasaka is authorized to solemnize marriage according to Buddhist marriage ceremony.

The words uttered by them are as under

Duties of the bridegroom

1. सम्माननाय	I will Honour my wife
2. अनवमाननाय	I will not disrespect my wife
3. अनितिचरीयाय	I will not do a bad thing and I will refrain from doing the same
4. इस्सरियवोस्सगेन	I will keep my wife happy by giving the necessary things of life
5. अलंकारानुप्पददानेन	I will treat my wife as equal in days of happiness and prosperity.

Duties of bride

1. सुसंविहितकम्मन्ता	I will take care of my family members.
2. सुसंघहित परिजना	I will show courtesy to my family members.
3. अनतिचारिणी	I will not do a bad thing and I will refrain from doing the same.
4. सम्मतं अनुरक्खणं	I will protect my house by all means.
5. दक्खा च अनलसा च सब्बकिच्चेसु	I will do my household works with due care and curiosity.
	Thus the marriage is solemnized.

(7) Marriage between Buddhist and Non-buddhist

A marriage solemnized according to the Buddhist ceremony between two major persons one of whom is a Buddhist and other is non-Buddhist, the couple shall be declared as Buddhist and all the concessions, facilities provided by Govt., the couple and their progeny shall be eligible and entitled to them as applicable to Buddhists vide *State Govt. G.R. Labour Social Welfare Dept. 12.8.1958.*

(8) Re-marriage (Pat-marriage/Vivah)

In the circumstances, when one of the spouses wishes to get re-married due to (i) death of the other party (ii) Divorce he/she shall be permitted to get re-married after clearing all the legal obligations (if any) as imposed by civil law.

In case of legal divorce, the obligation of providing maintenance to the other party, as directed by the competent court, shall be adhered to before getting re-married.

All conditions and restrictions, etc., applicable in connection with remarriage, prescribed in civil and criminal laws prevailing as to-day shall also be applicable to the Remarrying partners in Buddhist Marriages.

(9) Certificate of Buddhist Marriages

This certificate of marriage is issued according to provisions of Buddhist Marriage Act-2007 enacted by Government of Maharashtra.

Any *Upasaka or Bhante, Bhikkhu* can perform marriage as per Buddhist Ceremonies. He will have to issue certificate of solemnizing of marriage. On the basis of such certificate, invitation card, photograph of bridegroom and bride and witnesses to marriage, the sub-registrar of marriages duly filled in the proforma shall issue certificate of marriage to the applicants remitting fees admissible at that time such certificate is to be issued immediately.

(10) Registration of Buddhist Marriages

(1) For the purpose of facilitating the proof of Buddhist marriages, the Government may make rules providing that the

parties to any such marriage may have the particulars relating to their marriage entered in such manner and subject to such conditions as may be prescribed in a Buddhist Marriage Register kept for the purpose.

(2) Notwithstanding anything contained in sub-section (1) the state Government may, if it is of the opinion that it is necessary or expedient so to do, provide that the entering of the particulars referred to be in sub section (1) shall be compulsory in the state.

(3) The Buddhist Marriage Register shall, at all reasonable times, be open for inspection and shall be admissible as evidence therein contained and certified extracts therefrom shall on application, be given by the Registrar on payment of the prescribed fees.

(4) Notwithstanding any thing contained in this section the validity of any Buddhist marriage shall, in no way, be affected by the omission to make the entry.

"Bhavatu Saba Mangalam"

THE BUDDHIST SUCCESSION ACT - 2OO7

CHAPTER-I

PRELIMINARY

1. TITLE and Extent:

1. The title to the present Act states the Act relates to the law of succession among Buddhists. This Act shall be called the Buddhist Succession Act 2007.
2. It extends to the state of Maharashtra.

2. Application of Act:

This Act applies

(a) To any person who is Buddhist by religion.

(b) To any person who comes under the definition of Buddhist given in Buddhist Marriage Act-2007.

(c) A person who is converted on 14th Oct 1956 and thereafter to Buddhism and his offsprings.

(d) The enforcement of this Act shall be retrospective in its order.

Explanation: These following persons are Buddhist by religion, as the case may be.

(*a*) Any child, legitimate or illegitimate, both of whose parents are Buddhist by religion.

(*b*) Any child, legitimate or illigitimate, one of whose parents is a Buddhist by religion, and who is brought up as a member of the tribe, community, group or family to which such parent belongs or belonged.

(*c*) Any person who is a convert or reconvert to the Buddhism.

3. Definition and Interpretation

(1) In this Act, unless the context otherwise requires -

(*a*) *"Agnate"* one person is said to be an "agnate" of another if the two are related by blood or adoption wholly through males.

(*b*) *"cognate"* one person is said to be a cognate of another if two are related by blood or adoption but not wholly through males.

(*c*) "full blood", "half blood" and "uterine blood"

(*i*) Two persons said to be related to each other by full blood when they are descended from a common ancestor by the same wife, and by half blood when they are descended from a common ancestor but by different wives.

(*ii*) Two persons are said to be related to each by uterine blood when they are descended from a common ancestor but by different wives.

In this clause "ancestor" included the father and "ancestress" the mother.

(*d*) "heir" means any person, male or female, who is entitled to succeed to the property of an intestate under this Act.

(*e*) "intestate" a person is deemed to die intestate in respect of property of which he or she has not made a testamentary disposition capable of taking effect.

(*f*) "related" means related by legitimate kinship.

4. THE SCHEDULE

Class I Heirs	***Class II Heirs (in nine categories)***
(1) Mother	*Category I.* Father
	Category II.
(2) Widow.	(a) Son's daughter's sons.
	(b) Son's daughter's daughter.
(3) Daughter	(c) Brothers.
(4) Son	(d) Sister
	Category III.
(5) Widow of pre-deceased son	
	(a) Daughter's Son's son
(6) Son of a pre-deceased son	(b) Daughters' Son's daughter
(7) Daughter of a pre-deceased son	(c) Daughters' daughters' son
	(d) Daughters' daughter's daughter
(8) Widow of a pre-deceased son of a pre-deceased son	*Category IV.*
(9) Daughter of a pre-deceased son	(a) Brother's son
of a pre-deceased son	(b) Brother's daughter
	(c) Sister's son
(10) Son of a pre-deceased son of a pre-deceased son	(d) Sister's daughter *Category V.*
(11) Daughter of a pre-deceased	(a) Father's father
daughter	(b) Father's mother
	Category VI.
(12) Son of pre-deceased daughter	(a) Father's widow
	(b) Brother's widow.
(13) Son of pre-deceased daughter of	*Category VII.*
a pre-deceased daughter.	(a) Father's brother
	(b) Father's sister.
(14) Daughter of pre-deceased daughter of a pre-deceased daughter.	*Category VIII.*
(15) Daughter of pre-deceased son of	(a) Mother's Father.
a pre-deceased daughter	(b) Mother's mother.
	Category IX.
(16) Daughter of a pre-deceased	(a) Mother's brother.
daughter of pre-deceased son.	(b) Mother's sister

CHAPTER II

INTESTATE SUCCESSION

5. Devolution of Interest in Coparcenary Property

(1) The daughter of a coparcener shall.

(a) By birth become a coparcener in her own right in the same manner as the son.

(b) Have the same rights in the coparcenary property as she would have had if she had been a son.

(c) Be subject to the same liabilities in respect the said comparcenary property as that of a son.

(2) The Coparcenary property shall be deemed to have been divided as if a partition had taken place, and-

(a) The daughter is allowed the same share as is allowed to a son.

(b) The share of the pre-deceased son or a, pre-deceased daughter, as they would have got had they been alive at the time, of partition, shall be allotted to the surviving child of such pre-deceased son or of such pre-deceased daughter and

(c) The share of the pre-deceased child of a pre-deceased son or of a pre-deceased daughter, as such child would have got had he or she been alive at the time of the partition, shall be allowed to the child of such pre-deceased child of the pre-deceased son or a pre-deceased daughter, as the case may be.

Explanation: For the purposes of this section "Partition" means any partition made by execution of a deed of partition duly registered under the Registrar Act 1908 (16 of 1908) or partition effected by a decree of a court.

6. General Rules of Succession in the Case of Buddhist Male

The property of a male Buddhist dying intestate shall devolve according to the provisions of this chapter -

(a) Firstly, upon the heirs, being the relatives specified in class I of the schedule.

(b) Secondly, if there is no heir of class I, then upon the heirs, being the relatives specified in class II of the schedule.

(c) Thirdly, if there is no heir of any of the two classes, then upon the agnates of the deceased; and

(d) Lastly, if there is no agnate, then upon the cognates of the deceased.

7. Distribution of Property Among Heirs in Class I of the Schedule

The property of an intestate shall be divided among the heirs in class I of the schedule in accordance with the following rules.

Rule 1 - The intestate's widow, or if there are more widows than one, all the widows together, shall take one share.

Rule 2 - The surviving sons and daughters and the mother of the intestate shall each take one share.

Rule 3 - The heirs in the branch of each pre-deceased son or each pre-deceased daughter of the intestate shall take between them one share.

Rule 4 - The distribution of the share referred to in Rule 3...

(1) Among the heirs in the branch of the pre-deceased son shall be so made that his widow (or widows together) and the surviving sons and daughters get equal portions, and the branch of his predeceased sons gets the same portion.

(2) Among the heirs in the branch of the pre-deceased daughter shall be so made that the surviving sons and daughters get equal portion.

8. Distribution of Property Among Heirs in Class II of the Schedule

The Property of an intestate shall be divided between the heirs specified in any one entry in class II of the schedule so that they share equally.

9. Order of Succession Among Agnates and Cognates

The order of succession among agnates or cognates, as the case may be, shall be determined in accordance with the rules of preference laid down hereunder.

Rule 1 - of two heirs, the one who has fewer or no degrees of ascent is preferred.

Rule 2 - where the number of degrees of ascent is the same or none, that heir is preferred who has fewer or no degrees of descent.

Rule 3 - where neither heirs is entitled to be preferred to the other under Rule 1 or Rule 2 they take simultaneously.

10. Computation of Degrees

(1) For the purposes of determining the order of succession among agnates or cognates, relationship shall be reckoned from the intestate to the heir in terms of degrees of ascent or degrees of descent or both, as the case may be.

(2) Degrees of ascent and degrees of descent shall be computed inclusive of the intestate.

(3) Every generation constitutes a degree either ascending or descending.

11. Property of a Female Buddhist as her Absolute Property

(1) Any property possessed by a female Buddhist, whether acquired before or after the commencement of this Act, shall be held by her as full owner thereof and not as a limited owner.

Explanation: In this sub-section "Property" includes both movable and immovable property acquired by a female Buddhist by inheritance or devise, or at a partition, or in lieu of maintenance or arrears of maintenance, or by gift from any person, whether a relative or not, before, at or after her marriage, or by her own skill or exertion, or by purchase or by prescription, or in any other manner whatsoever, and also any such property held by her as stridhana immediately before the commencement of this Act.

(2) Nothing contained in sub-section (1) shall apply to any property acquired by way of gift or under a will or any other instrument or under a decree or order of a civil court or under an award where the terms of the gift, will or other instrument or the decree, order or award prescribe a restricted estate in such property.

The Supreme Court held in BAIVIJAYA v/s Thakuribai Chela Bhain AIR 1979 S.C. 993

This section recognizes equality of sexes and elevates the women from subservient position in the field of economy to a higher pedestal. Now the women can enjoy and have full powers as regards disposal of property held by them. They are to be taken as owners without putting any artificial limitations on their right of ownership.

12. General Rules of Succession in the Case of Female Buddhist

(1) The Property of a female Buddhist dying intestate shall devolve according to the rules set out in section 14.

(a) Firstly, upon the sons and daughters (including the children of any Pre-deceased son or daughter) and the husband.

(b) Secondly, upon the heirs of the husband.

(c) Thirdly, upon the mother and father.

(d) Fourthly, upon the heirs of the father and

e) Lastly, upon the heirs of the mother.

(2) Notwithstanding anything contained in sub-section (1).

(a) Any property inherited by a female Buddhist from her father or mother shall devolve, in the absence of any son or daughter of the deceased (including the children of any pre-deceased son or daughter) not upon the other heirs referred to in sub-section (1) in the order specified therein, but upon the heirs of the father, and

(b) Any property inherited by a female Buddhist from her husband or from her father-in-law shall devolve, in the absence of any son or daughter of the deceased (including the children of any pre-deceased son or daughter) not upon the other heirs referred to in sub-section (1) in the order specified therein, but upon the heirs of the husband.

13. Order of Succession and Manner of Distribution Among Heirs of a Famale Buddhist

The order of Succession among the heirs referred to in section 13 shall be, and the distribution of the intestate's property among those heirs shall take place, according to the following rules namely.

Rule 1 - Among the heirs specified in sub-section (1) of section 13 those in one entry shall be preferred to those in any succeeding entry and those including in the same entry shall take simultaneously.

Rule 2 - If any son or daughter of the intestate had pre-deceased the intestate leaving his or her own children alive at the time of the intestate's death, the children of such son or daughter shall take between them the share which such son or daughter would have taken if living at the intestate's death.

Rule 3 - The devolution of the property of the intestate on the heirs referred to in clause (b) (d) & (e) of sub-section in sub-section (2) of section 13 shall be in the same order and according to the same rules as would have applied if the property had been the father's or mother's or the husband's as the case may be, and such person has died intestate in respect thereof immediately after the intestate's death.

14. General Provisions Relatings to Succession

Full blood preferred to half blood. Heirs related to an intestate by full blood shall be preferred to heirs related by half blood, if the nature of the relationship is the same in every other respect.

15. Mode of Succession of Two or More Heirs

If two or more heirs succeed together to the property of an intestate, they shall take the property-

(a) Save as otherwise expressly provided in this Act, per capita and not per strips and

(b) As tenants-in-common and not as joint tenants.

16. Right of Child in Womb

A child who was in the womb at the time of death of an intestate and who is subsequently born alive has the same right to inherit to the intestate as if he or she had been born before the death of the intestate, and the inheritance shall be deemed to vest in such a case with effect from the date of the death of the intestate.

17. Presumption in Cases of Simultaneous Deaths

Where two persons have died in circumstances rendering it uncertain whether either of them, and if so which, survived the other, then for all purposes affecting succession to property, it shall be presumed, until the contrary is proved, that younger survived the elder.

18. Murderer Disqualified

A person who commits murder or abets the commission of murder shall be disqualified from inheriting the property of the person murdered, or any other property in furtherance of the succession to which he or she committed or abetted of commission of the murder.

19. Succession when Heir Disqualified

If any person is disqualified from inheriting any property under this Act, it shall devolve as if such person had died before the intestate.

20. Disease, Defect, etc. Not be Disqualified

No person shall be disqualified from succeeding to any property on the ground of any disease, defect or deformity or save as provided in this Act, any other ground whatsoever.

21. Failure of Heirs

If an intestate has left no heir qualified to succeed to his or her property in accordance with the provisions of this Act, such property shall devolve on the government, and the government shall take the property subject to all the obligations and liabilities to which an heir would have been subjected.

CHAPTER III

22. Testamentary Succession

Any Buddhist may dispose of by will or other testamentary disposition any property, which is capable of being so (disposed by him or by her) in accordance with the provisions of the Indian Succession Act 1925.

8

Deeksha Bhoomi of Ambedkar

C.D. Naik

Situated on the River Nag, Nagpur is the orange-growing capital of India. It was once the capital of the central province, but was later incorporated into Maharashtra. Long ago it was a centre for the aboriginal Gond tribes who remained in power until the early 18th century, and many Gonds still live in the region.

In the recent years there has been some desultory agitation for a separate Indian state of Vidarbha, which would have Nagpur as its capital.

On 14th October each year the town is host to the hundred thousands of Buddhists who come to celebrate the anniversary of Dr. Ambedkar's conversion to Buddhists in 1956. An estimated three million low caste Hindus followed him in converting to Buddhism that year.

Nagpur's History

Nagpur was supposed to be the capital of first Buddhist followers of Naga Tribe situated at the bank of river Naga, which is still flowing across the city. In hills and hillocks of Hidimba Tekadi, 40 kms. from Nagpur near Mansar, pieces of terracotta from Maurya, Shunga and Vakataka periods have been obtained by archeologists. The name Nagpur appeared for the first time on record in 10th century A.D. The Gond King Bakht Buland Shah of Devagad State founded Nagpur city on the bank of Nag river joined by 12 small hamlets known as Rajapur Barasa in 1702. His eldest son Raja Chand ascended the throne of Devagad in 1706 and he shifted his capital from Devagad to Nagpur. He constructed his fortress at Mahal surrounded by 3 kms. long wall and planned layout of Nagpur city. He ruled for 33 years. After him Bhosle dynasty of Deor under Raghuji dominated the place in 1742. Then Pendhari marauders burnt the city in 1765 and in 1811 again but Bhonsle developed the areas called Nawabpur, old Mangalwari, Shukrawari tank, Hansapuri, Jaripatka, Rajabaksha, Rambagh and Itwari. The city was lost to Britishers from the Marathas at the battle of Sitabuldi in 1817 and 1853, when it was incorporated into British residency. The first freedom struggle of 1857 laid down the foundation of many non-violent, non-cooperation movements. In 1861 Nagpur became capital of Central provinces. Three years later the Municipality of Nagpur was established.

The first train steamed out of Nagpur to Bombay was in 1867. In 1891 the seventh All India Congress Session under the chairmanship of P. Anandacharlu of Chennai was held at Lalbagh on 28th December. Eight years later plague took heavy toll in Nagpur. Two years later Cotton market and C.P. Club were founded with foundation of Indra in 1905, Punjabi line in 1911 and English daily 'The Hitavada' in the same year. In 1912 Vidhan Sabha was laid. The year 1920 saw laying down of new Congress Nagar colony near Dhantoli park on the conclusion of 35th All India Congress session, Nagpur under the presidentship of Shri Jamnalal Bajaj. On May 30, Dr. Ambedkar addressed The Untouchable conference chaired by Chhatrapati Shahu Maharaj. Mahatma Gandhi led the Congress since, three years later Pt. Nehru and Rajrishi Tandon involved themselves in protest rally of Jhanda Satyagrah Andolan and to mark this event Nagpur University was founded (1923). This was followed by the laying of Ramdaspeth and Lashkari Bagh, New Colony, and Dhantoli. In 1930 on 8-9th August All India Bahishkrit Classes Conference under the presidentship of Dr. Ambedkar was also held in Nagpur. Gondawana Club and Hindi Navbharat were started in 1934. Hindustani Lal Sena was founded by Maganlal Bagdi during the period between 1936 and 1938. In 1940 Netaji Subhash Chandra Bose's Forward Block Party organized its second All India session. When Bharat Chodo Andolan was vigorously running in "Nagpur in 1942 freedom fighter Shankar was hanged. On 13th December 1945 Dr. Ambedkar addressed public gathering and on 3rd September 1946 the Scheduled Caste Federation staged a satyagrah against Poona Pact."

Finally India got its freedom in 1947. All India Radio Station was founded in the city in the year. Nagpur was declared capital of Madhya Pradesh in 1950 and a year later Nagpur Municipality became Municipal Corporation, which later on 15.10.1956 gave its encomium to Dr. Ambedkar after his historical peaceful Dhamma revolution.

Bharatiya Jansangh came into being in 1951. On 2nd May 1954, Dr. Ambedkar visited Vidarbha Sahitya Sangha and on 14th October 1956 Dr. Ambedkar embraced Buddhism along with his five lakh followers at *Deeksha Bhoomi* followed by Nagpur Municipal Corporation's encomium conferred on him the following day. On 17th October 1957, the Nag Vidarbha Andolan Samiti was formed and a year later the third All India Congress party session was held at Abhyankar Nagar. It was in 1960 that Nagpur was transferred from Madhya Pradesh and it became the second capital to Maharashtra with first session of state legislature held there.

First Buddhist followers of Naga tribe were settled at the bank of Naga river in Nagpur. Dr. Ambedkar was in Nagpur at five times, first, when in 1930 on 8-9th August All India Depressed Classes Congress was held on fundamental rights and philosophy under his presidentship, second, when on 13th December 1945 Dr. Ambedkar addressed public gathering, third, when on 3rd September 1946 the Scheduled Caste Federation staged Satyagrah against Poona Pact, fourth when on 2nd May 1954 Dr. Ambedkar visited Vidarbha Sahitya Sangha, and fifth, when on 14th October 1956 Dr. Ambedkar embraced Buddhism along with his five lakh followers at Deeksha Bhoomi and when Nagpur Municipal Corporation gave its encomium to Dr. Ambedkar the next day. Thus Nagpur has been a well established city, politically active, historically documented and hollowed by visits of Dr. Ambedkar.

Need for Political Protection of Minorities Proposed by Ambedkar

While speaking on the Budget on February 1927 in the Bombay Legislative Council Dr. Ambedkar said, "If all communities are to be brought to the level of equality, then, the only remedy is to adopt the principle of inequality and to give favoured treatment to those who are below the level."

Writing his note of dissent to the report of the Simon Commission in 1927-28 Dr. Ambedkar said, "There will be a general agreement that the needs of the minority for the political protection are commensurate with the power it has to protect itself in the social struggle. That power obviously depends upon the educational status of the minorities. The higher the educational and economic status of a minority, the less is the need for it being politically protected. On the other hand the lower the educational and economic status of a minority, the greater will be the need for its political protection."

Starte Committee

Reservation in Government services, Assemblies and education were accepted both by the Central and Provincial Governments long before the inception of the Constitution of India. The Government of Bombay appointed under an ICS Officer, Mr. Starte, the Starte Committee in 1930. Its report highlighted the condition of the Depressed Classes as caused by pollution and isolation and suggested some special facilities in education, reservation and recruitment in the public services approved by the then Bombay Government in 1930 and accepted by the then India Government purely on the ground of the principle of social justice in 1934.

Eligibility Criteria

The criteria of eligible people for such political and social safeguard and social justice adopted by the Indian Government of the time and post-independent Constitution of India were two namely, (1) inability of the community to protect itself in the social struggle and (2) Community's backwardness in educational, economic and social status and position.

Principle of Reservation

Applying these principles to the Buddhist converts it is obvious that they are entitled to reservation and safeguards, concessions and facilities which they enjoyed before their conversion. In order to enable those who were denied rights and privileges, the necessity was felt and was accepted to give such people special representation by way of giving reservation and safeguards so that they can raise themselves in the social scale to enable them to give their consent to the Democratic Rule and to take part in the administration of the country. Besides this political foundation there was social philosophy behind this. The Indian Constitution not only has accepted the philosophy of fundamental rights, but has created a very powerful State as the central authority over and above the authority of the caste and the Indian Social System. The State, has been considered and determined in the constitution itself as a powerful instrument of changing the Indian society itself.

Based on the theory of fundamental rights and principle of reservation Article 46 of Indian Constitution and Article 35 of the Constitution of Burma respectively read: "The State shall promote with special care the educational and economic interest of (Indian Constitution) weaker section/(Burmese Constitution) weaker and less advanced section, (both Indian and Burmese Constitutions) of the people, and, (Indian Constitution) in particular, of the Scheduled Castes and the Scheduled Tribes, (both Constitutions) and shall protect from social injustice and all forms of exploitation." This has its origin in dissent note of Ambedkar to Simon Commission report on the ground of social justice referred to above. No other Constitution of world spoke about such protection clauses. Dr. B.N. Rao was the constitutional advisor to Drafting Committees both of the Indian and Burmese Constitutions. Directive principle under Article 46 of Indian Constitution is as justiciable as the Federal Principle of American Constitution and Principle of Sovereignty of Parliament under Constitution of United Kingdom and similar principle in the Constitution of Ireland. Chief Justice Shri P.B. Gajendragadkar of Supreme Court also decided in favour of its justifiability. Principle of constitutions presupposes the principle of social justice. Article 46 also enjoins the State to promote with special care the educational and economic interests of the weaker sections of the people besides protecting them from social injustice and exploitation. Article 15(4) reads that it would be open to the State to make special provisions for the advancement of any socially and educationally backward classes of citizens or for the Scheduled Castes and Scheduled Tribes. Article 46 directs the State and Article 15(4) obligates it under fundamental right of a citizen. Both are complementary. Article 16(4) as fundamental right of citizen under part XVI of Constitution provided for reservation in appointments and posts for the purpose of giving representation in the public services in favour of any backward class of citizens. Both Articles 15(4) and 16(4) speak of exercise of power by state to advance socially and educationally and in public service sector the backward class of citizens, implying SCs, STs and Weaker Section of the people under Article 46. Article 335 is related to this in that it mentioned taking into consideration the claims of the SCs and STs at the time of appointment in the public services. So Articles 330 and 335 are complementary to Articles 46, 15(4) and 16(4) in accepting the principle of the reservation for adequate representation in the legislature and in the public services etc. for economically and socially backward class of citizens or weaker sections of the people or SCs and STs.

Buddhist Converts as Weaker Section

New Buddhist converts are a weaker section. Weaker section of the people, according to Dr. Babasaheb Ambedkar's speech made in Parliament on 12th May 1951, includes the SCs and STs and means Backward Classes whether socially backward classes or economically backward classes as construed by Pandit Nehru and also interpreted by Basu in his commentary on the Constitution of India, Vol. I, p. 469.

Article 25 of Part III of Constitution of India read "For the purpose of providing for social welfare and reform [akin to promoting with special care the educational and economic interests (rights by Samond) of the weaker sections of the people in Article 46] the reference to the word 'Hindus' shall be construed including a reference to persons professing the Sikh, the Jain or the Buddhist religion. But Jains being Bania and businessmen and economically and socially better off they do not need protection in social struggle. Unlike them, the Buddhists are a weaker section in the social struggle and struggle for existence and stand in need of all concessions and facilities and safeguards to be guaranteed by the State under Constitution as per Articles 25, 46, 330, 335, 15(4) and 16(4) taken together. Then only will they be spearhead of the new movement for creating conditions for the establishment of the New Indian Society on the principles of justice, liberty, equality and fraternity.

Thus, before visiting Nagpur Dr. Ambedkar said, "If all communities are to be brought to the level of equality, then, the only remedy is to adopt the principle of inequality and to give favoured treatment to those who are below the level. There will be a general agreement that the needs of the minority for the political protection are commensurate with the power it has to protect itself in the social struggle. The lower the educational and economic status of a minority, the greater will be the need for its political protection."

The Starte Committee gave some special facilities in education, reservation and recruitment even before the inception of the Constitution of India.

Inability of community to protect itself against social struggle and backwardness of community in education, economic and social life made it eligible for special protection and safeguards. With this protection they can give their consent to be ruled by the politically dominant class.

Caste and social system are to be ruled by democratic political system. Constitutional principle is based on social philosophy of justice. Indian constitution in the forms of its

Articles 15(4), 16(4), 25, 46, 330, 335, Burmese constitution in its Article 35, Irish, American and English Constitutions accepted this philosophy for their backward sections of society whether they be in educational-economic-social life or/and from work participation point of view as are SCs/STs/Weaker/ Backward classes in India.

New Buddhists are a weaker section socially and economically as are the SCs and STs or Backward Classes. Hindu means Hindus, Buddhist, Sikh and Jain communities, the last being socially protected and the others in need of such special favour. Then only new society based on equality, liberty, fraternity and justice will take birth in India.

Treating the Buddhist group as SC/ST/Weaker/Backward section of Indian society His Excellency and Professor Shri Bhandare dealt with socio-economic, educational, political, religious and cultural problems of Buddhist community forty one years ago. He expected those in power and authority to enable birth of new regenerated society by promoting the conversion of Indian masses to Buddhism. Buddhist issue of status and identity is of lasting character. The Government of Maharashtra recognized the weaker social status of the converted Buddhist minority and there is need for the national central Government to follow the suit. Judicial thought of the world judges would decide in favour of their eligibility for special favour in above respects. Fundamental rights of citizen, Directive principles of Constitution and Human Rights consciousness of the world will not fail in putting the problems of the Buddhists in the context of those of the social categories like SC/STs of India.

Are the present Buddhists the members of the earlier Scheduled Castes? Why the scheduled castes enjoy political, social, economic and educational safeguards, benefits and concessions and facilities? Why were the Scheduled Castes given those special concessions and facilities?

It is generally accepted that even as all members of one religion observe same set of religious code of conduct even so citizens of one nation are supposed to abide by uniform set of ultimate purposes and pursuits. The SCs similarly observed all religious rites, festivities, gods and goddesses, scriptures, culture, and other precepts of Hinduism but despite this they were held polluting and forced to live in isolation. This treatment has been revolting against the ultimate national purpose of equality of status, and promotion of dignity of the individual and the unity of the nation. Conversion to Buddhism has reversed this inimical mind-set to fraternity of society under polity of democracy through Articles 14, 15, 16(1) and (4), 25, 38, 39, 43, 46, 74, 75, 79, 81, 330, 332, and 335 but it has been confined to the practitioners alone and it has not been generalised as SC/ST commission also corroborated the facts.

The Buddhist Community : Status and Difficulties

The problem is about the status and difficulties faced by the Buddhist community even after sixty years of their Independent nation. From non-Buddhist Hindu point of view they are as Scheduled Castes as they were untouchables before. However high aspiring and ennobling attitudes these people held in their day-to-day lives the others' attitude remained unchanged despite political upheaval and change of power in Uttar Pradesh from dominant castes to the Scheduled Castes and Buddhists. This chapter attempts to highlight the issues in the changed scenario.

The Buddhist minority problem, as far as it is a material one, is permanent issue since converts to Buddhism are not likely to retrace their step, and thus it cannot be left to the sweet will of any particular department of Government or to the Cabinet of any particular time. This was made clear by Prof. R.D. Bhandare's address delivered in Legislative Assembly Debates, Vol. No. 7, on 25th February 1958, p. 519).

Sukhdeo K. Thorat in his article on 'Economic Status of the Social Groups in Maharashtra: Emerging Issues' reported trend in consumption and poverty among the new Buddhists as under:

Poverty Level

The NSS survey for 1987-88 for the first time also provided the data for the neo-Buddhists (*i.e.* scheduled caste converted to Buddhism). This group constitutes a sizable portion of SC in the state. The level of poverty was the maximum among neo-Buddhists (61.50%) followed by 54% among SC and ST. The poverty level among general population works out to 35.72 per cent. Assuming that there was a marginal decline in the level of poverty between 1987-88 and 1993-94 little less than 60 per cent of neo-Buddhists may be still below poverty line. (p.7).

Unemployment

He further clarified about unemployment among the SCs and STs that in the case of unemployment rates based on usual status there is hardly any difference across social group. In fact the unemployment rate of SC/ST is slightly lower than other section in 1977-78 and 1983. This is not surprising as the NSS treat a person to be usually employed if he or she work for more than 180 days in a year. Since the SCs have limited alternative source of income other than wage employment, their participation in the work around the year would be certainty. (p. 6).

About how the neo-Buddhists were recorded as Scheduled Caste members the Census of India 1991 of Maharashtra by J.K. Banthia, Director of Census Operations, Maharashtra, Mumbai 1993 stated that "During the enumeration period of 1991 Census, about every individual information was asked whether he/she belonged to Scheduled Caste/Scheduled Tribe and the information was noted in the concerned Individual Slip. While recording a person as Scheduled Caste, it was ensured that he/she belonged to Hindu or Sikh or Buddhist or Nav/Neo Buddhist religion and the corresponding caste name found place in the list of the scheduled castes (p. xiv).

Summary

Buddhist problems are mainly five namely, (1) persistent inimical attitude of caste Hindus did not let them live as dignified Buddhists, (2) Even though the Hindus did not honour them as their own brethren the Buddhists are not to revert to their traditional religion unlike tribal converts to Christianity these days, (3) poverty among Buddhists is worse than that among SC/ST communities, it is even eighteen times greater than that existing among general population, (4)

Unemployment among SCs and STs is lower than that among other sections because working for even as less as for 180 days a year is also held as employment by NSS in case of only-wage-dependent persons like SCs, and (5) Buddhists are recorded as scheduled caste by census operators identifying them by their prior status of caste found in the list of Scheduled Castes.

Significance of Study

This study will resolve notional problem by underlying the need of practical measure on the part of political authority. Political power in the hands of the SCs will create conditions for social equality, even to the extent of changing Hindu mind-set. This implied the weak political will power of the present authority that let the subjected to prolong in subjugation to poverty and ignorance.

Study area commensurated with the status and problems of Buddhists of Nagpur. Samples represented urban and educated Buddhists with awareness and understanding of the situations surrounding them. In the year 2006 the Golden Jubilee of the historical Babasaheb Ambedkar's Deeksha Diwas Anniversary was pompously and massively celebrated at Deeksha Bhoomi and its adjacent areas. This was also high time to assess the changes taking place and taken place already in the lives of new Buddhist converts of this Nag city. Most of the samples were consulted at the holy pilgrimage of Deeksha Bhoomi and in the International Buddhist Convention held in VIP Deshpande hall in front of MLA hostel, Nagpur in that year.

Objective of the Study

This study has been conducted in keeping with the following main objectives:

1. To know the demographic profile of the Buddhist minority in Nagpur.
2. To understand the educational development of the Buddhist minority of Nagpur.
3. To underline the social mobility of Buddhist minority of the area.
4. To highlight the economic advancement of the Buddhist community after its conversion to Buddhist fold.

5. To analyse the data collected from the study area and discover impact of Buddhism on the socio-economic, cultural, educational, ethical, religious and political life of minority community in Nagpur, and
6. To draw conclusions based on the data and formulate suggestions for the inclusion in policies of implementing agencies.

Time and Budget

Primary data was collected during the 50th Golden Jubillee anniversary of Dr. Ambedkar's conversion to Buddhism in the year 2006 and the project was approved by the Head of the Institute in January 2008. Appropriate area, samples, tools and techniques were utilised for collecting data and drawing findings relating to the status and problems of Buddhist minority of Nagpur.

Growth Rate of Hindu and tribal*, Nagpur District

Census Year	*Hindus*	*Mean decennial growth-rate Hindus*	*Animists and Tribals*	*Mean decennial growth-rate Tribals*
1	*2*	*3*	*4*	*5*
1901	6,60976	..	38,497	-
1911	7,25,399	9.2	36,003	-6.6
1921	6,92,710	-4.06	52,062	36.4
1931	8,62,519	21.8	9,784	-136.7
1941	9,11,889	5.67	66,471	148.6
1951	11,44,411	22.6	Nil	Nil
1961	11,64,247	6,04,500	5,59,747	+1.7

*The population figures are as given by the censuses without regard to the transfer of territory during the decades.

Animists are another class of people who are not admitted among Hindus and are therefore suffering from pollution and seclusion like SCs/STs and Buddhists. The above table shows that in Nagpur District from the period of 60 years from 1901 to 1961 while Hindus were growing in number the tribal people were declining and in the year 1961 the tribal occupied less than half of the population of the Hindus. How this positive growth of the tribals took place remains unexplained.

Nagpur Population Constituents

People of Nagpur belong to different religious communities namely Hindus, Jains, Buddhists, Christians, Muslims, Jews, Sikhs, Zoroastrians, etc. The people largely comprise the society and culture of Nagpur. According to the statistics, the total number of men and women belonging to the different areas of Nagpur is 20,95,489 and 19,55,955 respectively. It is estimated that total urban population of Nagpur is about 21,29,500, which comprises about 4,10,000 households positioned in Nagpur. The given statistics included that about 25% of the total population of Nagpur comprised of the Scheduled Castes and Scheduled Tribes. To begin with, it can be said that Hinduism is the predominant religion of Nagpur. The Nagpur people are the staunch followers of Hinduism: a large part of the population of Nagpur comprises Hindus. The Hindus in Nagpur are divided into a number of castes. The Hindu people in Nagpur are categorized into following castes:

1. Ahirs, 2. Bahana, 3. Badhai, 4. Bhoyer, 5. Brahman, 6. Chambhar, 7. Dhimar, 8. Dhobi, 9. Govari, 10. Kalar, 11. Kayastha, 12. Kosti, 13. Kumbhar, 14. Kunbi, and 15. Mali, etc.

Among the people at Nagpur, Jains community covers a considerable part of the demographics. Furthermore, the Jains are divided into Digambars and Svetambars. The Jains in Nagpur are said to be a set of peace-loving people who avoid the destruction of animals. Beside the Hindus and Jains, the people of Nagpur contain Christians, Parsees and Muslims. Thus, the religion in Nagpur presents a distinct pattern: together with all the religions housed in Nagpur, Nagpur emerges a cosmopolitan district of Maharashtra being bestowed with the title of the 'winter capital of Maharashtra'.

Nagpur culture is an amalgamation of the various cultures prevalent within India. Nagpur culture is a cosmopolitan culture that projects the faiths and beliefs of different communities. The culture of Nagpur boasts of many different religions and beliefs.

Summary

The SCs and STs of Nagpur formed the 25 per cent of the total population of the area surrounded by about 75 per cent of the Hindus. Except for the small body mainly of Banias who follow Jainism the Hindus of the district belong to two main classes: (1) Brahmanic Hindus including Brahmans and other castes who worship Brahmanic gods, and employ Brahmans as their priests; (2) low-caste and tribal Hindus who mainly worship non-Brahmanic and animistic deities. This shows that 25 per cent of the SCs and STs are included among the Hindus despite the fact that their culture and religion are different from them.

If the Buddhists were enumerated as Hindus for the year 1961 their combined population which numbers 13,98,359 forms 92.4 per cent of the district population. It shows an increase of 111.5 per cent over the Hindu population of 1901 and a mean decennial growth rate 19.9 per cent over the Hindu population of 1951. This means that 2,34,112 Buddhists of the city were recorded as Hindus in 1961. They also are different from the Hindus from cultural and religious point of view. Buddhists are also included amongst the Buddhists. This is not strange but in keeping with the Central Government's strategy to include Buddhists among the SCs for social purpose of giving constitutional special favour to them.

Hindu Castes

The Hindu community is found divided into various socially differentiated groups better known as castes. In consonance with the changes in government policy, the census enumeration has eased to take cognizance of these groups since 1941. There were ninety or more castes enumerated in the district in 1931. Of these the most numerous castes in the district in 1931 were the Kunbis, the Mehras or Mahars, the Telis, the Gonds, the Kostis, the Brahmans, the Malis, the Dhimars, the Govaris, and the Barhais who constituted respectively about 19, 17, 8.5, 5.6, 5, 4, 3.6, 2.5, 23 and 1.6 per cent of the population.

Speaking generally about these castes the old District Gazetteer of Nagpur (1908) states: The most numerous castes in the district are the Kunbis constituting 20 per cent of the population, and the Mahars or Mehras 16 per cent. Brahmans are the largest proprietors and own 750 villages or a third of the total number and next to them come Kunbis with 440. The bulk of the population are of Marathi extraction, but in the north of the district there is a fair sprinkling of Kirars, Lodhis and Raghvis, who have come down from the Satpuda plateau, and these are the best agriculturists. Gonds are the only forest tribe, constituting 6 per cent of the population, but many of them have taken to work in the mines, and as coolies and porters in towns, and except in features are hardly distinguishable from Hindus. The remainders live principally in the tracts adjoining the Satpuda hills to the north.

Thus, the Mahar caste constituted 17 per cent of the population of the Nagpur area in 1931. This percentage is more than or at least equal to percentage of SCs and Buddhists to the total population of Maharashtra state.

Marriage Custom among Hindus

Dharrnasastra considers that it is obligatory for every person to marry, as, according to it vivaha (marriage) is one of the sansamskaras (sacraments sanctifying the body) through each of which every man and woman must pass at the proper age and time. But, though marriage is thus universally prescribed for all Hindus, the institution as such is hedged with several rules and restrictions which fall under two main heads, namely, endogamy and exogamy.

Marriage can be the most effective measures for bindinng the divided society by caste but this is not practised to the desired extent.

The Hindu marriage system is a system of prohibition on the basis of caste, subcaste, gotra, father's line and mother's line of degree of relationship despite the fact that cross-cousin marriages and niece-unle marriages are practised among the Brahmanas of the region.

Summary

The system of Hypergamy divides superior and inferior classes of people on the basis of gender and inviting dowry from female party to the male one as practised among the Brahmins, Marathas and Rajputs. When equality of persons is lost all distortions in contracting marriages followed.

Polygyny

Hinduism permits polygyny (The state of having more than one wife at a time is more aptly described a 'polygyny' than 'polygamy'.) The Smrtis not only prescribe, that a man who has entered grhasthasrama must not remain single and should take another wife without delay to keep up religious rites, but also ask to take another wife during the lifetime of the first one who had no son. But even then polygyny has been practised through the ages only by a few people. A Kunbi would take a second wife only if the first was childless or a bad character, or destitute of attractions. Polygyny was very rare among the Banias and it was generally the rule that a man must have obtained the consent of his first wife before taking a second one. Similarly, among the Kaikadis, the consent of the first wife must have been obtained to the taking of a second. In recent years, the spread of English education and assimilation of modern liberal ideas, have made almost all communities among the Hindus monogamous, though a few isolated cases, of polygyny could not be ruled out. However, the Hindu Marriage Act of 1955 has now completely reformed the law relating to Hindu marriage all over India and has made monogamy compulsory among all classes of Hindus.

For bringing equality of persons in Indian society Dr. Ambedkar had introduced the common Hindu Code Bill for which the Pt. Nehru as first Premier of India also committed himself to take it through the parliament but alas! conservative pressure suppressed the voice of equality and Dr. Ambedkar had resigned from his portfolio of Law Minister in the year 1951. According to the code bill no Hindu could have second wife as long as first wife was alive.

Dowry

In Hindu religious books are enumerated eight forms of marriage, *i.e.,* methods of consecrating a marriage-union of which, in modern times only two are in vogue, viz., the brahma and the asura. Conforming with the brahma form of marriage generally among the higher castes, a hunda (dowry—property which a woman brings to her husband) is paid by the bride's parents to the bridegroom. Among lower castes, the bride's parents usually take dej (bride-price) thereby conforming with the asura form. The monetary aspect in the settlement of a marriage may take, various forms, *e.g.,* among the Marathas, in a salankrta kanyadan, the bride's father, besides the ornaments he gives to his daughter, spends on many items of expenses on both the sides; in kanyadana, the expenses of the bride's father are much restricted; in varapaksa-vadhupaksa, the parties bear their own expenses, stand each other's manpan and the groom's party gives a rasbhog (feast) to all the villagers; in the hunda form the girl's father pays bridegroom-price to the boy's father, while in the dej form, as the proposal of the marriage comes from the boy's father, he has to pay a dej (bride-price) to the girl's father.

As long as dowry exists the plight of women is bound to aggravate. Whether Brahma method or Asura method either is dowry-maintaining mechanism. Bride's parents giving money to groom is Brahma method and pride's parent taking money from groom's parents is called Asura method. Both are evil methods. And Brahma one is more so.

Marriage Enactments

Social usage in relation to Hindu marriage has been considerably affected by various legal enactments passed, perhaps right from 1833 when the regulation prohibiting sati was declared, (1) A common form of civil marriage for all communities in India was provided by the Special Marriage Act III of 1872, which made it possible for an Indian of whatever caste or creed to enter into a valid marriage with a person belonging to any caste or creed, provided the parties registered the contract of marriage, declaring inter alia that they did not belong to any religion (Ghurye G.S., Caste and Class in India (1950), p.165.). This Act was amended by Act XXX of 1923, making it possible for Hindus, Buddhists, Sikhs and Jains (but not for Christians, Jews, Mahavardans and Parsees) to declare their religion and yet get their marriage registered, (2) The Child Marriage Restraint Act XIX of 1929) as amended by Act 19 of 1946 prohibited marriages of boys under 18 years of age, and girls under 14 years of age, (3) The Hindu Marriage Disabilities Removal Act XXVIII of 1946 validated marriages between parties (a) belonging to the same gotra or (b) belonging to different sub-divisions of the same caste; and now

(4) The Hindu Marriage Act of 1955 which abrogates and modifies all the past laws. It has made Hindu marriage now strictly adult and monogamous; has done away with the caste and gotra restrictions which limited the field of marriage; and has set down definite conditions under which a degree of nullity and further of dissolution of marriage could be obtained.

As marriage from the Hindu point of view created an indissoluble tie between the husband and the wife, divorce was not known to the general Hindu law. Neither party to a marriage could, therefore, divorce the other unless divorce was allowed by custom. The Indian Divorce Act, 1869 provided inter alia for dissolution of marriage, but it applied only to cases where "the petitioner or respondent professed the Christian religion" (S. 2 of the Act). However, according to the Hindu Marriage Act, 1955, reliefs by way of judicial separation, declaration of nullity of marriage and divorce are recognized (Ss. 10 to 13).

This was to take place earlier than the year 1950 had the Hindu Code Bill been adopted by the Indian parliamentarians. The said code bill was adopted by the Buddhists as their own method of marriage as is evident from Maharashtrian MLA Dr. Nitin Raut-prepared and circulated brochure on Buddhist Marriage Act.

Fertility

On national level the fertility rate is 2.81 children born/woman as per 2007 estimate. The TFR (Total number of children born per women) according to Religion in 2001 was : Hindus -2.27, Muslims - 3.06, Sikhs - 1.86, Christians - 2.06, Buddhists - 2.29, Jains - 1.50 , Animists and Others— 2.99, Tribals - 3.16, and Scheduled Castes - 2.89. This shows that Muslim, Animist and others, Tribals and SCs have more fertility rate than that of the national level.

Studies reveal that among the urbanised citizens of Nagpur Teachers form the highest group followed by Doctors and Engineers. lt is needless to stress that in our samples also we have found professional and technically qualified respondents including scholars, teachers, doctors, engineers and literates above the level of matriculation. Rural Nagpur is backward in educational categories and they are members of the Hindu castes, among whom the Mahars are influenced by the teaching of Buddha and Dr. Ambedkar enabling them to migrate to urban areas and get education and services. Prof. Bhandare in his booklet entitled *The Problems of the Indian Buddhists* (Mumbai 1966) explained that the philosophy behind reservation and safeguards was originally intended not for any religious group but exclusively for such masses of people who suffered from difficulties and disabilities, on account of the factors of pollution and isolation. And Buddhists are such people beside the SCs and STs, who continue to suffer from them and are compelled to live in a state of isolation and segregation and are therefore quite powerless and miserable. Indian constitution covers these provisions to establish political, economic and social democracies. (ibid. pp. 26-27).

Religious Demography from 1951-61 to 1991-2001 and Political Consequences

Prof. C.D. Naik opined that in every village Scheduled Castes and Scheduled Tribes are surrounded by Hindu majority people. Buddhists also are more vulnerable to local situation even though their number increased on national reckoning in general and Maharashtra State and Nagpur District in particular.

According to the census of 1961 the total population of the Maharashtra State was 3,95,53,718, out of which the total population of the Scheduled Castes was 22,26,914 (5.62 per cent) and that of the Scheduled Tribes was 23,97,159 (6.06 per cent) and that of the new converts to Buddhism was 27,89,501 (7.07 per cent). Thus the demographic change of percentage of Buddhists compared to SCs and STs was a new phenomenon and it existed only in Maharashtra due to conversion movement.

As for the population by religion in the year 1951 and 1961, the following table is illustrative.

For the decade between 1951 and 1961

Name of community	*Population in million in 1951*	*Percentage in 1951*	*Increase in population in million in 1961*	*Increase in percentage in 1961*
Buddhist	0.2	0.1	3.3	0.7
Christian	8.4	2.4	10.7	2.4
Hindu	303.6	85.0	366.5	83.5
Jain	1.6	0.4	2.0	0.5
Muslim	35.4	9.9	46.9	10.7
Sikh	6.2	1.7	7.8	1.8
Other	1.8	0.5	1.6	0.4
Total	357.3	100	438.9	100

Source: The Statistical Outline of India, Table 10, Tata Industries Private Ltd, p. 12.

The numerical strength of the various religious communities and sects in the district as returned by the Census of 1961 is as under:

Urban/Rural population of Religious Communities in Nagpur District, 1961

		Urban		*Rural*	
S.N.	*Community*	*Males*	*Females*	*Males*	*Females*
(1)	Parsees (Persons 840)	487	353		
(2)	Buddhists	57,73	54,856	61,084	0,199
(3)	Christians	6,744	6,265	358	322
(4)	Hindus	3,04,661	2,69,049	2,99,839	2,90,698
(5)	Jains	3,258	3,082	615	567
(6)	Jews	15	28		
(7)	Muslims	41,047	35,762	5,750	5,505
(8)	Sikhs	2,106	1,773	86	43
(9)	Zorostrians	487	353		
(10)	Tribals	86	73		
(11)	Non-Tribals		2		
(12)	Religion not stated	24	56	28	13
	Total	4,16,401	3,71,299	3,67,760	3,57,347

These include 54,388 (m. 27,906; f. 26,482) belonging to Scheduled Castes; no person has been returned as belonging to Scheduled Tribes, but 159 (m. 86; f. 73) are separately returned as Tribals.

In 1951, under the head of 'Other religions' were shown 'Tribals' and 'Non-Tribals'; the district had then no 'tribals'; the Non-tribal religions included 38 (m. 25; f. 13), Khojas, 15. (m. 12; f. 3) Bohoras and 8 (m. 8; f.-) Kabirpanthis.

The following Census data for the year 1991 throws light on social, economic, genderic and educational conditions of Dalit Buddhists.

SC Population 1991

SC population increased in 1991 compared to earlier censuses because according to the Constitution of India, SCs could belong to only Hindus and Sikh (Jains not mentioned. It may be because in Nagpur the Jains are nearly all Marvadi Banias and are engaged in trade and banking; Consequently they are much wealthier than other castes) religions and not to Buddhism but, as a result of the Constitution (Scheduled Castes) Orders (Amendment) Act 1990 those SCs who returned their religion as Buddhist or Nav/Neo Buddhist have also become eligible in Maharashtra to be enumerated as Scheduled Castes along with 'Hindus' and 'Sikh' provided their caste name found place in the list of the SC applicable to the state in which they were being enumerated.

During the last decade ST population has increased by 0.08 points only. A member of a ST may belong to any religion. A person will be reckoned as belonging to ST only if in his/her tribe name appeared in the list of STs applicable to the State.

Primary Census Abstracts for SC/ST began to be presented since 1981 along with PCA for general population but these special PCAs for SC/ST will not be presented at the village level. Nor will they present information as to area and number of occupied residential houses. The following table shows some information regarding SC/ST in State, Nagpur District-Urban/ Rural with gender and work classification.

Percentage of SC/ST population in State and District

SC in State in %	*SC in Nagpur* District in %	*ST in State in %*	*ST in Nagpur* District in %
11.9	18.84	9.27	13.92

Source: Census Report 1991.

Explanation: Out of thirty districts of Maharashtra, Nagpur has the highest percentage of SC/ST population. Although SC population is concentrated in rural areas of all the districts of Maharashtra it is not so in Nagpur district unlike ST population. Thus, conversion to Buddhism has urbanizing impact on SCs of the district. Percentage of SC population to total population in Nagpur District is 18.84 in 1991 while it was only 7.05 in 1881. In Nagpur District as in every other district percentage of SC population has increased.

Percentage of Literacy rate for SCs and STs

State Average SC Literacy Rate in %	*SC Literacy Rate in Nagpur District in %*	*ST Literacy Rate in Nagpur District in %*
56.46	71.08	36.78

Source: Census Report 1991.

Explanation: Thus it is obvious from above table that SC literacy rate in Nagpur is higher than state average and that of ST literacy rate also.

Work Participation of SC and ST

Work Participation of SC in State in %	*Work Participation of SC in Nagpur District in %*	*Work Participation of ST in State in %*	*Work Participation of ST in Nagpur District in %*
42.82	35.95	52.23	42.81

Source: Census Report 1991.

Explanation: Work participation rate of SCs for Nagpur District has been lower than that of State average and that of ST work participation in the District also. Occupational Classification of SC/ST in Nagpur and Main Workers in primary sector services are as under:

Occupational classification of SCs & STs I

As Agricultural Labourers		*In Other Services*		*In Livestock etc.*	
SC Agricultural Labourers in Nagpur District in %	ST Agricultural Labourers in Nagpur District in %	SC in Other Services than primary sector in Nagpur in %	ST in Other Services than primary sector in Nagpur in %	SC in livestock, forestry, hunting, plantation, orchard, allied activities in Nagpur in %	ST in livestock, forestry, hunting, plantation, orchard, allied activities in Nagpur in %
26.40	35.44	17.98	9.43	1.41	2.31

Source: Census Report 1991.

Occupational Classification of Ss and STs II

In Household Industry		*In Mining and Quarrying*		*Transport, trade and commun*	
SC in Household Industry in Nagpur District in %	ST in Household Industry in Nagpur District in %	SC in Mining and Quarrying in Nagpur District in %	ST in Mining and Quarrying in Nagpur District in %	SC in Transport, trade and communica- tion in Nagpur in %	ST in Transport, trade and communica- tion in Nagpur in %
1.63	6.16	2.48	1.88	8.45	4.10

Source: Census Report 1991.

Occupational Classification of SCs and STs III

In Trade and Commerce		*In Construction*		*In Cultivation*	
SC in Trade and Commerce In Nagpur District in %	ST in Trade and Commerce in Nagpur District in %	SC in Construction in Nagpur District in %	ST in Construction in Nagpur District in %	SC in Cultivation in Nagpur District in %	ST in Cultivation in Nagpur District in %
8.50	7.45	8.68	4.70	12.63	18.30

Source: Census Report 1991.

Explanation: In Nagpur SC main workers are mostly engaged in agricultural labour and in other than primary sector services. ST workers are mostly engaged in primary sector as shown in the above table.

State and District SC Sex Ratio

State SC Sex Ratio Per 1000 males	State SC Sex Ratio among total workers	State SC Sex Ratio among main workers	State to SC Sex Ratio among marginal workers	Nagpur SC Sex Ratio per 1000 males	Nagpur SC Sex Ratio among total workers	Nagpur SC Sex Ratio among main workers	Nagpur SC Sex Ratio among marginal workers
1	2	3	4	5	6	7	8
944	695	601	5145	935	485	442	2324

Source: Census Report 1991.

State and District ST Sex Ratio

State ST Sex Ratio Per 1000 males	State ST Sex Ratio among total workers	State ST Sex Ratio among main workers	State ST Sex Ratio among marginal workers	Nagpur ST Sex Ratio per 1000 males	Nagpur ST Sex Ratio among total workers	Nagpur ST Sex Ratio among main workers	Nagpur ST Sex Ratio among marginal workers
1	2	3	4	5	6	7	8
968	879	742	7970	—	940	598	4035

Source: Census Report 1991.

State General population sex ratio

State General Sex Ratio Among Total Workers	State General Sex Ratio among main workers
1	2
593	482

Source: Census Report 1991.

Explanation: Higher sex ratio among marginal workers indicate preponderance of females over males. Compared to general population total and main workers sex ratio SC sex ratio for those classes is much higher and ST sex ratio for the same is the highest. This accounted for lower status of women in Hindu society. As for the Dalit Buddhists equality of men and women is the principle of associated living among all Buddhists whether in Nagpur, India or abroad.

Classification of SC population of Nagpur in household, persons, gender, infants and literacy

SC Households	*SC Persons*	*Males*	*Females*	*Persons of Age 0-6*	*Literates*
1	2	3	4	5	6
1,24,180	6,19,226	3,19,940	2,99,286	1,00,349	3,68,656

Source: Census Report 1991.

Classification of SC population of Nagpur in primary sector and other works

Total main Workers of Category I-IX	*Cultivators*	*Agro-labourers*	*Livestock etc.*	*Mining and Quarrying*	*Manufacturing etc. in household*
7	*8*	*9*	*10*	*11*	*12*
2,11,171	26,667	55,749	2976	5245	3433

Source: Census Report 1991.

Classification of SC population of Nagpur in primary sector and other works

Manufacturing etc. in other than household industry	*Constructions*	*Trade and Commerce*	*Transport, Storage and Communication*	*Other Services as public utility etc.*	*Marginal Workers*	*Non-Workers*
13	*14*	*15*	*16*	*17*	*18*	*19*
25001	18,323	17,956	17,846	37,975	11,454	3,96,601

Source: Census Report 1991.

Explanation: In the above primary census Abstract table reference to main worker means one who engaged in any economically productive activity for 183 days or six months or more during the year preceding the date of enumeration. Primary sector I-IX occupations are (1) Cultivators, (2) Agricultural Labourers, (3) Workers in livestock, forestry, fishing, hunting and plantations, orchard and allied activities, (4) Mining and quarrying, (5a) Manufacturing, Processing and repairs in household industry, (5b) Manufacturing, processing, servicing and repairs in other than household industry, (6) Constructions, (7) Trade and Commerce, (8) Transport, storage and communication.The other services include public utility services like electricity or gas or water supply, sanitary services; central, state or municipal employees, professional services; trade or labour associations, recreational services etc. and non-workers refer to those who had not worked at all any time in the year preceding the date of enumeration.

Classification by Nagpur (U.A.) and Nagpur Corporation

Classification of SC population of Nagpur Corporation in Household, persons, gender, infants and literacy

	SC Households	*SC Persons*	*Males*	*Females*	*Persons of Age 0-6*	*Literates*
	1	*2*	*3*	*4*	*5*	*6*
UA	62,671	3,25,102	1,68,008	1,57,094	51,241	2,07,984
Corp	6,0577	3,15,640			51,241	2,01,829

Source: Census Report 1991.

Classification of SC population of Nagpur in primary sector and other works

Total Main Workers of Category I-IX	*Cultivators*	*Agro-labourers*	*Livestock etc.*	*Mining and Quarrying*	*Manufacturing etc. in household Industry*
7	*8*	*9*	*10*	*11*	*12*
88,092	327	658	957	582	1,113
85,351	317	646	940	577	1,102

Source: Census Report 1991

Classification of SC population of Nagpur in primary sector and other works

	Manufacturing etc. in other than household industry	*Constructions*	*Trade and Commerce*	*Transport, Storage and Communication*	*Other Services as public utility etc.*	*Marginal Workers*	*Non-Workers*
	13	*14*	*15*	*16*	*17*	*18*	*19*
UA	15,516	13,598	14,019	14,763	26,559	2,286	2,34,724
Corp	14,438	13,251	13,778	14,487	25,815	2,216	2,28,073

Source: Census Report 1991.

Explanation: From the above table it is seen that Nagpur urban area SCs in above categories stand higher than they are in these respect in Nagpur Corporation.

Buddhist Population

In 1951, there were only 149 (m. 63; f. 86) Buddhists but their number had increased to 2,34,112 (m. 1,19,057; f. 1,15,055) in 1961. This sudden increase of the Buddhists was obviously due to the return of a large number from the 'Scheduled Castes', particularly from the Mahars, of 1951 as Buddhists (Neo Buddhists) in 1961. The 'Scheduled Castes' who numbered 2,23,546 in 1951 have decreased by 1,89,158 in 1961. Many of them who might have been returned as Buddhists (Neo Buddhists) are shown as forming a community separate from that of the Hindus.

According to 1991 census total Indian population was 836 million, out of which were 130 million SCs, 60 million STs, and 424 million OBCs. The Buddhists were 0.76% of total population. SCs were 15%. Total population of Buddhists was 6.3 million. There are 25 states and Union Territories where Buddhists, are less than 1%, and 16 districts have not a single Buddhist. Maharashtra has 6.39% Buddhists.

Then only the North East (excluding Assam and Nagaland) has an average of about 5 per cent of traditional Buddhist population, Himachal 1.24% - perhaps due to Dalai Lama, top most is Sikkim with 27.18%. Laddakh is not mentioned. The

States of Bihar, Rajasthan, Andhra, Tamil Nadu, Karnataka, Haryana, U.P., Gujarat, Kerala, Orissa, Punjab and surprisingly Nagaland and Assam has negligible population of Buddhists.

Concentrating only on Maharashtra, we find that Mahars are 6.45 per cent, non-Mahar SCs are 4.64% and registered Buddhists are 6.39 of total population. Nine Districts of Vidarbha and three of Marathwada only have more than average of 6.39 per cent, Akola being highest of 16.79%. Mumbai has first highest number (5,57,089) and Nagpur district second highest (4,93,208) number1.

Mahars

Mahars or Mehras formed about 17 per cent (1931) of the population. "Looked down upon as outcastes by the Hindus, they are hampered by no sense of dignity or family prejudice. They are fond of drinking but are also hard workers. They turn their hands to anything and every thing, but the great majority of them are agricultural labourers. If there is only one well in the village he may not use it but has to get his water supply from where he can. His sons are consigned to a corner in the village school and the schoolmaster, if not superior to caste prejudices, discourages their attendance. Nevertheless Mahars will not remain for years down-trodden in this fashion and are already pushing themselves up from this state of degradation. In some places they have combined to dig wells and in Nagpur have opened a school for members of their own community (Nagpur Settlement Report, para 58.) Occasionally a Mahar is the most prosperous man in the village. Several of them are money-lenders in a small way and a few are malguzars.

A large number of the Mahars have turned to Buddhism following the lead given by Dr. Ambedkar and call themselves as neo-Buddhists. In schools, colleges and in Government services a number of seats are reserved for them and economic aid is given. Conscious and painstaking efforts by social workers to create a proper social attitude as also by the members of their own community to come up in various spheres have helped to overcome the former prejudices, and a new trend has begun.

SC/ST Commission's observation on Status of SCs and STs

According to SC/ST Commission report of 1958-59 and 1960-61 the following facts were observed:

1. As many as 56.75 per cent SCs and STs experienced discrimination in regard to seating arrangement and use of common utensils.
2. 56.8 per cent of respondents expressed hesitation in visiting public places because of resentment of caste Hindus.
3. 31.4 per cent respondents would not visit public places because of their economic dependence.
4. The religious isolation of SC/STs still persists in considerable degree which is obvious from the comparatively smaller percentage of non-Harijans associating the SCs/STs in religious activities.
5. The degree of awareness of untouchability (Offences) Act has been found to be higher among non-Harijan respondents *i.e.* 77.7 per cent as compared to the SC/ST respondents among whom it was found to be 66.6 per cent.
6. The evil of untouchability exists among the untouchables themselves and 18.3 per cent respondents admitted practising untouchability against lower castes.
7. Based on religion the ordinary Hindu only relaxes the rules of untouchability where he cannot observe them. He never abandons them, for the abandonment of untouchability to him involves a total abandonment of the basic religious tenets of Hindus. Based on religion, untouchability will present as all other religious notions have done.

Notional Removal of Untouchability

In addition to above Prof. Bhandare also pointed out that although the rigours of pollution have been loosened and lessened to some extent under the modern conditions untouchability in its notional aspect is not changed to any extent at all (p. 11). As for conversion it has to be said that Dr. Ambedkar converted himself to Buddhism because of his genius desire and urge for the spiritual and cultural resurgence and regeneration. He and his followers converted to Buddhism to change their outlook and notional aspect rooted in irrational dogma of caste and untouchability of Hinduism. This does not change the attitude and notion of the Hindus towards converts though.

Compared to the scheduled castes the Buddhists are in worse political position because of the wrong construction and misunderstanding of the real nature, scope and purpose of the special provisions incorporated in the constitution of India and also the basic principles underlying the principles of social justice and economic justice adumberated in the constitution of India (p.16).

New converts to Buddhism should be allowed to have reservations, political, social and economic which are contemplated and given to the scheduled castes and the scheduled tribes under the constitution of India and also other concessions and facilities to enable them to derive benefits arising out of these reservations and concessions and facilities under the principle of social justice. (Bhandare, ibid. p. 24).

In pursuence of the recommendation of the Indira Gandhi Committee, the Prime Minister on September 25 to October 1, 1961 called a National Integration Conference to which representatives of all major political parties, educationists, scientists and social workers were invited. In spite of these important measures, the popular mind is apt to comprehend and interpret the problem in a very narrow sense that the problem mainly concerns adjustment among communities professing various faiths or speaking different languages.

The most important aspects of the problem of national integration are the integration of the Scheduled Castes with the Caste Hindu society and that of the tribals with the general population of the country. Untouchability is an extreme form of casteism and therefore, quickest ways have to be devised to do away with both simultaneously.

According to Prof. Bhandare there was some change in the attitude towards untouchability in its literal sense (ibid. p. 10). But Dr. Babasaheb Ambedkar said (Note on Indian Franchise Committee Report 1932, Vol. I, p. 204), "If this is a correct statement of the facts of the life, then the difference between untouchability in its literal and notional sense is a distinction witch makes no difference to the ultimate situation, for (as the extract from the Census Report 1921, of Bihar and Orissa shows) untouchability in its notional sense persists even where untouchability in its literal sense has ceased to obtain. This is why I insist that the test of untouchability must be applied in its notional sense."

In his note of dissent submitted to the Indian Franchise Committee Dr. Ambedkar explained that "The system of caste and the system of untouchability form really the steel-frame of the Hindu society. This division cannot easily be wiped out for the simple reason that it is not based upon rational, economic and racial grounds. On the other hand the chances are that untouchability will endure for long into the future than the optimist reformer is likely to admit on account of the fact that it is based on religious dogma."

Buddhis Population Growing in India

One reason for the current interest in Buddhism is the success of those who became Buddhists in the past. 72.7% have a basic education compared with the national average of 52.21% and the community is increasingly confident, self reliant and free from negative social norms. The new Buddhists refuse to work within the ritually polluting and ritually duties traditionally associated with their caste, such as handling dead bodies: a strategy that works when people are able to find alternative employment outside the village. However, even if new Buddhists are successful in joining upon ritually more or less neutral professions, they are looked down[2].

Demographic Information of Population
Census information for 2001

Composition	*Hindus*	*Muslims*	*Christians*	*Sikhs*	*Buddhists*	*Jains*	*Others*
	1	*2*	*3*	*4*	*5*	*6*	*7*
% total of population 2005	80.4%	13.4%	2.2%	1.9%	1.1%	0.4%	0.5%
10-Yr Growth% (est '91-'01)	20.3%	29.5%	22.6%	18.2%	24.5%	26.0%	103.1%
Sex ratio* (avg. 944)	935	940	1009	895	955	940	100

Composition	*Hindus*	*Muslims*	*Christians*	*Sikhs*	*Buddhists*	*Jains*	*Others*
	1	*2*	*3*	*4*	*5*	*6*	*7*
Literacy rate (avg. 79.9)	75.5	60.0	90.3	70.4	73.0	95.0	50.0
Work Participation Rate	40.4	31.3	39.7	37.7	40.6	32.9	48.4
Rural sex ratio	944	953	1001	895	958	937	995
Urban sex ratio	922	907	1026	886	944	941	966
Child sex ratio (0-6 yrs)	925	950	964	786	942	870	976

Source: The First Report on Religion: Census of India 2001.

According to 2001 Census Hindu (82.5%), Muslim (11.4%), Christian (2.31%), Buddhists (0.8%), Sikh (1.93%), Jains (0.41%), and others or not stated (0.76%) formed the religious classification of Indian population.

Mandar Phanse, CNN-IBN described that according to the 2001 census there are 7.95 million Buddhists in India out of a population of 1 billion, making it the country's fifth-largest religion. The true figure is far higher - between 20-30 million, but many do not register as Buddhists for fear of losing government concessions that are due to low-status Hindus. "We have 405 New-Buddhists in our village, 69 from the Matang community, they say there were only 105 of us in 1991 and in 2001 census, we are not there. This means we don't get any relief or benefit from government. We are supposed to get 20 per cent of the Panchayat budget of Rs. 3 lakh per year". — Census wipes out dalits in Maharashtra. These Buddhists include a number of groups. There are scattered survivors of the period when Buddhism flourished in India such as the Baruas of Assam, Chakmas of Bengal, the Saraks of Orissa and the Himalayan Buddhists of North-East India; there are also ethnic overlaps from Nepal, Thailand and Burma, such as Tamangs and Sherpas, there are converts who have been influenced by the Maha Bodhi Society, the Dalai Lama and so on; and there are refugee Tibetan Buddhists in different settlements. Finally they are the followers of Dr. Ambedkar, who constitute over 90% India's Buddhists.

Every year Dalits and Buddhists gather at Nagpur to remember 14th Oct 1956 conversion event. They number anywhere from 8,00,000 to 10,00,000. According to solar calendar, this is the day when Dr Ambedkar led the biggest conversion sans bloodshed or allurement in the history of the world. On that day alone, around 5,00,000 Dalits had converted to Buddhism leaving behind the cobwebs of caste ridden Hindu society.

Media Black out on Dalit News

In the year 2006, an estimated 2 million, yes, a whopping 20,00,000 people gathered from across the world to mark the 50th year of Dhamma Chakra Pravartan Din on 2nd October! According to local reports, some 2,00,000 Buddhist Bhikkhus (Monks) wearing saffron clothes, forming a 6 km long chain took the procession turning the entire orange city into saffron and blue. The Celebrations lasted for more than a week.

Now, for an Indian media that is always looking for something sensational - that's a huge gathering, isn't it? And how many white collar Journalists holding Handy Cams from the leading electronic media turn up, including your own? None! Reason?

Like the Upper caste villagers boycott Dalits in villages, their caste Hindu counterparts in the media boycott almost everything that is related to Dalits. Ghatkopar, Seoni, Jajjhar, Kherlanji - the shame continues!

Crime against Dalits

On Sep 29, in one of the most gruesome and dreadful incidents of Dalit atrocities, Bhaiyyalal / Bhotmange, a Dalit-Buddhist farmer in Kherlanji (Bhandara, Maharashtra) witnessed his wife Surekha (44), daughter Priyanka (18), sons, Roshan, 23, and Sudhir, 21 being killed by the Landlords in front of the villagers. Worst, the mother and daughter were first paraded naked; gang raped, and then sticks were pushed into their private parts. The sons were stabbed repeatedly and their private parts mutilated. And what was their fault? Surekha had dared to fight for getting *back* a portion of their farm, which was grabbed by the landlords.

India's National Crime Records Bureau working under the jurisdiction of Ministry of Home Affairs has reported that in the year 2005 alone, 26,127 crimes were committed against SC/STs including 1172 rape against Dalit women and 669 cases of Murder (Reference: http://ncrb.nic.in). To summarise, every day, while three Dalit women are raped and two Dalits are murdered, two Dalit homes get torched. If you add to this the thousands of unreported cases, the picture is abysmally inconceivable[3]!

Handover to Buddhist Management the Mahabodhi Mahavihar : A Request

We therefore request the UN to activate the convention concerning the Protection of the World Cultural and Natural Heritage (UNESCO) adopted on 16th November 1972 and entered into force on 17th Dec. 1974. It was ratified by 159 countries including India. The convention provides that the heritage committee shall supervise the protection of items recognised by the convention as those of outstanding universal value from the point of view of history, art, science and aesthetics. We also request the United Nations to direct India to obey the Universal Declaration of Human Rights (1948) on the rights of persons belonging to national, ethnic, religious or linguistic minorities and handover entire managemant of Mahabodhi Mahavihara by suitable amendment to the Bodh Gaya Temple Act 1949 (Bihar Act of 17th of 1949) - (as modified up to 8th Feb. 1955) and help prevent confrontation between the Buddhist and Hindu Brahmins over the issue of Mahabodhi Mahavihar. With profound regards. Yours truly, (Bhadant Arya Nagarjuna Shurei Sasai)[4].

World Conference Against Racism : Indian Govt Stand

Under the title "UN Prepcom for WCAR, Geneva May 1-5, 2000 and Dalit "Traitors" Yogesh Varhade classified the Dalits into two categories namely (i) Honest and (2) Dishonest. This is clear from his letter cited below: To Dalit Warriors around the Globe: Jaibhim!

I just returned from Geneva UN Prepcom for World Conference Against Racism (to be held in September 2001). In the last 10 years of participation of Ambedkar Centre for Justice and Peace at many UN forums to highlight our problem, I never found that India was ever interested in promoting Dalit activists, scholars etc.

To my great surprise for this Prepcom for World Conference Against Racism at Geneva, India (indirectly financed and) supported the Dalit Delegation to attack our efforts to address the major workshop on "Casteism". India uses International Institute of Non-Aligned Studies and Indian Council of Education as fronts to voice its policy. The "Traitors" among the Dalits were sponsored by these organizations.

Among the Dalit Activists Groups participated were: Ambedkar Centre for Justice and Peace-Yogesh Varhade Dalit Solodarity Forum - Mr. Paul Diwakar, Ruth Manorama, Henry Thagraj, Martin Macwan, Priest Yesu from TN, Mimroth lawyer from Rajasthan working in Delhi Dalit Media Network - Dr. Sridhar, TN Human Rights Watch-Smita Narula.

Ms. Meira Kumar said in her intervention"... there is no real problem in India on Caste System since the laws are in place and there are strong constitutional provisions. It is the creation of the west that there is a problem (of untouchability and caste system)." She refused to circulate the copy of her intervention when asked by NGOs.

Mr. Pakhiddey and Choudhary, Narang, Tamata participated in the NGOs workshop discussion on themes for Asia-Pacific and Middle East Regional Workshop.

Mr. Martin Macwan and Ruth Manorama did the intervention on behalf of Dalit groups. I could not do the statement as I went through Canadian NGO, with consultative status, who had 12 other delegates to intervene. Dr. Shridhar, a young doctor, activist in Dalit Media Network, from TN also did intervention on Dalit issue. Smita Narula, Human Rights Watch did the same on behalf of her NGO.

In NGO Forum I insisted that since the Caste System and Practice of Untouchability affects quarter billion population, it is the largest and biggest discrimination, segregation, destitution on Earth and it must have major theme and workshop at Regional Prepcom in Tehran before final World Conference in South Africa. Anything less will not be acceptable. DSF Paul Diwakar, Martin Macwan, Mimroth, Henry Thagraj etc. all were also supporting the theme- "Caste System".

BJP sponsored puppets were trying to stop discussion on Caste System because India sees the serious consequences to its "so called largest democracy in the world" image alongwith the real truth about Hinduism. Also India worries about future Draft Declaration in the World Conference in 2001 in South Africa and solutions to Caste System in it.

Pakhiddey insisted that he was opposed to having a theme on "Caste System" because he said, "Dr. Ambedkar mentioned that we are of the same race" Caste is not a discrimination. Even the Brahmins have 354 sub-castes. They are also discriminated".

Mr. Pakhiddey should do some reading on the literature of Babasaheb, specially his last speech at Nagpur on 14-15th October 1956 during the Conversion to Buddhism.

There Babasaheb clearly stated, explaining why he selected Nagpur for Conversion that "Nagpur was the centre of Naga Kingdom and Culture. There is a river known as Nag River around this city, I heard...Nagpur name also came from Nag People. At one time Nagas were the warriors and rulers of India...Nagas were the staunch followers of Buddhism...After Aryan invasion, there were many wars between them. India's history is nothing but the struggle for supremacy between Buddhism and Brahminism. They annihilated Nagas by hook or by crook... We heard the story of saving a Nag, the serpent, by Agastya Rishi in the Hindu literature. That was not the nag serpent but Nag people...we are supposed to be the descendants of that Naga Person..." This clearly states that we, the Dalits, are different from Indo-Aryans.

There is a need for our people in Delhi to give some lessons to this "TRAITOR" and others like him who studied on the scholarship created by our liberator.

Committee on Elimination of Racial Discrimination (CERD)

For the information of our readers: In 1996 August, Committee on Elimination of Racial Discrimination (CERD), while discussing Country Report India submitted to Treaty Bodies, heard the claim of India that situation of Scheduled Castes and Scheduled Tribes does not fall under the Scope of the Convention and ruled that it does fall under the CERD Convention. Ambedkar Centre had lobbyed very hard and majority of 18 Experts were totally in favour of Dalits. The report was very critical of India and it gave many strong recommendations to implement immediately.

Two most important recommendations were: (1) "Continuing campaign to educate the Indian Population on Human Rights... aimed at eliminating the institutionalised thinking of High-Caste and Low-Caste Mentality".

(2) "... just and adequate reparations to people suffering from the acts of discrimination... belonging to caste or tribe." More details on 3 major Conventions and Treaty Bodies of UN who gave very strong recommendations to India on Dalit problem will be available on "www. Ambedkar.Org" very soon.

As our saviour, one and only liberator, Babasaheb, Dr. B.R.Ambedkar said "Our battle is for Justice, reclaiming the human personality... Justice is on our side. We are bound to succeed." Let us have a faith in our strength and unity. There is a need for more Dalit Groups to work in International Arena with firm belief in our cause and commitment till we succeed. Dalit Solidarity Forum, with the support from Churches, is doing good work in internationalisation in some parts of Europe. But for better results we need to bring more serious workers globally and sooner than later civil society in the west will have to come to our rescue. It is the only choice they have to keep the stability in South Asia and world peace-dismantle this hidden Apartheid! Yours in the mission for a just society, Yogesh Varhade[5].

Conspiracy against Buddhist Political Share as of 2008 for Representing the Buddhists

According to Buddhist and SC Rights Association of Maharashtra an E-mail appeal message regarding reconsideration of constituency reorganisation Commission's recommendation was sent to the President of India for sending the same to the Parliament for its review because of serious discrepancies committed therein. Because of separate column of census 2001 tabulation for displaying Buddhist population on the basis of religion the state Commission calculated the population of SCs excluding that of the Buddhists and allotted five reserved seats in the State Council and 29 reserved seats in State's lower House based on the exclusive proportion of SCs to total State population of the State and thus deprived the political representation of sixteen percent SC population inclusive of Buddhists of the state and their right for eight seats in the Council and forty seven seats in the Assembly. Such error put the social group of SC and Buddhist at loss when Zilla Parishad, Panchayat and village panchayat elections were held earlier. Now state legislative elections will also curtail their seats in the name of constituency reorganisation commission's resolution to be finalized soon. This is in violation of Constitutional Amendment Act 1990 and recognition of the Buddhists at par with the SCs for social policies in India in general and Maharashtra in particular.

Earlier to this incident such instance took place in case of the representation of the tribes also. The reserved seats of the tribes were reduced due to elimination of the four north-eastern states Jharkhand, Assam, Manipur and Arunachal Pradesh from electorate reorganisation there by the Central Cabinet.

For details on this matter please newspaper clippings in Marathi may be researched.

Primary Source and Data Analysis for the Project

REPORT ON STATUS AND PROBLEMS OF BUDDHISTS MINORITY IN NAGPUR

Profile of the respondents: Age-wise distribution of Respondents

The sample of the study covered 63 respondents among them 88.89 per cent were male and 11.11 per cent were female. The age-wise distribution of the respondents illustrates that majority of the respondents *i.e.* 63.49 per cent did not mention their age during the interview. The number of the respondents of age group 30-40 years constitute 14.29 per cent of total respondents followed by the age group 40-50 and 50-60 years comprising 9.52 per cent each. A marginal number of respondents were from the age group of 20-30 years and 60 years accounted for 1.59 per cent each.

Educational Status of the Respondents

As far as the educational status of the respondents is concerned 39.68 per cent of them did not indicate their educational qualification in the schedule. But those responded to the question regarding education reflects that most of them were highly qualified. It is evident from the data given that 23.81 of total respondents were postgraduates followed by 19.05 having professional and technical degrees/diploma in various disciplines and 7.94 per cent were holding M.Phil/Ph.D. and other sorts of Higher qualification. 7.93 per cent of the respondents were graduates and only 1.59 per cent constituted the category having SSC level education. Not a single person in the domain of the study undertaken was found illiterate or below HSC level.

Occupation of the Respondents

The study shows that occupation of professorship/ lectureship/ teachership was found to be dominated among all disciplines or professions with 23.89 per cent and the profession of private and government service accounts for 26.99 per cent, rest of the respondents were found to be engaged in other occupations.

4.76 per cent of total respondents were social/religious leaders and, farmers and monks accounted for 3.17 per cent each. The students and retired persons were found in same number and this number reckons for 3.17 per cent. The Doctors and poets constituted the same percentage of sample and it was a marginal number of the total respondent's i.e. 1.59 per cent. The remaining 26.99% of the respondents did not respond to the question regarding their profession.

Problems as stated by the Respondents

As data respondents having one to four member families were 3 couples 4.76% and four to eight and eight to twelve member couples 1/1.59% each respectively. The rest of the 58/ 92.06% respondents did not respond in this regard.

Problems as Stated by the Members of Buddhist Minority

S.No.	*Type of Respondents*	*No. of Respondents No. / %*
1.	No Homogeneity in cultural and Social rites, rituals (Marriage etc.)	13/20.64
2.	Don't appear as a distinct community	8/12.69
3.	Belief in Hindu customs and traditions	24/38.10
4.	Lack of trained monks and training camps	11/17.46
5.	Monks do not perform their duty	8/12.70
6.	No effective organization for spreading ideas of Buddha and Ambedkar	12/19.04
7.	Vihars are not utilized for Dhamma Prachar and discussions	11/17.46
8.	People do not join social and Dhamma gatherings	9/14.29
9.	Lack of unity/co-operation due to caste/sub-caste ego and weak organization	26/41.27
10.	No knowledge and acceptance of Bauddh rites e.g., Panchsheel/22 Oaths	24/38.19
11.	Lack of education	19/30.16
12.	Unavailability of their own educational institutions	13/20.64
13.	Poverty, unemployment/slavery/crimes in slums etc.	22/34.92
14.	Don't have their own industrial unit/companies	5/7.94
15.	Drinking habit	5/7.94
16.	Living modern and fashionable life	1/1.59
17.	No unity among Boddh organizations and monks	4/6.35
18.	No social movement like those of Phule and Ambedkar	1/1.59
19.	No unity and co-operations between political and social leaders	13/20.64
20.	Small in number and disunity, hence could not achieve political power	3/4.76
21.	No traditions and culture of their own	7/11.11
22.	Educated and wealthy are apathetic to Buddhism or unaware	10/15.87

S.No.	*Type of Respondents*	*No. of Respondents No. / %*
23.	Unawareness about their rights	2/3.17
24.	Leaders are not interested toward spread of Buddhism	6/9.52
25.	Buddhist counting by Govt. personnel is not fair	2/3.17
	Total	63/100

The Hindu society has been instrumental in suppressing, exploiting, degrading and discriminating a large chunk of population. This is the population which belongs to the fourth Varna of Hindu social system 'Chaturvarna' the Shudra and the another section is Varna Bahya *i.e.* untouchables or Dalits of today and women. The oppression by the upper castes has been the prime factor, which led the people of lower castes to leave Hinduism and take shelter under the shade of any other religion or faith.

The untouchables have been the most badly affected victims by inhuman orthodox traditions of Hinduism. Consequently, this community has ever been in motion to take itself out of Hinduism. The process was activated by Dr. Babasaheb Ambedkar embracing Buddhism on 14th October, 1956. The process of conversion of untouchables from Hindu faith to Buddhism has been continuing since then. The Dalit converts in any of the faith *e.g.* Islam, Buddhist, or Christianity have been facing some of the acute problems due to various factors.

Problems

This study, is very much concerned with the Buddhist converts, therefore we would deal with their problems only.

1. *Poverty* : As it is well known fact, that almost all Dalits castes have been in immense poverty due to various restrictions on them by the dominant castes of Hindus. After conversion, this problem of poverty could not be resolved. It is evident from the study. The table 8.4 illustrates that 34.92% of the total respondents responded that the main problem being faced by the Buddhist converts has been of poverty. (Quereshi Ayyaj Ahamad 1995, Wasnik, R.K.1996 and Bhadoria Kiran 1999).

2. *Unemployment* : This is further aggravated by unemployment and squandering money in drinking and celebrating useless rites, rituals and other ceremonies. The most crucial problems as stated by the respondents and one that comes on the front of discussion, is the problem of disunity, non-co-operation between converts and non-converts and between the different sub-castes of Dalits. The 41.27% of the respondents offered their opinion in favour of this problem and considered that this fact of disunity and non co-operation is one of the biggest hurdle in the way of development of all Dalits including converts.

3. *Illiteracy* : The inadequacy of the education among Dalit masses has been one of the prime issue for centuries. The problem of illiteracy has slightly improved after the independence but compared to other categories of society it can't be said satisfactory. In this regard, 30.16% of the respondents considered that lack of education among the converts is a major issue to be looked into.

4. *Ignorance of Buddhist Rites* : The Buddhist minority is the group of society that has come from the lowest rung of Hindu society. Their own culture and modes of life were grabbed and destroyed through applying the sanctions through social, religious and political forces, this group therefore imitated and followed the Hindu traditions, rites, rituals and started worshipping of Hindus Gods and Goddesses. This process of following Hindu traditions is still in practice. The 38.10% of the respondents consider it as a problem for Buddhist minority as it raises a strong impediment in the way of becoming a worth potential and pure Buddhist culture. The one other reason behind this, which the respondents consider important, has been the general illiteracy and ignorance about the Buddhists rites and rituals.

5. *Heterogeneity of socio-cultural Rites* : Of the respondents 20.64% think that the heterogeneity of social and cultural rites and rituals is the main problem before the Buddhist minority. They think that this is one of the most important problem, the Buddhist minority is facing. According to them, the people of this group cannot make themselves unite and run their cult

forward successfully as per the wishes and ideology of Dr. Babasaheb Ambedkar.

6. *No Distinct Culture* : Because of this heterogeneity of culture and adhering to the values of their old religion *i.e.* Hinduism, Buddhist minority does not reflect a distinctness of their own culture. This was the view of 12.69% of the respondents. There is no sufficient number of trained Buddhist monks and teacher to teach Buddhist minority the teachings of Buddha and rites and rituals of Buddhism. This was found the consideration of 17.46% of people. This want of trained monks / teachers and training camps leaves no alternative before the people of this community except following their old Hindu traditions. The Hindu rites have already been ingrained in the mind of Dalit people and the scarcity of teachers and training force them to be engaged in the old Hindu belief and customs and rites. 38.10% of total respondents accepted that the acceptance and follow up of Hindu belief (which are almost the superstitions) is a big problem as well as a challenge to this minority group.

7. *Scarcity of Monks* : The respondents told about the scarcity of monks, training camps/places but this problem further aggravates when the existing small number of monks do not perform their duty as per the need of this minority group. This was stated by 12.70% of respondents. Dr. Ambedkar puts his view that neither the Bhikkhu Sangha guides the people nor does it serve them (Jatava. D.R.: Critics of Ambedkar). The reason for such sort of behaviours is either due to the ignorance of monks or their apathy towards accepting and spreading the values of Buddhism. The most of the monks seem to be not conscious about their position in the society as they come from the lowest stratum of Hindus society, which had been their traditional culture. It is perhaps owing to the reason that they assume themselves too inferior to dream high so as to stay at the top of society. As (Marx, and R.N. Mukerji & Arunansu Ghosal; 2006, p.78) stated that the ideas of ruling class in every age are the ruling ideas *i.e.* the class which is the dominant material force in society is at the same time dominant intellectual force. Next problem that the respondent felt was the problem of unavailability or scarcity of organisations to

spread the thought and philosophy of Ambedkar and Buddha 19.04% of respondents were of this view.

8. *Non-utilisation of Vihars to spread Buddhism* : The respondents told that the monks as well as Vihars were less in number yet these places are not being fully utilised to spread Buddhism and preach the people. The number of respondents, who uttered none or less utilization of Vihars, constitutes 17.46% of the respondents.

9. *Low presence in Buddhist Gatherings* : Since the proper efforts are not made by the Buddhist monks to create awareness among the masses of Buddhist minority as well as non Buddhists scheduled castes to make them realise the importance of their own culture and ideology, the Buddhist converts do not seem to be interested to join the social and religious gatherings. The poor economic condition is one of the reasons for it, but the awareness is the main thing. Therefore, the low presence or absence is another problem as stated by the 14.29% of respondents.

10. *Lack of Education* : The importance of education is well known in the all around development of society as well as individual. But as already mentioned low level of literacy is one of the main problem before converts as well as non-convert SCs. A large proportion of respondents which constitutes 30.16% were found to have asserted that the lack of education is the acute problem the Buddhist minority faces.

11. *Absence of Buddhist Education Institutions* : All religious communities are well aware about their educational needs and fulfilment of these but owing to various reasons the converts and non converts SC do not have their own educational institutions. 20.64% of respondents consider them as one of the biggest problem before Buddhist minority.

12. *Absence of Unity* : The norms and values of Hindu social order do not let the different castes and groups unite and work with co-operation. No group or caste can escape the evil features of this social order. 20.64% of the respondents said there exists no unity and co-operative feeling among the political leaders representing the community.

13. *Lack of Awareness of problems and Conditions of Buddhists* : The educated persons of the converts can do a lot for the improvement of Buddhist minority, but the 15.87% of the respondents were of the view that the educated and prosperous persons are either apathetic or unaware about the problems and conditions of Buddhist minority.

14. *Absence of Culture and Traditions* : Because there is no sufficient number of monks / religious places / Vihars etc. to make the people know about the rites and rituals of Buddhism, therefore the Buddhist minority faces a problem of not having their own culture and traditions. 11.11% of respondents consider this as one of the main problem before the Buddhist minority.

15. *Dalit Leader's Non-Support to Change* : 9.52% of the respondents hold that the leaders are not interested to spread their religion *i.e.* Buddhism. Rajsakher V.T. analyses this sort of mentality of Buddhist or non Buddhist SC leaders. He (Rajsakher; 1995, p. 17) equating SCs to the neegros of USA, establishes that for the fear of loosing their place in socio-political arena, the Dalit leaders feel a comfort in existing scenario and they do not dare any change. He further maintains that the Dalit leaders are not the leader of Dalits but of their parties and parties are regulated by the Hindus. 7.94% of respondents hold the view that the non existence of industrial units and companies of the Buddhist minority is the another problem, and the same number of persons i.e. 7.94% say that the drinking habit of the people of this community is taking them to the reverse direction of progress. It not only makes their money spend but also kills their ambitions to go on to the relatively higher level in society.

16. *Lack of Coordination* : The monk and Buddhist organisation have no co-operation and co-ordination between them. No proper plans are there to lead Buddhist minority in a proper and desired direction. This was uttered by 6.35% of respondents covered under study. A small fraction of respondents e.g. 4.76% say that the Buddhist minority is less in number and scattered here and there and it in itself becomes a problem hampering their empowerment and development. 3.17% respondents proposed unawareness about their rights as a problem before Buddhist minority.

17. *Unfair Count of Buddhist Population* : The same percentage of people, i.e., 3.17% persons responded that government officials do not take fair steps when counting and registering the number of Buddhist minority.

Suggestions given by the respondents to resolve the above mentioned problem

S.No.	*Type of Respondents*	*No. of Respondents and %*
1.	There should be more training centers and camps for both followers and Monks	7/11.11
2.	There should be organizations like Christian missionaries to propagate Buddhism from childhood	27/42.86
3.	Educated person especially youth must help to spread Dhamma	3/4.76
4.	New avenues of education must be searched and poor be given preference and aid	9/14.29
5.	Need of their own educational and Dhamma Institutions	15/23.81
6.	Need of special movements to uproot the habits of drinking and money squandering	7/11.11
7.	People be encouraged to come in Vihars and other social gatherings	9/14.29
8.	Buddha and Ambedkar ideas are panacea, hence be spread through seminars/organizations	11/17.46
9.	Vihars must do the job of Dhamma and social reform	7/11.11
10.	Need of an economic zone of Buddhists (Industries/ companies)	9/14.29
11.	Unity and co-operation between political and social leaders	5/7.94
12.	Destruction of caste/sub-caste and ego, unity and co-operation be there	12/19.04
13.	Abandonment of worshipping of Hindu Gods/Goddesses and spread of 22 oaths and implementation	4/6.35
14.	All Bauddh places/Vihars etc. be given to Indian Buddhists	2/3.17
15.	There should be our own traditions (civil codes and marriage acts etc.)	10/15.89

S.No.	*Type of Respondents*	*No. of Respondents and %*
16.	Social movements like Phule's and Ambedkar's be launched	1/1.59
17.	Seminars and discussion on Buddha and Ambedkar's Thoughts	3/4.76
19.	Research centers and Institutions for the problems of Dhamma and its followers	3/4.76
20.	All Buddhist countries must come forward to help Indian Buddhists	4/6.35
21.	OBC be taken under the umbrella of Buddhism	1/1.58
22.	Buddha and his Dhamma be made compulsory to all Monks	4/6.35
23.	Old methods of enlightenment be searched and spread	1/1.59
	Total	63/100

References

1. Dr. K. Jamanadas, *Some Self Introspection on Future of Buddhism*, November 07, 2001 Send e-mail to dalits@ambedkar.org with questions or comments about this web site. "Shalimar", Main Road, Chandrapur, (Maharashtra), 442 402. Tel: (07172) 55346
   E-mail: kjdas@nagpur.dot.net.in
2. *An Overview of India's Buddhist Movement*, Friday, October 06, 2006.
3. An Open Letter To Rajdeep Sardesai, By Ravikiran Shinde, 31 October, 2006.
4. President All India Buddha Gaya Mahabodhi Mahavihar Action Committee, Indora Buddha Vihar Nagpur, India. 440004 Ph. 0091-712-642575 e-mail: shuraisasai@rediffmail.com
5. President, Ambedkar Centre for Justice and Peace, For www.ambedkar.org from UN, Posted on 2001-08-10.
6. *Social Thought from Comte to Mukherjee*; (2006). R.N. Mukerjee and Arunansu Ghosal, Vivek Prakashan, New Delhi.
7. *Dalit: The Black Untouchables of India*, V.T. Rajshekar; (1995), Clarity Press, Inc. Roswell RDNE, Atlanta.

8. *The Critics of Dr. Ambedkar*; (1997), D.R. Jatava, Surbhi Publication. Cited from Buddha and the Future of His Dhamma, p. 17.
9. *ibid*, pp. 21-22.
10. J.K. Banthia, Director of Census Operation, Maharashtra, Part II-B(ii), Series-14, PCA for SCs, Mumbai 1993.

9

Ambedkar's Spirit of Indian Constitution and Social Organisation

C.D. Naik

Ambedkar as Law Minister

Dr. Ambedkar performed his governmental and opposition role perfectly well and effectively during his stay in the Parliament from 1947 to 1951. His exemplary contribution is and will be inspiring for generation to come. There has never been such a cabinet member of the Government who compromised with his principle and with promotion of the weaker sections of society and resigned for the love of adherence to their cause. His character and scholarship both are of versatile standing and worth emulating for each and every politician in this country.

Dr. Ambedkar was very much concerned about the character of the Member of the Parliament. This aspect did not receive much attention before and is therefore of very much consequence. If social democracy is to pave way in Indian life then character of citizen and that of the representative has great significance in the political life of a country. Morality is the foundation of social, political as well as religious life of the people. A sense of morality is vital for building a fraternal bond with which to tie all brothers and sisters of all the classes and sections of the society.

Speaking in respect of Law Ministry of 1951 Dr. Ambedkar told that a Central Agency was created for the conduct of cases in the Supreme Court on behalf of the Central and State Government and its expenditure was to be shared between the Government of India and the Government of the participating States. Dr. Ambedkar was associated with legal affairs as a member of Bombay Legislative Council from 1927, as witness before the Simon Commission in 1928, as participant in the three Round Table Conferences during the period from 1930 to 1932, where, at the Second Round Table Conference, he repeatedly clashed with Gandhi, who later signed the historic Pune Pact, and recognized Dr. Ambedkar as the only true spokesman of the depressed classes and became Labour Member equivalent to Cabinet Minister in July 1942 of the Viceroy's Executive Council.

Ambedkar's Appointment as Law Minister

Dr. Ambedkar was elected to the Constituent Assembly by the Bombay Legislature Congress Party. As an elected member of the Constituent Assembly of India Ambedkar was chosen as the Chairman of the Drafting Committee on 29th August 1947. Another Member Shri T.T. Krishnamachari mentioned about the contribution of Ambedkar to Indian Constitution in these words :

"Though a committee of seven members was formed, one of them resigned. Another was nominated in his place. Another member died. No one took his place. One of the members was very busy with government work. Owing to ill health two other members were far away from Delhi. As a result, Dr. Ambedkar alone had to carry the entire burden of preparing the draft of the Constitution. The work he has done is admirable."

Nehru appointed Ambedkar as the Minister of Law on 3 August 1947. As the Minister for Law, Dr. Ambedkar, placed the draft Constitution before the Constituent Assembly after one year, two months and six days (on 4th November 1948). He gave satisfactory answers to many questions raised concerning the Constitution. Article 17 of the Constitution wiping out 'untouchability' was approved twenty five days later (on 29th November 1948).

Dr. Ambedkar as law minister visited Sri Lanka and attended First World Fellowship of Buddhist's Conference in 1950.

- Burma as opposition leader in 1954, and
- Nepal in 1956 where he spoke on Buddha and Karl Max depicting the superioty of Buddhas method of peaceful revolution over Karl Max method.

Presenting the Draft Constitution before the Constituent Assembly

While responding to the debate on constitution in the Constituent Assembly Dr. Ambedkar dwelt on the Indian history of freedom and its consequences and warned the new Indian nation in the following words:

"India has lost her freedom only owing to treason of her own people. Raja Dahir of Sindh was defeated by Mohammad Bin Khasim. The only reason for this defeat was that the generals of the Sindh army took bribes from Dahir's men and did not fight for the king. It was Raja Jaichand of India who invited Mohammad Ghori to fight against Prithviraj. When Shivaji was fighting for the freedom of the Hindus, other Maratha leaders and Rajputs were fighting for the Mughals. When the Sikhs were fighting against the British, other leaders did nothing... Such things should not happen again; therefore, everyone must resolve to fight to the last drop of his blood, to defend the freedom of India."

The Constituent Assembly appointed him to the Drafting Committee, which elected him as a Chairman on 29th August 1947. In February 1948 Dr. Ambedkar completed the Draft Constitution of Indian Republic. On Oct 4th, 1948 Dr. Ambedkar presented the Draft Constitution to Constituent Assembly. On 26 November 1949 Constituent Assembly adopted the Constitution.

Resigning from Nehru's Cabinet

Two years later after adoption of Constitution on September 9, 1951 Dr. Ambedkar resigned from the Nehru Cabinet because, in spite of the earlier declaration in the Parliament by the Prime Minister Pt Jawaharlal Nehru, that his Government would stand or fall or he himself would sink or swim with the Hindu Code Bill Cabinet withdrew its support to it. On 19th September 1951 though the bill was reduced to only two items viz. *the marriage and divorce* and was discussed in the Parliament it was not through even then and inevitably on 11th October 1951 Dr. Ambedkar walked out of the House. After resigning from Nehru's Cabinet Ambedkar contested Lok Sabha election as an opposition leader in 1952 and 1954 but was defeated in both these elections and acted as Member of the Council of States (Rajya Sabha) since March 1952.

Dr. Ambedkar's Published Works

Even though Law Minister Dr. Ambedkar was busy in his pursuit of literary production and publication of 1947-*States and Minorities,* 1948-*'The Untouchables',* and *Maharashtra as a linguistic Province*; 1950- *The Buddha and the Future His Religion;* 1951-*The Rise and Fall of Hindu Women*, and *Merits of Buddhism*, 1951-*Buddha Upasana Patha* his contributions as Law Minister cannot be exaggerated.

Constitution

On *the constitution (First Amendment) Bill* Dr. Ambedkar is reported to have said[2] 2. (P.D., Vol. 12, Part II, 16th/18th May 1951, pp. 8814-15/9004-32) that in the situation of Supreme Courts and High Courts interpreting constitutional article provisions in such a way as to impede the advancement of the weaker sections development which was not the intention of the constitution father, nor reflecting the spirit of it was inevitable to make amendments and restore the right view.

His Contribution to the Chapter on Fundamental Rights

Dr. Ambedkar is honored as the Principal Architect of the Indian Constitution. The Fundamental Rights and the Directive Principles of State Policy are his special contributions. If the chapter on Fundamental Rights, particularly its cardinal articles on Equality before the Law, Equality of Opportunity and the Right to Life (and Livelihood) as interpreted by the Apex Court are indeed held sacred, then read with Articles 37, 38 and 39 of the Directive Principles they are the guiding spirit of the Constitution and immutable.

Dr. Ambedkar pressed repeatedly with the Chairman of the Constituent Assembly to incorporate his proposals in the Chapter on Fundamental Rights of the Constitution and not disallow them on 'technical grounds'. He argued that it was a matter in which the labouring classes in general and the scheduled castes in particular, are vitally concerned. That is the precise reason why it was not permitted in the justifiable part of the Constitution but relegated to the Directive Principles. The PS Appu Committee observed in its report on Land Reforms in 1972, that the hiatus between precept and practice, between policy pronouncements and actual execution has been the greatest in the domain of land reforms.

Reservation for Backward Classes in Public Services and Educational Institutions

The necessity for the amendment of Article 15 arose on account of the judgements delivered by the Supreme Court in two cases which came up before them from the Madras State. One case was *Madras vs. Shrimati Champakam Dorairajan* and the other was *Venkataraman vs. the State of Madras.* In the case of Venkataraman the article involved was Article 29, clause (2). In the one case the question involved was the reservation for backward classes in public services and in the other case, the question involved was the reservation for backward classes in educational institutions.

It was said by the Supreme Court that Article 29, clause (2), did not have a saving clause like clause (4) attached to article 16. As the House will remember under clause (4) of article 16, a special provision is made that Article 16 shall not stand in the way of the Government making a suitable provision for the representation of backward classes in the service. Such a provision of course is not to be found in Article 29. With regard to Article 16, clause (4), the Supreme Court came to the conclusion that it involved discrimination on the ground of caste and therefore it was invalid. Ambedkar found this judgement to be utterly unsatisfactory. There was no disparagement of the learned Judges at all. The judgement did not appear to be in consonance with the articles of the Constitution. That was his point.

In his view in Article 29, clause (2), the most important word is 'only'. No distinction shall be made on the ground *only of race, religion or sex.* The word 'only' is very important. It does not exclude any distinction being made on grounds other than those mentioned in this article and he respectfully submitted that the word 'only' did not receive the same consideration which it ought to have received.

Then with regard to Article 16, clause (4), Ambedkar's submission was this that it was really impossible to make any reservation which would not result in excluding somebody who had a caste.

It was to be borne in mind and it is one of the fundamental principles which is stated in Mulla's last edition on the very first page that there is no Hindu who has not a caste. In this connection Dr. Ambedkar in the course of his practice told the presiding judge in very emphatic terms that *I am bound to obey his judgement but I am not bound to respect it.*

His Contribution to the Chapter on the Directive Principles of State Policy

The Directive Principles of State Policy, were held to be legally unenforceable at the time the Constitution was adopted in the name of "We the People..". However Directive Principles of State Policy have a mandatory character, as the injunction to the State. In the Constitution First Amendment Bill debate also Dr. Ambedkar explicated how obligatory this constitutional part is despite being unjustifiable as some prefer to invoke it like that.

Now the point has to be borne in mind that in Article 46 of the Directive Principles an obligation has been laid upon the government to do everything possible in order to promote the welfare and the interest of what are called the weaker sections of the public by which Dr. Ambedkar understood to mean the backward classes or such other classes who are for the moment not able to stand on their legs—the scheduled castes and the scheduled tribes. It is therefore incumbent not merely on the Government but upon this Parliament to do everything in its hands to see that article 46 is fulfilled and if that fulfillment is to come, how one can escape an amendment so as to prevent article 29, clause (2), and Article 16, clause (4) being interpreted in the way in which it has been interpreted and being made to block the advancement of the people who are spoken of as the weaker class. That is the necessity for amending Article 15.

Article 19, an article which gave rise to great excitement among the Members of the House. Clause (3) (1) (a) of the Bill amends the original clause (2) of Article 19. As Members will see this sub-clause proposes to add three heads: Relations with foreign States, Public Order, and Incitement to offence.

A question was asked as to what was the necessity for introducing three new heads. The necessity has arisen out of certain judgements which have been delivered by the Supreme Court as well as by the Provincial High Courts.

There are the judgements of the Supreme Court in Ramesh Thapar's case and in *Brij Bhushan's case*, the judgements of the State High Courts especially the Punjab High Court in Master Tara Singh's case and *Amarnath Bali versus the State of Punjab*. There are two judgements: Shilabala Devi versus the Chief Secretary of Bihar of the Patna High Court and Bynes versus the Stat of *Madras* of Madras High Court.

In *Ramesh Thapar's* case what was involved was the validity of the Madras Maintenance of Public Order, 1949. Brij Bhushan's case involved the validity of the East Punjab Public Safety Act, 1949. Master Tara Singh's case involved the validity of sections 124A and 153A of the Indian Penal Code. Amarnath Bali's case involved the validity of section 4 of the Indian Press (Emergency Powers) Act of 1931. Shilabala Devi's case also involved the validity of section 4 of the Press Act and the same was involved in the case of Bynes versus Madras State.

All these cases have resulted in the decision that they are void laws, that is to say, in view of the provisions contained in clause (2) of Article 19, the courts have held that all these Acts, however valid they might have been before the Constitution came into existence, are bad laws now, because they are inconsistent with the Fundamental Rights.

Press Act: Section 4

This is what Section 4 of the Press Act says:

"Whenever it appears to the Provincial Government that any Printing Press, in respect of which any security has been ordered to be deposited under section 3 is used for the purpose of printing or publishing any newspaper, book or other document containing any words, signs or visible representations which "—"(a) incite to or encourage, or tend to incite to or to encourage, the commission of any offence of murder or any cognisable offence involving violence, or (b) directly or indirectly express approval or admiration of any such offence or of any person, real or fictitious, who has committed or is alleged or represented to have committed any such offence or which tend directly or indirectly. (c) to seduce any officer, soldier, etc...

It means that under the decision of the Provincial High Courts it is now open to anybody to incite, encourage, tend to incite or encourage the commission of any offence of murder or any cognizable offence involving violence.

Is it a satisfactory position that any person should now be free to incite or encourage the commission of offences of murder or any cognizable offence involving violence? Is it a desirable state of affairs that our Constitution should leave us in this desperate position that we could not control the right of free speech which has been granted by clause (1) of article 19 and it should be so unlimited that any person should be free to preach murder or the commission of any cognizable offence.

Public Safety Laws made by Supreme Court

The same thing has now occurred with regard to the public safety laws or the laws made by the various States for the maintenance of public order, because they also have been held by the Supreme Court to be not open to any limitation by virtue of the Constitution. The Supreme Court has made a distinction between the security of the State and the maintenance of public order. They say that it may be open for Parliament to make a law for the security of the State but it is not open to parliament to make a law for the maintenance of public order. Is the House prepared to allow the right of freedom of speech and expression to be so untrammeled, to be so unfettered, that any man can say anything and go scot-free, although such speech creates public disorder? If the judgements of the Supreme Court and the High Courts stand as they are, then the only consequence that follows is that we shall never be able to make a law, which would restrict the freedom of speech in the interests of public order and that we shall never be able to make a law which would put a restraint upon incitement to violence. Consider whether the void created in our legislation by the decisions of the Supreme Court and the Provincial High Courts should be allowed to remain in the name of freedom of speech.

Constitution of India Vs Constitution of USA

Why the Supreme Court and the various State High Courts say that Parliament has no right to make a law in the interests of public order or in the interests of preventing incitement to offences? That is a very important question and refer very briefly to the rules of construction which have been adopted by the Supreme Court of the United States—and the House will remember that if there is any Constitution in the world of a country of any importance which contains Fundamental Rights it is the Constitution of the United States, and those of us who were entrusted with the task of framing our own Constitution had incessantly to refer to the Constitution of the United States in framing our own Fundamental Rights. There are many Members, who are familiar with the Constitution of the United States. How does the constitution of the United States read? Hon. Members will realise that apparently there is one difference between the Constitution of India and the Constitution of the United States so far as the Fundamental Rights are concerned. The Fundamental Rights in the Constitution of the United States are stated in an absolute form; the Constitution does not lay down any limitation on the Fundamental Rights set out in the Constitution.

Limitations on Fundamental Rights

Our Constitution, on the other hand, not only lays down the Fundamental Rights but also enumerates the limitations on the Fundamental Rights, and yet what is the result? The result is this, that the Fundamental Rights in the United States, although in the text of the Constitution they appear as absolute, so far as judicial interpretations are concerned they are riddled with limitations of one sort or another. Nobody can in the United States claim that his Fundamental Rights are absolute and that the Congress has no power to limit them or to regulate them. In our country we are in the midst of a paradox; we have Fundamental Rights, we have limitations imposed upon them, and yet the Supreme Court and the High Courts say, "You shall not have any further limitations upon the Fundamental Rights."

Interpreting the US Constitution

Now comes the question; how does this result come to be? Come to the canons of interpretation which have been adopted in the United States and by the Supreme Court and High Courts in our country. As hon. Members who are familiar with the growth of the Constitution of the United States will know, although the Constitution of the United States is a bundle of bare bones, the United States Supreme Court has clothed it with flesh and muscle so that it has got the firmness of body and agility which a human being requires. How has this happened? This has happened because the U.S. Supreme Court, although it was the first Court in the world which was called upon to reconcile the Fundamental Rights of the citizen with the interests of the State, after a great deal of pioneering work came upon two fixed principles of the Constitution.

Police Power

One is that every State possesses what is called in the United States "police power", a doctrine which means that the State has a right to protect itself whether the Constitution gives such a right expressly or not. The "police power" is an inherent thing just as our Courts have inherent powers, in certain circumstances, to do justice. It is as a result of this doctrine of "police power" that the United States Supreme Court has been able to evolve certain limitations upon the Fundamental Rights of the United States citizens.

Implied Power

The second doctrine which the United States Supreme Court developed and which it applied for purposes of interpreting the Constitution is known as the doctrine of "implied powers". According to the decisions of the Supreme Court if any particular authority has been given a certain power, then it must be presumed that it has got other powers to fulfil that power and if those powers are not given expressly then the Supreme Court of the United States is prepared to presume that they are implied in the Constitution.

Interpreting the Indian Constitution

Now, what is the attitude which the Supreme Court has taken in this country in interpreting our Constitution? The

Supreme Court has said that they will not recognise the doctrine of the "police power" which is prevalent in the United States. The judgements of the Supreme Court, are dealt with in the case known as *Chiranjit Lal Chowdhuri versus the Union of India* otherwise known as *the Sholapur Mills case.* You find the judgement of Mr. Justice Mukherjee expressly rejecting this doctrine which in the text of the judgement occurs on page 15. They say they will not apply this doctrine. The reason why the Judges of the Supreme Court do not propose to adopt the doctrine of "police power" is this, that the Constitution has enumerated specifically the heads in clause (2) under which Parliament can lay restrictions on the Fundamental Right as to the freedom of speech and expression and that as Parliament has expressly laid down the heads under which these limitations should exist, they themselves now will not add to any of the heads which are mentioned in clause (2). That is in sum and substance, the construction that you will find in the case of Thaper's judgement which was delivered by Mr. Justice Patanjali Sastri. He has said that they will not enlarge it and therefore as the Constitution itself does not authorise Parliament to make a law for purposes of public order according to them Parliament has no capacity to do it and they will not invest Parliament with any such authority. In the case on the Press Emergency Laws also they have said the same thing—that in clause (2) there is no head permitting Parliament to make any limitations in the interests of preventing incitement to an offence. Since section 4 of the Press (Emergency Powers) Act provides for punishment for incitement to the commitment of any offence. Parliament has no authority to do it. That is the general line of argument which the Supreme Court Judges have adopted in interpreting the Constitution.

With regard to the doctrine of implied powers, they have also more or less taken the same view. There is ample scope for recognising the doctrine of implied powers, and our *Directive Principles are nothing else than a series of provisions which contain implicitly in them the doctrine of implied powers.* These Directive Principles are made a matter of fun both by judges and by lawyers appearing before them. Article 37 of the Directive Principles has been made a butt of ridicule. Article 37 says that these Directives are not justifiable that no one would be entitled to file a suit against the Government for the purpose of what we call specific performance. That is not the way of disposing of the Directive Principles. What are the Directive Principles? The *Directive Principles are nothing but obligations imposed by the Constitution upon the various Governments in this country—that they shall do certain things, although it says that if they fail to do them, no one will have the right to call for specific performance.* But the fact that there are obligations of the Government, stands unimpeached. If these are the obligations of the State, how can the State discharge these obligations unless it undertakes legislation to give effect to them? And if the statement of obligations necessitates the imposition and enactment of laws, it is obvious that all these fundamental principles of Directive Policy imply that the State with regard to the matters mentioned in these Directive Principles has the implied power to make a law. Therefore, my contention is this, that so far as the doctrine of implied powers is concerned, there is ample authority in the Constitution itself to permit Parliament to make legislation, although it will not be specifically covered by the provisions contained in the Part on Fundamental Rights.

The various provisos attached to the various fundamental articles need not be interpreted further as though they were matters of strait-jacket as if nothing else is permissible. On account of the declaration by the Supreme Court that this Parliament has no capacity to make a law in certain heads, the question before the House is this: can we allow the situation to remain as it is, as created by the judgements, or we must endow Parliament with the authority to make a law?

SOCIAL ORGANIZATIONS

Organizations Established by Dr. Ambedkar and their Objectives and Programmes

In line with Buddha's Bhikkhu Organization which was based on the slogan of weal and welfare programmes for the people Dr. Ambedkar established his social, and political organisations as follows: 1. Depressed Classes Society, (2) People's Education Society, (3) Bahishkrit Hitakarini Sabha, (4) ILP, (5) SCF and (6) RPI. Ambedkar started the Bahishkrit

Hitkarini Sabha and the Samaj Samanta Sangh for the uplift of untouchables. He led processions and dharnas for his community, demanded separate electorates for them, parted ways with Gandhi, violently differing with Gandhi's approach toward the Untouchables, and finally, left the Hindu fold, embracing with thousands of his followers the more egalitarian faith of Buddhism.

This is what Jawaharlal Nehru wrote of the commitment of Ambedkar to the untouchables: "Dr. B.R. Ambedkar would be remembered mostly as the symbol of revolt against all the oppressing features of Hindu society. In a way he symbolized the hopes and aspiration of the oppressed and the Untouchables."

Our Humanity is cultivated through our emotions. Each day we should look not only to be moved by others, but also to move them through kindness, patience and caring, said venerable Master Sing Yunon. Dhammachakra Pravartan Din, October 15, 2002, Juhu Scheme, Mumbai.

In July 1924, he founded the Bahishkrut Hitkarini Sabha that aimed to uplift the downtrodden socially and politically. The Sabha campaigned for scrapping the caste system from the Hindu religion, started free school for the young and the old and ran reading rooms and libraries. Dr. Ambedkar took the grievances of the "untouchables" to court and gave them justice. People affectionately called him "Babasaheb." Ambedkar formed the Independent Labour Party in 1936 and contested the provincial elections. Ambedkar and his candidates won at many places and fought against untouchability.

As a leading Dalit scholar, Ambedkar had been invited to testify before the Southborough Committee, which was preparing the Government of India Act 1919. At this hearing, Ambedkar argued for creating separate electorates and reservations for Dalits and different religious communities. In 1920, he began the publication of the weekly *Mooknayak (Leader of the Dumb)* in Mumbai. Attaining popularity, Ambedkar used this journal to criticize orthodox Hindu politicians and a perceived reticence in the Indian political community to fight caste discrimination. His speech at a Depressed Classes Conference in Kolhapur impressed the local state ruler, who shocked orthodox society by dining with Ambekdar and his untouchable colleagues. Ambedkar exhorted his Mahar community to abandon the idea of sub-castes, and held a joint communal dinner in which the principle of segregation was abandoned. Upon his return from Europe, Ambedkar established a successful legal practise, and also organised the Bahishkrit Hitakarini Sabha *(Group for the Wellbeing of the Excluded)* to promote education and socio-economic upliftment of the depressed classes.

In 1926, he became a nominated member of the Bombay Legislative Council, and led a *satyagraha*—non-violent protest and civil disobedience as pioneered by Mahatma Gandhi—in Madh to fight for the right of the untouchable community to draw water from the main water tank of the town. On January 1, 1927 Ambedkar organised a ceremony at the Koregaon Victory Memorial near Pune, which commemorated the Indian soldiers who died during World War I. Here he inscripted the names of the soldiers from his Mahar community on a marble tablet. In a Depressed Classes Conference on December 24, he condemned the ancient Hindu classical text, the *Manusmriti (Laws of Manu)*. Condemning it for justifying the system of caste discrimination and untouchability, Ambedkar and his supporters burned copies of the texts. In 1927, he would begin his second journal, the *Bahiskrit Bharat (Excluded India),* later rechristened as *Janata (The People)*. He would be appointed to the Bombay Presidency Committee to work with the all-European Simon Commission in 1928. This commission had sparked great protests across India, and while its report was ignored by most Indians, Ambedkar himself wrote a separate set of recommendations for future constitutional reforms. He was injured in an accident that occured during a visit to Chalisgaon on October 23, 1929. Hoping to help the untouchable community, which was facing a social boycott from orthodox Hindus, he was confined in bed there till the end of the year.

In 1936, Ambedkar founded the *Independent Labour Party*, which won 15 seats in the 1937 elections to the Central Legislative Assembly. Ambedkar oversaw the transition of his political party into the All India Scheduled Castes Federation, although it performed poorly in the elections held in 1946 for the Constituent Assembly of India. Since 1948, Ambedkar had been suffering from diabetes. He was bed-ridden from June to October in 1954 owing to clincial depression and failing eyesight. He had been increasingly embittered by political issues, which took a toll on his health. His health worsened as he furiously worked through 1955. Just three days after completing his final manuscript, Ambedkar died in his sleep on December 6, 1956 at his home in Mumbai.

RPI:

Republican Party of India founded at the Last Leg & Life by Dr. Ambedkar saw both its glorious and doctining phases. About the latter Shri Teltumbde commented as follows:

> It is a tribute to the political consciousness of dalits that while they starved and bled themselves over the issue of unity of these leaders, it never occurred to them to ask, even in a whisper, a question about the source of their material well being! Many blatantly indulged in the acts contrary to their profession for amassing wealth - some set up liquor factories and still remained the front rank leaders of the Buddhists, some allied with the rank casteist and communalist and still claimed to be ardent Ambedkarites. What counted was money and power. Paradoxically, the more affluent ones seemed to fit the bill better as they looked bigger 'sahebs', adding an additional aura to their leadership. Apart from the naked might of money in the electoral politics that tended to situate the moneyed men at the pedestal of power, the leadership model outlined above certainly contributed to their sustenance. With the money power they could invest into cultivation of their cronies and in turn command a better return in the wake of electoral parleys. As a result, the so-called giants who claimed the legacy of Ambedkar became contented with the identity of the parenthesised alphabets of their names after the RPI. They did not even worry about the fact that the formations represented by these parenthesised identities were basically a mere coagulation of their own sub-castes, in their respective geographical areas.

BSP

BSP as political organization was founded by Shri Kanshi Ram by caste (Chamar) in 1970s beginning with the social organization called BAMCEF. The political aim of the BSP is to capture the political master key to unlock each and every lock of social, cultural, economic, employment, trade, land and educational doors on the basis of vote-banks of the backward classes in India, who account for 85 per cent of population dominated by 15% Savarnas.

Findings on Application of Ambedkar's thoughts in Social Organization in Indore, Ujjain and Dewas Districts

1. Most of the organizations depend on donations as their main source of financial support.
2. The social activities of the organizations include the following: Co-operate in social functions (23/25%), to enhance social awareness and social organizations (11/11.95%), Female awareness, respect and empowerment of women (11/11.95%), to make opportunities of work available to the members of the SCs and STs (10/10.87). To help the poor in need and make them aware of their rights (7/7.60); to assist poor students financially and promote educational opportunities for them (6/6.52%); to remove habits of gambling/drinking alcohol and encourage clean habits (4/4.34%). Other activities (15/16.30%).
3. The organizations performed the following religious activities: Propagate Buddhist religion, donations to religious activities, to endevour to remove superstitions (45/48.91); celebrating religious festivals, birth of great men like Kabeer, Ravidas and Ambedkar, related to temples, devotions (23/25%), and others (24/26%).
4. Cultural activities of organizations cover celebration of life events of Buddha, Babasaheb etc. (32/34.78%); national days, drama, singing, yoga, mediation, sport, dance, competition, worship, entertainment etc (37/40.21%) and other (23/25%).

5. Political activities of the organizations are focused on political awareness of rights, Dalit organizations and membership (31/33.70%); training and gains of political consciousness, voting power, to support Dalit political parties, training to Panchayat representatives and public awareness campaigns (30/32.60%) and other (31/33.70%).
6. Economic activities of the NGOs include to make known governmental schemes, bank loans and utilize the same, to form SHGs and maintain them (25/27.15%); to encourage economic development (15/16.31%); to provide jobs for families broken and impoverished and extend to them small amount of loans (10/10.88%); to form womens saving groups and help them stand on their own feet, training for making domestic items and typing, computer education, distribute books and copies for intelligent and poor students (25/27.17%) and other (17/10.49).
7. Educational activities of the above organizations are: to hold students competition and distribute educational aids (20/21.74%); to promote higher education (16/17.39%), propagate education, female education and prize for intelligent students (15/16.30%); to organize evening classes, adult education, distribute educational material, hostel facilities, schooling in slums, for handicapped, all round development, environmental education (20/21.73%).
8. Dr. Ambedkar's thoughts were propagated by the organization by adopting various methods of which Bheemsong, Buddhist speeches, camp are used (29/29.35%); by publishing small booklets and distribute them among people and open public libraries (20/21.74%). Seminar/symposium, debate competition, singing and drama (11/11.96); celebrate birth and life events of Dr. Ambedkar, hold meeting to explain to public about their mission and discuss thoughts of Ambedkar (14/15.21%). And other (20/21.74).

9. As a result of their social, economic, political, religious, cultural and educational activities the organizations achieved these results: people have learnt about sacrifices of Dr. Ambedkar changed their lives accordingly in respect of 20/21.74 per cent. Public awareness was enhanced and people got interested in Buddhism in case of 24/26.9 per cent. Obtained jobs through training and loan facilities, especially for women, reduced burden of marriage customs by public marriage organizations (19/20.65%); assistance was taken by children and women for educative activities, negative social customs were got rid off and carrying human soil on the head was stopped in respect of 20/ 21.74 per cent. Other 10/10.87%.
10. According to the majority of the organizations social life is possible only if the SC/ST communities provide their unbroken services for the rest of the society.
11. However the hurdles they faced in their performance of application of Dr. Ambedkar Thought in the existing social and cultural issues were namely superstition, illiteracy, nil knowledge about Ambedkar, economic difficulties, opposition by general people, lack of literature regarding Babasaheb in simple language and free of cost, time and money, political issues (55/ 59.78%) and other 37/40.21 per cent.

Suggestions/Recommendations

1. Active and useful organizations may be financially assisted by public and Government agencies.
2. Thoughts of Dr. Ambedkar and Buddha may be circulated through educational institutions, public libraries, religious places, community centres and government offices as indispensable for unity and solidarity of social groups.
3. Social application of Ambedkar's philosophy and Buddhism is the need of the hour and it should be undertaken by NGOs and other agencies in the interest of national and international interests.

4. Further researches in the similar topics may be conducted to update the findings and learn more effective ways and means of affecting richer and better social and cultural life of communities.
5. The relevance of ideology of Ambedkar to the contemporary social and cultural issues is revealed by the fact that by the virtue of his ideas social justice and equality, restructuring society, removal of casteism, promoting education and change, women's empowerment, economic prosperity amidst reservation to the deprived classes are possibilities of the present time in general and of places in Indore, Dewas and Ujjain Districts in particular.

References

1. Joseph Raz "The Authority of Law: Essays on Law and Morality" 1983.
2. Dr. Ambedkar as Law Minister and Member of Opposition in Indian Parliament 1947-51, Vol. 12.

10

Educational Policies and Programmes for Dalit : Present Scenario

Prof. Satyapal Katakar*

Education is a very important factor in human life. The very definition of education indicates its importance. According to Buddha, "Education is enlightenment", for Dr. Babasaheb Ambedkar it is "Power of realization" and according to John Dewey, "What nutrition are to physiological life, education is to social life".[1] In India a handful people of high castes were educated and masses were kept in ignorance in the name of religion in order to exploit them. Consequently, even after independence, education was monopoly of few people. In order to bring these socially, economically and educationally backward people in the mainstream of the nation our constitution made special provisions for them. In a general term, weaker section includes those who are weaker with a specific reference to economic and political development, social development, educational development, physical development, intellectual development etc. Thus, it includes Scheduled Castes, Scheduled Tribes, Other Backward Classes, women, physically and mentally challenged people etc.[2] Dr. Ambedkar called weaker sections as the depressed people, oppressed people, backward classes, broken people and in this category he included Dalits, Tribes, Criminal Tribes etc.[3] The Government of India has been making various educational policies and programmes for weaker sections but Dr. Babasaheb Ambedkar was the first one who advocated special policies and facilities for weaker sections. He gave protection to their rights in the form of our Indian Constitution. While making the special provisions for these people, he had lot of expectation from it, for example economic and educational progress of these sections. So it is important to examine to what extend we succeed in realizing Dr. Babasaheb Ambedkar's dream regarding the upliftment of weaker sections.

Dr. Babasaheb Ambedkar wrote lot of books on various subjects but he did not write any specific book on his educational philosophy. Nevertheless, his educational philosophy is expressed in his articles on education which is published in his weeklies like 'Muknayak', 'Janata' and 'Samata', in speeches he delivered at meetings and conference of students, teachers, in his suggestions on the Bombay University Reform, his debate on the Bombay University Act Bills in Bombay Legislative Council etc. His philosophy of education is so valuable that we need to adopt it in the present education system to make it an ideal society and the nation's welfare.

Contribution to the University Reforms Committee

On 15th August 1924, Dr. Babasaheb Ambedkar gave written testimony before the University Reform Committee. He was one of the intellectual to whom they sent their questionnaire containing as many as fifty-four questions but Dr. Ambedkar responded only to some questions that reval his idea of higher education. It contains aims and functions of university, discrepancies of the existing education system and university's role in a society. While talking about aims and function of the University Dr. Ambedkar says that, the University is not merely the place of teaching, learning, conducting examinations and conferring degrees. University education must be society-oriented, scientific, shaping the personality of a learner and unbiased, irrespective of the interest of any particular class. He strongly recommended that unless those backward classes were involved in the process of decision-making and policy formulation in the Senate Body of the University, their interest of education could not be protected and promoted. He asserted that one of the fundamental functions of the University is to provide facilities for bringing higher education to the door of the needy and the poor.[4]

Contribution to Bill on Education Grants

On 12th March 1927 while discussing the Bill on, 'Grants for Education', in Mumbai Legislative Council, he brought to the notice of the Government that due to the privatization of the primary and secondary education by recovering the expenditure by charging its cost on its recipients and in a form of fees respectively, the backward classes will suffer a lot since they are economically weaker than other classes, so it is essential to make such education available to them at minimum cost. Dr. Ambedkar urged the Government to spend extra money on the primary education in order to stop the high rate of dropout students. Unless Government spent extra money on the primary education, the whole amount spent on primary education will be wasted. He argued that the aim of primary education would not be fulfilled merely by the enrolment of students in primary education.

Minimum Level of Competency Goal

Education must develop minimum level competency in him. Unless students develop minimum level competency they should not leave school. In 1990, Government appointed a committee to start minimum level learning programme and Prof. R.H. Dave was its chairperson. In 1995, the committee's programme was recognized and in 1997 it was brought in effect. It is clear that Dr. Ambedkar is the founder of this policy. If we had made it earlier, the development of weaker sections must have been faster than the present condition. Ambedkar knew that for educational progress of these classes they are in need of special facilities and provisions. As we know, Ambedkar's this view took shape under Article 45 in the 'Directive Principles of State Policy', which state 'free and compulsory educations to the children of six to fourteen years age'. In 2001, according to 93rd Constitution Amendment this provision was included in the Fundamental Rights under Article 21C.[5] While stating the importance of education to the Backward Classes people, Dr. Ambedkar says, "The Backward Classes have come to realize that after all education is the greatest material benefits for which they can fight. We may forego material benefits of civilization, but we cannot forego our right and opportunity to reap the benefits of the highest education to the fullest extent".[6] Dr. Ambedkar gave prime importance to education. He believed that even if we get independence notwithstanding the fact that three-fourth of the population is drenched in ignorance, our representative system will be a sham and there would be a rule of wealth against poverty and of power against weakness.

Dr. Ambedkar makes it clear that education is not only important for the upliftment of weaker sections but also for the success of democracy in India.

The Starte Commission

In 1928 Ambedkar was one of the members of the Starte Committee appointed by the Bombay Government to enquire into the educational, social and economical condition of the Depressed Classes and Aboriginal Tribes of the Presidency and recommend measures for their upliftment. The Starte Commission later in March 1930 submitted its report and in the context of education, Dr. Ambedkar recommended an increase in scholarship and hostels for the Depressed Classes students attending Secondary schools, provision of scholarship for industrial training of apprentice in Mills and Railway workshop and scholarship for studying abroad.[7] Our Government's policies and programmes for weaker sections clearly reflect Dr. Ambedkar's thoughts on education for weaker sections.

Importance to 'Shil' : Good Character

Dr. Ambedkar equally gives importance to Shil that is good character. He believed that the use of knowledge depends upon a man's Shil. Knowledge is like a sword, in the hand of a man with Shil, it may be used for saving him in a danger but in the hand of a man without Shil, it may be used for murder, so knowledge without Shil is dangerous, because compared to illiterate man, educated person can use his knowledge to cheat others and it is harmful. Dr. Ambedkar was highly influenced by his Professor John Dewey's pragmatism. He believed that our education system should adopt this philosophy in order to make it society oriented.

Hindu Code Bill and Women Empowerment

Empowerment of women is talk of today, but Dr. Ambedkar realized it long before and he put it in action by introducing 'Hindu Code Bill' in the Parliament on 5th February 1951 as the first Law Minister in independent India. He was aware of the poor condition of women in our society and knew that for the development of nation, empowerment of women is essential. But unfortunately most of the Parliament Members rejected the Bill. Dr. Ambedkar's disappointment was sore. He resigned his seat from the Cabinet on 27th September 1951. The value he attached to this Bill is clear from his resignation speech, where he says, "The Hindu Code Bill was the greatest social reform measure undertaken by the Legislature in the country... to leave inequality between class and class, sex and sex which is the soul of Hindu society untouched and go on passing legislation relating to economic problems is to make farce of our Constitution and to build a palace on a dung heap".[8] Dr. Ambedkar argued that women must get education equal to men and there should be no discrimination between them, for this reason he advocated co-education. At that time, it was believed that co-education would spoil boys and girls students. Dr. Ambedkar said that if a man keep control on his passion even in the company of women and if woman cannot deflect from the path of virtue even in the company of men, then it is called true morality. Thus, his definition of morality was very broad and of high level. Dr. Ambedkar gave attention to every weaker section people.

Designing of Fundamental Rights in Provisions relating to Abolition of Untouchability

Dr. Ambedkar knew that in this caste-ridden society, the rights of weaker sections need legal protection. Thus, he was careful to secure the rights of the Depressed Classes and every individual of weaker sections. He paid especial attention in designing the Fundamental Rights in the constitution because of the peculiar socio-economic condition, which are unshakably deep rooted the ruling castes of India. In this connection, he elaborately dealt with the provisions relating to abolition of untouchability in Article 17.

Article 15 that states prohibition of discrimination on ground of religion, race, sex, caste, place of birth. Article 16 gives equality of opportunity in matter of public employment. Article 23 and 24 prescribe prohibition against exploitation, of traffic in human being, and forced labour. Article 46 under 'Directive Principle of State Policy' prescribes that the state shall promote with special care the educational and economical interests of the weaker sections of the people and in particular, of the Scheduled Castes and Scheduled Tribes and shall protect them from social injustice and all forms of exploitation. Article 335 under 'Special Provisions Relating to Certain Classes gives claims of Scheduled Castes and Scheduled Tribes to services and posts in the central and state governments. Article 338 under 'Special Provisions Relating to Certain Classes' prescribes national commission for Scheduled casts to investigate their social, economic and educational condition and to protect them from exploitation. Article 340 under 'Special Provisions Relating to Certain Classes' recommends an appointment of a commission to investigate the condition of the Other Backward Classes. For the protection of the Minorities in India, Article 29 under 'Fundamental Rights' gives protection to their language, creed and culture of Minority as well as Article 30 gives right to them to establish education institutions and its administration. Apart from these, there are several articles that give protection to weaker sections.

Propagation of Education among Weaker Sections

To propagate education among weaker sections he established 'The Depressed Classes Education Society' in 1928 and 'People Education Society' on 8th July 1945 which opened Siddhartha Art and Science College in 1946 in Bombay, Milinda College of Art and Science in 1950 in Aurangabad and Sidhartha Commerce and Economic College in 1953. Dr. Ambedkar's thoughts on education will always be our guiding light to make our education system as an instrument of every individual's development as well our nation's development. Dr. Ambedkar was not only a brilliant economist, politician, social thinker but also an expert educationist whose educational philosophy is valuable in every context of life.

Education Commissions and Policies

To improve the standard of education and to propagate it among weaker sections Government of India has appointed various education commissions with the passage of time. Thus, it is important to see what recommendations they have given in this regard and to what extent it has helped weaker sections in education.

University Education Commission (1948-49). It was the first Commission in the field of education in independent India. It was appointed in 1948 under the chairmanship of Dr. Radhakrishnan. The objects of this Commission were to study contemporary universities and to find out their shortcomings, to determine the aims of higher education, suggest the measures for raising the teaching standard of higher education etc.

Secondary Education Commission (1952-53). According to the recommendation of the Central Advisory Board of Education of 1951, the Government appointed the commission under of Lakshmanswami Mudaliar, then Vice-Chancellor of Madras University. The objects of this Commission were to study the organization and administration of secondary schools of every province of India and suggest measures for their reform, to study secondary education curriculum and suggest reform, to study examination system of secondary education of every province of India and suggest remedies etc.

National Education Commission (1964-66). The Government in 1964 appointed a commission for advice on the national pattern of education and the general principle policy for the development education of all stages. The chairman of UGC Dr. Kothari was appointed as the chairman of this Commission. The Commission started its work on 2nd October 1964 and submitted its report on 29th June 1964. The Commission suggested that education should be related to life and need of person, the process of modernization should be speed up and the development social values etc. The Commission made especial recommendations for weaker sections under 'Equalization of Education Opportunity'.

National Policy on Education (1986). 'The National Policy on Education' announced in 1986, marked the significant steps in the history of education in post independent India. It took steps for the advancement of weaker sections in education. In fact, it is renewal of National Policy on Education 1968.

Revised National Policy on Education 1986 (1992). With the National Policy on Education in 1986, its implementations and results will be reviewed by every five years, in the meantime the National Front Government appointed Ram Murti Committee in 1990 and Janardhan Reddy Committee in 1992 to review the policy.

Education Policies and Programmes for Weaker Sections

Pre-Matric-Post Matric Scholarships for Weaker Sections

Dr. Ambedkar made it clear that for the success of our democracy, literacy would be the first condition so the high rate of illiteracy became major problem in India and Government set out to make various educational policies and programmes for weaker section due to their low percentage of enrolment in every stage of education. For advancement of education among SC, ST and OBC people Government started Pre-Matric and Post-Matric Scholarship for them. Surely, these students benefitted from it, especially in case of Pre-Matric scholarship, it secured their retention in secondary schools. The drawback of this policy is that most of the time students get their scholarship at the end or after completion of their academic year. Thus, the very purpose of awarding scholarship is neglected due to the delay. Student could not utilize this amount to fulfill his educational needs. The same condition is of Post-Matric scholarship. The maintenance amount of Post-Matric scholarship should be increased so that students can fulfill their educational needs. To make this policy more effective Government should award it per month so that the object of awarding scholarship will be fulfilled. Government is providing scholarship to students belonging to minority but the number of scholarship is so limited that very few students get this scholarship. While making education programmes and policies government should take care that majority students will be benefitted from it.

Construction of Hostels

In order to enable and encourage students belonging to Scheduled Castes to attain the quality education, the scheme of construction of hostels was started in 1989. This scheme was revised and renamed as "Babu Jagjivan Ram Chhatravas Yojana" in 2008. The object of this scheme is to provide residential accommodation facilities to Scheduled Castes boys and girls studying in middle school, higher secondary school, colleges and universities. According to this scheme, 266 Boys' hostels and 111 Girls' hostels were built in 2003-04. In the following two years, this number was decreased to 110 Boys' hostels and 14 Girls' hostels in 2004-05 and in 2005-06, the number of hostels were 88 Boys' hostels and 56 Girls' hostels. In 2006, 109 Boys' hostels and 204 Girls' hostels and in 2007, 114 Boys' hostels and 187 Girls' hostels were built. This scheme helped especially to rural Scheduled Castes students to study in urban places. (web source)

National Overseas Scholarships for SC Students

To promote the higher study in SC students and to enable them to study abroad the Central Government started, "The Central Sector Scheme of National Overseas Scholarship" in 2007-08. According to this scheme, the financial assistance of fifty thousand overall is provided to the selected candidates for pursuing higher studies abroad in specified field of Master level courses and Ph.D in Engineering, Technology and Science. The awards under the scheme are not available in discipline of Agriculture, Medical Science, Humanities and Social Sciences. Thirty awards per year are available under the scheme with twenty-seven awards for SC, two awards for Denotified Nomadic and Semi-Nomadic Tribes and one award for Landless Agricultural Labourers and Traditional Artisans. (Web source) It is noteworthy that Government is taking efforts to promote higher study in SC students by giving financial assistance to study abroad. Every year thirty students will be going abroad for higher study.

Drawbacks

The conditions for getting the scholarship produce questions, is it really helping the poor students among SC who cannot bear the big amount to study abroad? The first condition to get this scholarship is that a student has to secure the admission in Foreign University or institute. Those students who are intelligent but whose economic condition is not sound cannot take up entrance exam and attend interview in foreign countries in order to get admission and Government does not provide any help in this regard. The second important factor is, this scholarship is awarded only for Engineering and Technology and all other courses are excluded from it. It underestimates the value of Humanities, Social Sciences and other subjects. It is accepted that today's world is the world of industry and technology but does not our country need brilliant economists? Does not our country need political philosophers and social thinkers? Sayajiraje Gaikwad, the King of Baroda gave scholarship to Dr. Ambedkar to study abroad and our country got a brilliant economist, political philosopher and social thinker. Therefore, it is important that Government should give this scholarship to other courses as well. The third drawback of this policy is its selection procedure. The candidates who apply for this scholarship is called for interview and the merit list is prepared to make the short list of candidates. In case of tie up of two or more candidates the one who is eldest in age as per the date of birth, the priority is given to this candidate. The criterion of age seniority is wrong one. Dr. Ambedkar dismissed this criterion for filling the high posts vacancies in any employment. In the University Reform testimony he says, "The principle of seniority has become sacred convention that all upper grade vacancies are filled by this and not on the basis of intellectual ground and the field of education is not exception to it[10]. In view of Dr. Ambedkar person's intellectuality and creativity count more than seniority. In the 'National Overseas Scholarship' selection, criteria should be an intellectuality of the candidate and his economic condition. Government should help students in taking up entrance examination of foreign universities, so that the poor students will be benefitted by this scheme. Dr. Ambedkar as the Member of Parliament argued and demanded that weaker sections and especially Scheduled Castes students should get financial assistance to study abroad because they are backward and poor and cannot bear the high cost of foreign education. For the development of these people Government should restart the scheme of sending the backward classes students foreign to study higher education. The policies which Government is implementing now, was first of all advocated by Dr. Ambedkar.[11]

Rajiv Gandhi National Fellowship

To increase opportunities available to Scheduled Castes and Scheduled Tribes students in research work the Central Government started the "Rajiv Gandhi National Fellowship" in 2005 that provides financial assistance for pursuing research work in Science, Humanities, Social Science, Engineering and Technology in all recognized Universities and Research Institutes of India. There are one thousand three hundred and thirty three slots for Scheduled Castes students and six hundred sixty-seven slots for Scheduled Tribes students. To increase the participation of women in research work, 50% of the fellowship is awarded to women candidates. According to these scheme twelve thousand per month for initial two years and fourteen thousand per month for remaining tenure is awarded to those who are pursuing research work in Humanities and Social Science with the contingency of ten thousand per annum for initial two years and twenty thousand five hundred per annum for remaining tenure. Those who are pursuing research work in Science, Engineering and Technology are awarded fourteen thousand per month for initial two years and fifteen thousand per month for remaining tenure with the contingency of twelve thousand per annum for initial two years and twenty thousand five hundred per annum for remaining tenure. The selection is made on the basis of merit. The drawback of this scheme is that Government makes delay in distributing the scholarship and scholars have to wait for months to get it. There are lot of needy people who want to pursue higher education and to enable them to study, it is needful that the number of slots should be increased. Government should make the policy to secure jobs of high-educated weaker section people. (web source)

In our Indian Constitution Article 41 under 'Directive Principles of State Policy' prescribes that the state shall within the limits of its economic capacity and development make effective provision for securing the right to work, to education and to assistance in cases of unemployment, old age, sickness and disablement. To bring this provision in effect, the Ministry of Social Justice and Empowerment started the 'National Scholarship for Persons with Disabilities' which provides financial assistance of seven hundred per month and four hundred per month for the hostellers and day scholars respectively who are pursuing Post-Matric/ Post-Secondary technical and professional courses. For pursuing M. Phil and Ph.D in professional and technical courses, the amount of thousand per month for the hostellers and seven hundred per month for day scholars is given. As we compare this scholarship scheme with other scholarship schemes, the amount given in this scheme is insufficient that can hardly fulfill their needs. This scholarship programme is meant to promote education in these students and make them able to live common life like any individual in society. However, the criterion for the continuation of this scholarship is strict one. The continuation of the scholarship for the next year depends on successfully completing the course in the preceeding year with minimum 50% marks. For these people to pursue education itself is a big challenge and put the condition of 50% in the preceeding examination is too strict to enable them to continue the scholarship. For educational development of weaker sections, Government has been making various policies and programmes and for the success of these policies, Government should make sure that these have reached up to the lowest strata of society. In October 2008, the Supreme Court gave verdict on reservation for OBC students in higher education. According to this verdict, OBC students got 27% reservation in IIT, IIM and Central Universities.[12] It is important to examine to what extend weaker sections have achieved progress in education in the present scenario.

Present Scenario in Education System

Today the world has become a global economy; an open market that ultimately leads to intense competition in every sphere of life and education is not exception to it. At such time, Government has to carry out double responsibilities at the same time. It has to cope with the present system of economy and bring the nation at the forefront of development and at the same time it has to take care that weaker sections are not left behind in this competition. Table 1 will help us to understand their condition in education field.

Table 1. Estimated Population by Age Groups (2005)

(in % age)

Stages of Education	*Relevant Age Groups*	*All Categories Students*	*SC*	*ST*
Primary	06-11	12.1	2.1	1.1
Upper Primary	11-14	7.4	1.2	0.6
Elementary	06-14	19.4	3.4	1.7
Sec/Senior Secondary	14-18	9.4	1.5	0.8
Higher Education	18-24	12.4	1.9	0.9
All Education	06-24	41.3	6.8	3.4

Source: www.Scribd.Scribd.com/doc/11569307/Education-Statistics-2005-06.

From the Table 1, it is clear that the SC and ST students are still struggling to make their progress in education. There is a wide gap between the all categories of students of every stage and SC and ST Students. Their share in overall percentage of every stage is very low that itself indicates the poor condition of these people in education despite the fact that the Government are implementing various schemes for them. It is important to give attention to women's education since they constitute one of the factors in weaker sections. Table 2 makes clear their progress in education.

Table 2. Percentage of Girls Enrolment to Total Enrolment by Stages of Education

Year	*Primary I-V*	*Middle VI-VIII*	*Sec. / Hr. Sec. Intermediate IX-XII*	*Hr. Education Degrees and above level*
1980-81	38.6	32.9	29.6	26.7
1990-91	41.5	36.7	32.9	33.3
2000-01	43.7	40.9	38.6	39.4
2001-02	44.1	41.8	39.5	39.9
2002-03	46.8	43.9	41.3	40.1
2003-04	46.7	44.0	41.1	39.7
2004-05	46.7	44.4	41.5	38.9
2005-06	46.6	44.7	42.0	38.3

Source: http://www.education.nic.in/stats/ES-Glance%202005-06.pdf

It is clear that women are making progress in education due to the efforts taken by Government and NGOs. We need to take more efforts to increase their participation and to balance gender parity in education. The backwardness of weaker sections in education is due to drawbacks in educational policies and programmes, unawareness among these people about these policies and the most importantly the privatization in education system. The privatization in education has created the contradictory situation, on the one hand, the number of educational institutes is increasing every year and on the other hand, the enrolment of women and those belonging to SC, ST are still very much under representation. At the time of independence, our country had twenty universities and six hundred thirty six colleges.

Today we have more than three hundred universities and over twenty thousand colleges. This will be increasing every year for example in 2008, one hundred and twenty one institutes got recognition as Deemed Universities. (web source) As we observe this data, the percentage of private unaided institutions has increased with the advanced stage of education, at the primary level it is only 7.1% but at the senior secondary level, it is 32.3%. On the contrary, the percentage of Government schools is being reduced with advance stage of education. It reveals the reason behind the contradictory situation in education. The private institution at every stage swelling the figure of total number of educational institutions but their high fee is beyond the consideration of weaker sections, thus they cannot get access in these institutions. The privatization of higher education and professional courses has badly affected weaker sections.

Privatization of Education : Impact on Dalits

Privatization of educational institutions claims to increase quality and ease Government's financial burden. But many educational scholars and writers show that it is not the case. The underlying philosophy of privatization is that anything related to the public sector is inefficient and anything related to the private sector is efficient and desirable. Accordingly, privatization is being pursued in all sectors of economy including education as a means of improving efficiency and easing financial stress. But overall efficiency of the system may indeed suffer and financial gain may not be sizeable.[13] In general, it is argued that education as public good has suffered in India and that the privatization is proceeding apace with public higher education sector funds being reduced. Neo-liberal policy and globalization have increasingly taken hold in India, leading to a doubling of higher education sectors, a rapid increase in private institutions and number of problems related to access, quality and equity in education.

It is noteworthy to remember that Dr. Ambedkar in 1924 while writing testimony on the Bombay University Reform, questioned the quality maintained by the private educational institutes while imparting higher education. He says, "At present the teachers are attached to the colleges and their pay and status are regulated by the authorities governing the colleges. But the colleges do not seem to be making the appointment solely from the sense of obtaining the most qualified persons nor regulating their grades, tenure, pay and promotion in such manner as to open a career to the best and most qualified members of the staff.[14] He rightly points out that in private educational institutes self-interest is more important than quality and equity in education. Apart from the problem of quality and equity, it has given rise to many other problems. As education is privatized, less privileged youths are denied access to professional and technical education. It is this denial and exclusion from education and jobs make them prey to fundamentalist right wing forces.[15] It is quite true that exclusion from education and unemployment leads man to follow wrong path but from the recent events happened in India it shows that in the name of protection of culture and religion, terrorism taking its root in India and even highly educated people are part of it. While making education policy and curriculum instead of national value and scientific views if we give more importance to culture and religion, it will lead to the beginning of terrorism. In our schools and colleges when we give undue importance to religion, students perceive that their religion is superior to other and it is under threat so in order to protect their culture and religion they choose the path of terrorism. Therefore it is important that while making education policy scientific views and philosophy of Dr. Ambedkar should be adopted.

Today Dalits are lagging behind in every field of life. In order to bring them in the mainstream of nation, education is the most effective instrument. It is the most vital input for the growth and prosperity of nation. It has the power to transform human being into human resources. It is important that while making educational policies, aims and goals decided by our constitution must be given priority, that is, "...To secure to all its citizens Justice, social, economical and political.... Equality of status and of opportunity and to promote among them all

Fraternity assuring the dignity of the individual and the unity and integrity of the Nation..." The success of democracy lies in people and our education must be such that brings all round development of personality of a learner, that inculcates national values in a learner, that will lead to nation's unity and integrity. While making educational policies nation's welfare must be given priority and welfare of nation is not complete unless weaker sections are educated and empowered. It is responsibility of our Government and their organizations like NCERT and SCERT which make education policy and curriculum from primary to higher secondary level and NCTE, AIU, UGC, AICTE, Bar Council of India, Medical Council of India, Council of Architect, Central Council of India, Pharmacy Council of India, Indian Nursing Council, the Council of Higher Education and Distance Education Council that make education policy and curriculum for higher education from undergraduate level to Ph.D. to make educational policies as such that enable our students to compete in this global economy world and develop in him a sense of responsibility toward his nation and people. We have achieved a little success in this regard because in our society even highly educated and high post people do not think beyond their caste and community. In private unaided professional colleges the students of SC, ST, OBC, NT, VJA were not getting any freeship or scholarship so it was hard time for the poor students to complete their course. In 2002, some initiative was taken to get these students full reimbursement in Medical, Engineering, Agricultural, Pharmacy and Nursing College. The author met Government officials and wrote requisition letters to them in order to make them understand the importance of freeship in professional courses for weaker sections. Along with students, he gave requisition letter to Maharashtra Legislative Assembly. He also wrote requisition letters to officers of education department and to the President of India, Minister of Education and others. The former President Honourable Mr. Abdul Kalam took notice of this problem and drafted a letter to Maharashtra Government to solve the problem immediately. In Maharashtra in all private unaided professional colleges, the students of SC, ST, NT, VJA are getting the full reimbursement and OBC students got 50% fees concession in the above mentioned professional courses. Government should imply this policy in all states of India that will help weaker sections students to pursue professional courses and higher study.

It is need of our time that we, followers of Dr. Ambedkar should come together, collaborate, and cooperate to solve the problems of our nation and its people. It is our responsibility to take Dr. Ambedkar's thoughts to every common man of this country then only our nation will be strong enough to face the challenges of 21th century and will become a developed nation.

References

"Parliamentary Debate in Rajyasabha, August-September, 1954".

Ambedkar, B.R. *Dalitanche Shikshan* Trans. and Ed. Devidas Ghoreswar. Nagpur: Samata Prakashan Samata Sainik Dal, 1994.

Basu, Durga Das. *Introduction to the Constitution of India*. 18th Ed. New Delhi: Prentice Hall of India Pvt. Ltd., 1998.

Chand, Tara, *Development of Education System in India.* New Delhi: Anmol Publication Pvt. Ltd., 2004.

Keer, Dhananjay, *Dr. Ambedkar: Life and Mission.* Bombay: Popular Prakashan, 1971.

Krestovics, Maik and Steve O Michael. *Financing Higher Education in Global Market.* New York: Algora Publication, 2004.

Kundale, M.B. *Shekshnic Tatvadyan aani Shekshnic Samajshastra.* (Educational Philosophy and Educational Sociology) 10th ed. Pune: Shreevidya Prakashan, 2003.

Moon, Vasant, ed. Dr. Babasaheb Ambedkar Writings and Speeches. 2nd vols. Bombay: Education Department Maharashtra, 1982.

Mukhopadhyay, Marmar and Parhar, Madhu. *Indian Education:* Development since Independence. Calcutta: Vikas Pub. House, 1999.

Naik, C.D. Thoughts and Philosophy of Dr. Ambedkar. New Delhi: Sarup and Sons, 2003.

Sharma, Prakash Sanjay. *B.R. Ambedkar: A Crusader of Social Justice*. Jaipur. RBSA Pub., 2003.

Shiva, Vandana. *India Divided Diversity and Democracy under Attack*. Bangalore: Seven Stories Press, 2005.

Shukla, P.D. The New Education Policy in India. New Delhi: Sterling Publisher Pvt. Ltd., 1985.

Oza ed. Chronicle Year Book, Noida: Chronicle Publication Pvt. Ltd., 2009.

Web Sources:

www.socialjustice.nic.in
www.scribd.com
www.eciucqtion.nic.in
www.ugc.nic.in

References

1. M.B. Kundale. *Shekshnic Tatvadyan aani Shekshnic* Samajshastra. (Educational Philosophy and Educational Sociology) 10th ed. Pune: Shreevidya Prakashan, 2003, p. 6.
2. Tara Chand, *Development of Education System in India*. New Delhi: Anmol Publication Pvt. Ltd., 2004, p. 177.
3. Vasant Moon.ed. *Dr. Babasaheb Ambedkar Writings and Speeches*. 2nd Vols. Bombay: Education Department Maharashtra, 1982, p. 41.
4. *Ibid.,* pp. 296-312.
5. N.N. Oza ed., Chronicle Year Book. Noida: Chronicle Publication Pvt. Ltd., 2009, p. 146.
6. Vasant Moon.ed. *Dr. Babasaheb Ambedkar Writings and Speeches*. 2nd vols. Bombay: Education Department Maharashtra, 1982, p. 62.
7. Dhananjay Keer *Dr. Ambedkar: Life and Mission*. Bombay: Popular Prakashan, 1971, p. 132.
8. Sanjay Prakash Sharma *B.R. Ambedkar: A Crusader of Social Justice*. Jaipur. RBSA Pub, 2003, p. 162.
9. Dhananjay Keer *Dr. Ambedkar: Life and Mission*. Bombay: Popular Prakashan, 1971, p. 124.
10. Vasant Moon ed. *Dr. Babasaheb Ambedkar Writings and Speeches*. 2nd Vols. Bombay: Education Department Maharashtra, 1982, pp. 303.
11. Parliamentary Debate Rajyasabha August-September, 1954 in B.R. Ambedkar. *Dalitanche Shikshan*. Trans. and Ed. Devidas Ghoreswar. Nagpur: Samata Prakashan Samata Sainik Dal, 1994, pp. 1140-41.

12. N.N. Oza, ed. Chronicle Year Book. Noida: Chronicle Pub. Pvt. Ltd., 2009, p. 155.
13. Maik Krestovics, and Michael Steve O *Financing Higher Education in Global Market*. New York: Algora Publication, 2004, p. 286.
14. Vasant Moon, ed. *Dr. Babasaheb Ambedkar Writings and Speeches*. 2nd Vols. Bombay: Education Department Maharashtra, 1982, p. 303.
15. Vandana Shiva. *India Divided Diversity and Democracy under Attack*. Bangalore: Seven Stories Press, 2005, p. 77.

11

Pali Grammar

C.D. Naik*

On reading Bharatsinha Upadhyaya's Pali Sahitya Ka Itihas we come across the lines that Acharya Buddhaghosha used Panini's ashtadhyayi in *interpreting Buddhavacana,* which is unbelievable. Because in the same source it was questioned and surmised that in technical sense *Pali might have no grammar* or nirukti-shastra[1] except rules to explain terms in Tipitaka called Veyyakarana before the *time of Buddhaghosha.* The interesting thing about grammar was Lord Buddha's exhortation to his disciples to preach dhamma of perfect and pure celibacy both in spirit and letter.[2] In addition to this the knowledge of letters was appreciated while stating that the meaning of wrongly placed letters and words lead to wrong sense and that of properly placed letters and words to good sense.[3] Thus in Sthaviravada tradition there is balance in relations between meaning and words. Letters are defined as clothings of meaning in yasma panetam (vyanjanam) attham vyanjayati, tasma evam vuttam"ti.[4] In Dhammapada also a wise one is required to know language, poetics and grammar in order to get rid of fetters. As far as non-canonical Pali literature goes the most authoritative Milinda-Panha's *Bahiranidanakatha* tells of the Elder Nagasena that he first studied Buddha-word in letters and later grasped it by meaning. With regard to Pali literature the German poet Gette's remark *that literature is humanization of universe* is cent per cent applicable to Pali literature also.

Legal Code: Books in Pali Text

However, historically speaking the two Buddhist countries namely Sri Lanka and Burma have been preservers of Pali literature and carriers of new patterns of literary crafts from early centuries to the present age. Take for example the Hindu Code of *Manusmriti* which is one of the Hindu sacred books against which Dr. Ambedkar revolted and drafted the Constitution of India on just universal humanized norms and late Hindi and Pali Buddhist monk scholar Bhadant Anand Kausalyayan wrote *Manusmriti Jalai Gai Kyon*, had prototype parallel in Buddhist Pali literature in Burma known as Thammathat composed by Dhamma-Vilas (Sariputra) during the reign of the King Narapati-Si-Thu (1167-1202).

Later in the thirteenth century the Burmese King Vagaru's Legal code book by name *Manu-Sar* was translated into Pali in sixteenth century. In the seventeenth century Dhammavilasa Dhammasattha came in the edition of Manu-Dhammasattha. In the eighteenth century Vanna Kyav-Din's *Man-Vannana* was very popular in this genre. Such legal code books were culminated in the nineteenth century by Rajbal Kyav-Din's composition of Mohavicchedani in Pali versified form. This book was based on law of Succession in Dayabhag tradition and is in particular comparable to Dr. Ambedkar's Hindu Code Bill based on the integration of both Dayabhaga and Mitakshar legal norms prevalent in East India until the fiftees.

The authors of such works as the Dathavansa, the Saddhammopayana, and the Mahabodhivansa made use of Pali words derived from Sanskrit Amarakosa and used them as Pali. However the list of such Pali words thus derived from Sanskrit would not be a long one.

When about a thousand years afterwards, some pandits in Ceylon began to write in Pali they were so familiar with the method of writing on palm leaves that the works belonging to this period were not intended to be learnt but to be read.

Dr. Ambedkar's Contribution Includes the sixteenth volume of Writings and Speeches of Dr. Babasaheb Ambedkar published by Government of Maharashtra on *Pali Grammar and Pali Dictionary.*

Pali Literature and Grammar

In the above mentioned two Buddhist countries again the tradition of literature related to grammar commenced. Today whatever literature of grammar is in Pali, is classified into three branches namely.

1. Kaccayana-grammar and its auxiliary literature.
2. Moggallana-grammar and its auxiliary literature.
3. Aggavamsa's Saddaniti and its auxiliary literature. The first one belonged to the seventh century and has 675 formulae, divided into 8 chapters, each describing four matters namely.
   - (i) Sutta (formula, rule)
   - (ii) Vutti (description of Vritti to simplify formulae)
   - (iii) Payog (Use) and
   - (iv) Nyasa (mukhamattadeepani or interpretative notes) all four composed by Kaccayana, Sanghannandi, Bramadatta and Vimalabuddhi respectively.[6]

Kaccayana-grammar is the earliest grammar of Pali literature. Its author is Katyayan, who was different from others of same name such as one of the Buddha's chief disciples (600 B.C.), Panini's Ashtadhyayi sutras commentator (300 B.C.) and the author of nettipakarana and petkopadesa.

In 1171 (Buddha Era 1715) Cchapada wrote commentary on Kaccayana-Grammar called Suttaniddesa or Kaccayana-sutta-niddesa.

Unlike Kaccayana-vyakarana the Moggallana grammar and its subsidiary literature was far better in depth and completeness having 817 formulae and six parts covering sandhi, samasa, stri-pratyaya, taddhiya, kridant and verbs. But the former and latter both are supposed to be following in the footprints of their precedents of sakkatagandha (sanskritgrantha) such as Katantra-grammar (400 A.D.) and commentary of Panini's Ashtadhyayi called Kashika vritti (700 A.D.).

I-tsing's Testimony on Role of Panini's Grammar in Indian Education

In Chapter xxxiv of his Record of the Buddhist Religion, I-tsing also gives us information about the method of learning followed in Indian educational establishments. According to him Sanskrit grammar was always one of the basic studies of a scholar. I-tsing says: "The old translators (of Sanskrit into Chinese) seldom tell us the rules of Sanskrit language... I trust that now a thorough study of Sanskrit grammar may clear up many difficulties we encounter whilst engaged in translation.[7] It is clear from commentaries such as those of Yasomitra that Panini's grammar formed a part of the basic training of a young scholar. A scholar was required to study Panini's sutras, Dhatupatha, Astadhatu, Unadi-sutras, Kasikavrtti, Curni (perhaps the same as Patanjali's Mahabhasya), Bhartrhari's sastra, Vakyapadiya and Pei-na or Bedavrtti, logic (Hetuvidya), metaphysics (Abhidharma-kosa), Nyaya-dvara-tarka-sastra, inferences (anuman), and Jatakamala.[8] The priests learn besides all the Vinaya works and investigate the sutras and sastras as well. They oppose the heretics as they would drive beasts (deer) in the middle of a plain and explain away disputations as boiling water melts frost".[9] In India, there are two traditional ways in which one can attain to great intellectual power. Firstly, by repeatedly committing to memory the intellect is developed; secondly, the alphabet fixes one's ideas. In this way, after a practice of ten days, a scholar feels his thoughts rise like a fountain, and can commit to memory whatever he has once heard (not requiring to be told twice). This is far from being a myth, for I myself have met such men".[10]

Post-Buddhist Literature

According to N. Aiyaswami Sastri the age of the Gita is post-Buddha period as it refers to Buddhist ideas like the instructions regarding proper food, timely sleep and timely waking,[11] which undoubtedly refer to some of the most important Buddhist teachings born of the Buddha's own personal experiences. The opinion refered to in the lines of tyajyam dosavad ity eke karma prahur manisinah[12] "some wise men say that the wrongful action is to be abandoned" is exactly what the Buddha held. The Anguttara, for example, says that the Buddha confessed himself to be an advocate of inaction in the sense that he argued in favour of abandoning wrongful act.[13] The fourfold food, "annam caturvidham" mentioned in verse XV, 14, corresponds to that of Buddhist literature (cattaro ahara). And it is hard to believe that the original Mahabharata could have consisted of the whole of the Bhagavadgita. Nonetheless, it is possible that the Gita was composed in Panini's time, 500-450 B.C., for the grammarian alludes definitely to Bhakti and the Bhagavata religion.

Perhaps, the most indisputable evidence in favour of placing Panini in the post-Buddha period is his references to Maskariparivrajaka, who was in all probability Makkhali Gosala, the reputed religious leader of the Ajivaka sect.[14] R.G. Bhandarkar is of the opinion that it was composed not later than the beginning of the 4th century B.C. Radhakrishnan pleads for 500 B.C. in his Indian Philosophy[15]. Prof. Belvalker expressed in a personal talk to N. Aiyaswami that he would be inclined to assign to it a date prior to the Buddha. It is now the generally accepted view that the worship of idols among the Hindus is as old as Panini (500-450 B.C.).

Buddhaghosa's commentaries contain much of the matter as old as Tipitaka itself and are rich in history and folklore and abound in varied information which throws abundant light on the social and moral conditions of ancient India. His own creation, the Visuddhimagga is called as an Encyclopaedia of Buddhist Doctrine.

Besides the Pali literature *Dipavamsa* and *Mahavamsa* are first in importance followed by *Milinda Panha*, the Questions of King Milinda who is identified with certainty with Bactarian King (Minander).

Dr. Ambedkar so loved Milinda Panha with its main characters, Milinda and Nagasena that he established Milinda Mahavidyalaya in Nagasena Grove in Aurangabad by his Peoples Education Society, and promoted the study of Pali language and literature and now it has been producing notable scholars there in that domain.

Ambedkar's Pali Dictionary

Ambedkar's first M.A. Dissertation on *Ancient Indian Commerce* referred to Jataka sources for prosperous ancient Indian commercial relations with foreign countries and described how Indian artisans formed into various guilds. In his *The Buddha and His Dhamma* Ambedkar culled his material from various canonical and commentarial Pali literature. He adopted Buddhist spirit of *Bahujana Hitaya Bahujana Sukhaya* in the drafting of Indian constitution. He codified the two different social-legal traditions existing in India called Dayabhaga and Mitakshar into one unified *Hindu Code Bill* for regulating unequal status of man and woman and establishing justice for both of them in matters of property, marriage, divorce, succession, adoption, widow remarriage, and civil rules of rites and ceremonies of betrothal.

About the periods of Jatakas T.W. Rhys Davids marked two currents in Buddhist stories, earlier folklore and its subsequent Pali versification both combined together in the Jatakas. He also wrote about Robert Caesar Childers' first volume of his Pali Dictionary published in 1872 that, "It is somewhat hard to realize that he had at his command a few pages of the canonical Pali books". When scholars had leisure to collect and study the data to be found in this pre-Sanskrit literature it threw as much light on the history of ideas and language as the study of names and places threw upon the political divisions, social customs, and economic conditions of ancient India.

Rhys Davids also made clear the importance and significance of Pali Dictionary project when he wrote, "Anybody familiar with this sort of work will know what care and patience, what scholarly knowledge and judgement are involved in the collection of such material, in the sorting, the sifting and final arrangement of it, in the adding of cross references, in the consideration of etymological puzzles, in the comparison and correction of various faulty readings, and in the verification of references given by others, or found in the indices".

Dr. Ambedkar was past 50 when he started the compilation of the *Pali Dictionary*. It was an effort contrasted to the effort of Dr. Samuel Johnson who attempted his dictionary of English on the threshold of becoming the world language in 1755.[16] Describing the difference between the living and the dead languages the editor, Vasant Moon noted that, "Pali, though the *lingua franca* of the Buddhist world, is a dead language. In support of a living language, authority for correct sense and words, is always at our elbow, in the chat of our domestics or in the converse of the passengers at our street door, in colleges of learned and in stables of menials; in lanes of a city and in remote hamlets. That is not the case in respect of a dead language which has many pitfalls. Words and phrases of a dead language, are exercises in reconstruction of history, they are passages to times past and pathways to the sociology and culture of the ages gone by. The dictionary of the Pali language taken up by Dr. Ambedkar for compilation when he was 50, shows his indomitable spirit to look into the past, in order to know the present and to see the light for the future."

Conclusion

In the community in India which is newly restored to Buddhists in the world when even the so simplest Pali aphorism as '*atta dipo bhava*' cannot be expected to print correctly on their wedding card the Pali Grammar by Babasaheb Ambedkar is a no small help. It also follows the Grammar tradition of Kaccayana, Moggalana, Rupasiddhi and Saddaniti by giving all possible contents of a grammar, especially parts of speech.

Compared to the world famous Sanskrit Grammar by Holy Faith[17] covering as many as 175 pages and A.K. Warder's 464 page-*Introduction to Pali*[18] the Pali Grammar of Dr. Ambedkar fills the ocean into a pot by covering all fundamental rules of grammar within 88 pages only.

It is to be investigated whether the Pali grammarians followed in the footprints of Panini, Katyayana and Patanjali or as they say thirteen pre-Panini and ten post-Panini Sanskrit Grammarians, and whether the Pali language was closer to Prakrit vernaculars developed from the beginning from its supposed founder Valmiki to his successors Trivikram Pandit (1400 A.D.), Srutasagar, Shubhacandra, Laxmidhar, Chandrapandit, Sheshnag, Lankeshvar all in (1600 A.D.) and Ramtarka Vagish and Markandeya in the 17th century[19] or it had its own course of development in the Kosalan and Magadha Kingdoms then and the Theravada Buddhist nations afterwards.

In a time when Pali scholarship is limited to the old great authors with its new young followers adhering to duplicate their works this book is unique and milestone in the contemporary revival movement of Pali and Buddhism in India and abroad.

References

1. (nirutti-interpretation of Pali Tipitaka terminology as per rules of grammar).
2. (See mahavagga-sattham savyanjanam kevalaparipunnam parisuddham brahmacariyam pakasetha).
3. (Anguttara-nikaya, pancakanipata, tatiya saddhamma sammosa-sutta).
4. (Buddhaghosha, Atthasalini).
5. (Verse//19//Tanhavaggo, Canto 24).
6. Bharatasinha Upadhyaya, Pali Sahitya Ka Itihas, Hindi Sahitya Sammelan, Prayag, 2000, p. 747 and Minayef ed. Journal of Pali Text Society, Gandhavansa, p. 59 from Bharatasinha Upadhyay, Pali Sahitya Ka Itihas.
7. Prof. P.V. Bapat, ed. 2500 years of Buddhism, Publication Division, Ministry of Information and Broadcasting, Government of India, New Delhi, 1959, 4th rep. 1976, p. 168.
8. P.V. Bapat, ed. *ibid.,* (pp. 176-77).
9. P.V. Bapat, ed. *ibid.,* (p. 181).
10. P.V. Bapat, ed. *ibid.,* (pp. 182-83).
11. (Majjhima, VI, 16-17).
12. (Majjhima XVIII, 3).
13. (Anguttara, I, 62, IV, 183).
14. (Cf. V.S. Agrawala, Panini, etc., pp. 358-60).
15. (I, p. 524).
16. (M.i,231(sutta, No. 35):Imesam Sanghanam Gananam seyyathidam Vajjinam, Mallanam, etc.
17. (Geeta, 9,32).
18. See Arthur Waley, New Light on Buddhism in Medieval India (Melanges chinois et bouddhiques), Vol. I (1931-32), pp. 354-376.
19. Holyfaith, Sanskrit Vyakarnana with a Smile, Holy Faith International, New Delhi.
20. A.K. Warder, Introduction to Pali, PTS, Routledge and Kegan Paul Ltd, London, 1974.
21. Acharya Devi Shankar Misra and Dr. Rajkishor Sinh, Sanskrit Sahitya Ka Itihas, Lucknow.

Other Sources

1. Vasant Moon ed., Dr. Babasaheb Ambedkar: Writings and Speeches, Vol. 16, Education Department, Government of Maharashtra, Mumbai 1998.
2. Rahula Sankrityayan, Pali Sahitya Ka Itihasa, Lucknow 1963, 3rd ed. 1992.
3. Bhadant Anand Kausalyayan, Unnattisa Din mein Pali, Nagpur 1987.
4. Dr. B.R. Ambedkar, The Buddha and His Dhamma, Mumbai 1957.
5. T.W. Rhys Davids and William Stede, The PTS's Pali-English Dictionary, London 1921-25, 5th ed. 1972.
6. Rhys Davids, Buddhist India, Motilal Banarsidass, Delhi, 1971.
7. H.B. Rangaree, Pali Is the Mother of Sanskrit, Nagpur 1994.
8. Jagdish Kashyapa, Moggallana Vyakaran in Hindi.
9. Bhadant Anand Kausalyayan, Dhammapada, Sarnath 1938, Nagpur 1993.
10. Bhadant Anad Kausalyayan, Bouddha Jeevan Paddhati, Buddha Bhoomi Prakashan, Nagpur, 3rd rep. 2000.

BIBLIOGRAPHY

1. Dr. B.R. Ambedkar, The Buddha and His Dhamma, Mumbai 1957, rep. 1997, 2001
2. B.R. Ambedkar, The Untouchables, Mumbai 1948
3. B.R. Ambedkar, Buddha and Future of His Dhamma, 1951
4. B.R. Ambedkar, Rajyasabha, August-September 1954, Parliamentary Debate
5. D.R. Jatav, The Critics of Dr. Ambedkar, Surabhi Publication 1997
6. H.S. Olcott, The Poor Pariah, Madras 1893
7. Nagendranath Bose, Modern Buddhism and its Followers in Orissa
8. Arnold J. Toynbee, A Study of History, vol. IV, Oxford 1940
9. C.D. Naik, Social and Political Thought of Dr. B.R. Ambedkar, New Delhi, 2007
10. C.D. Naik, Buddhist Development in East and West since 1950, New Delhi 2005.
11. V. Moon ed. The Writings and Speeches of Dr. Babasaheb Ambedkar, Vol. I, Education Department, Government of Maharashtra, Mumbai 1979
12. V. Moon ed. Ibid. Vol. III
13. V. Moon ed. Ibid. Vol. II, Bombay 1982
14. V. Moon ed. Ibid., Vol.16, Mumbai 1998
15. Baatr Dorj Bazarov, Buddhists in the USSR, New Delhi 1979
16. Stcherbatsky, Central Conception of Buddhism
17. P.C. Ranasinghe, Buddha's Explanation of the Universe, Ceylon 1957
18. E. W. Hopkins, The Great Epic of India, 1920
19. P.L. Narasu and Winternitz Maurice, The Great Epic of India, vol. I, Calcutta 1927

20. P. Laxmi Narasu, A Study of Caste, Madras 1922
21. W.W. Hunter, Indian Empire 1983
22. Walter Elliot, The Untouchables, New Delhi 1948
23. Jivanayakam, The Right Hand and left Hand Castes, Nagarcoil 1913
24. Hunter, Indian Empire
25. Edgar Thurston, Castes and Tribes of Southern India, vol. VI, Government Press, Madras 1909
26. H. Dharmaratna, Buddhism in South India, Ceylon 1968
27. Baburao bagul, Dalit Sahitya Ajache Kranti Vigyan, Nagpur 1981
28. Vincente Fatone, The Philosophy of Nagarjuna, 1st ed., Delhi 1981, rep. 1991
29. E. Lamotte, History of Indian Buddhism: From the Origin to the Shakya Era, tr. Sara Webb-Boin, 1988
30. Andrea Loseries Leick, Tibetan Mahayoga Tantra on Ethno-Historical Study of Skulls, Bones and Relics, Delhi 2008
31. Snellgrove 1959
32. Robinson 1979
33. Nagarjuna, Uhapoha, Lucknow 1955
34. Dr. Ram Kumar Ram, tr. F.T. Stcherbatsky, Bouddha Nyaya, Varanasi 1969
35. T.W.W. Rhys Davids ed. Yogavacara's Manual, London 1896
36. G.C. Pande, Studies in Mahayana, India, Central Institute of Higher Tibetan Studies, Sarnath, Varanasi 1933
37. Hirakawa Akira, A History of Indian Buddhism, From Sakyamuni to Early Mahayana, tr. Paul Groner, rep. Delhi 1998
38. Andrew Skilton, A Concise History of Buddhism, Birmingham 1994
39. Edward Conze, Prajaparamita Literature, Delhi 2000
40. D.T. Suzuki, Studies in the Lankavatara Sutra, Taipei 1991
41. Thich Nhat Hanh, The Heart of the Buddha's Teaching, N.Y. 1988
42. Sangharakshita, A Survey of Buddhism, Pune 1996

43. Nanamoli and Bodhi, M.655, Mass. 1955

44. P.V. Bapat, @500 years of Buddhism, Delhi 1959, 4th rep. 1976, 1997

45. W. Pachow, Comparative Study of Pratimoksha, Delhi 2000

46. R. Spence Hardy, Manual of Buddhism in its Modern Development, new Delhi 1996

47. Garma C.C. Chang tr. Paramita of Ingenuity, A Treasury of Mahayana Sutra, Delhi 2002

48. H.V. Guenther, Yuganadha, The Tantrik View of Life, Benaras 1952

49. H.V. Glasenapp, Die Entstehung des Vajrayana, Zeitschr.d.deutch morgenland.Gesellschaft, vol. 90, 560, Leipzig 1936

50. Advayavajra, Caturmudra, Yuganadha

51. Prajnopaya-Vinischaya-Siddhi, Two Vajrayana Works, Gaikwad Oriental Series, No. XLIV

52. Bhadant Anand Kausalyayan, Dhammapada, Pakinnavaggo canto 21, Verses 294, 295, Nagpur 1938

53. W.V. Evans-Wentz, Tibetan Yoga and Secret Doctrines

54. Guru Gampopa, The Twelve Indispensable Things

55. Hans Wolfgang Schumann, Buddhism, An Outline of its Teachings and Schools, USA 1973

56. Lusthaus, Dan, Buddhist Philosophy, Chinese

57. Donald S. Lopez, Jr., Philosophy, East and West, Buddhist Hermeneutics: A Conference Report, University of Hawaii Press, vol. 37, No. 1, January 1987

58. Nathan Katz, Philosophy, East and West, prasanga and Deconstruction: Tibetan Hermeneutics and the yana Controversy, vol 34, no. 2, University of Hawaii Press April 1984

59. R.N. Mukerjee and Arunansu Ghosal, Social Thought from Comte to Mukherjeee, New Delhi 2006

60. V.T. Rajshekar, Dalits: The Black Untouchables of India, Clarity Press, Inc. RDNE, Atlanta 1995

61. J.K. Banthia, Director of Census Operation, Maharashtra, Part II-B(ii), Series-14, PCA for SCs, Mumbai 1993

62. M.B. Kundale, Shaikshanik Tatvadnyana aani Shaikshanik Samajshastra, 10th ed., Pune 2003

63. Tara Chand, Development of Education System in India, New Delhi 2004

64. N.N. Oza ed. Chronicle Year Book, Noida 2009

65. Dhananjay Keer, Dr. Ambedkar: Life and Mission, Bombay 1971

66. Sanjay Prakash Sharma, B.R. Ambedkar: A Crusador of Social Justice, Jaipur 2003

67. Devidas Ghodeswar ed. Dalitanche Shikshan, Nagpur 1994

68. Maik Krestovics, and Michael Steve O, Financing Higher Education in Global Market, New York 2004

69. Vandana Shiva, India Divided Diversity and Democracy under Attack, Bangalore 2005

70. Bharatsinha Upadhyaya, pali Sahitya Ka Itihas, Prayag 2000

71. Arthur Waley, New Light on Buddhism in Medieval India, (Melanges chinoi et bouddhiques), vol. I, 1931 - 32

72. Holyfaith, Sanskrit Vyakarana with a Smile, New Delhi

73. A.K. Warder, Introduction to Pali, London 1974

74. Acharya Devi Shankar Misra and Dr. Rajkishor Sinh, Sanskrit Sahitya Ka Itihas, Lucknow

75. Rahul Sankrityayan, Pali Sahiya Ka Itihas, Lucknow 1963, 3rd ed. 1992

76. Bhadant Anand Kausalyayan, Unnatisa Din mein Pali, Nagpur 1987

77. B.A. Kausalyayan, Dhammapada, Sarnath 1938, Nagpur 1993

78. B.A. Kausalyayan, Bouddha Jeevan Paddhati, Nagpur, 3rd rep. 2000

79. T.W. Rhys Davids and William Stede, The PTS's Pali-English Dictionary, London 1921-25, 5th ed. 1972

80. Rhys Davids, Buddhist India, Delhi 1971

81. H.B. Rangaree, Pali Is the Mother of Sanskrit, Nagpur 1994

82. Jagdish Kashyap, Moggalana Vyakaran, (Hindi)

Scriptures

1. Revelation 19:20, Rev. 20:8
2. Dhammapada 129, 130
3. DN. II, 49, vol. L
4. D.II, MI
5. Vajrasuci, Shloka 22-27
6. Avatansaka (The Flower Ornament Scripture)
7. Anangavajra, Prajnopaya-Vinischaya-Siddhi,v. 25,
8. Yuganadha,
9. Guhya Samaja Tantra
10. Buddhaghosa, Atthasalini
11. Tanhavaggo, canto 24, verse 19
12. Majjhima, VI, XVIII
13. Anguttara I
14. V. S. Agrawal, Panini
15. Itivuttaka
16. Geeta, 9:32

Sutras

1. The Sutra of Hui Neng, Shanghai, November 21st, 1929
2. Garma CC Chang, Maharatnakuta Sutra (Treasury of Mahayana Sutra)
3. Tatiya Saddhamma Sammosa sutra, Pancakanipata, Anguttaranikaya

Cases

1. Hon'ble J.J. Bhau Wahane, Criminal Case No. 246/89, Suresh Rathi Vs. State of Mah.
2. Judgement of the Supreme Court (Full Bench), P.B, Gajendragadkar, C.J., K.N. Wanchoo, H. Hidayatullah, Rajhubar Dayal and J.R. Mudholkar, Punjabrao Vs. Dr. D.P. Meshram, AIR 1965, 1179 delivered by Hon'ble J.R. Mudholkar
3. Judgement of the Bombay High Court of Judicature at Bombay bench at Nagpur in Smt. Shakuntala Vs. Nilkanth and Others, Criminal Appeal No. 29 of 1970 decided on 25th October 1972 by Justice Masodkar

4. Babi W/o Jayant Jagtap Vs. Jayant Mahadeo Jagtap, Criminal Appeal No. 815 of 1979, the Bombay High Court Judicatur,Bombay, Hon'ble R.S. Bhonsale J. decided and delivered the judgement on 28-29 January 1981, Maharashtra Law Journal, p. 815, 1981
5. Rekha Vs. Ashok and others, II 1985 Divorce and matrimonial Cases Criminal Revision No. 5 of 1984 decided on 18th September 1984 with Hon'ble Dhabe J. present.

Internet surfing

1. IFM corporate, 5.10.2008
2. Dr. Anad Teltumbde, Globalisation and the Dalits, 5.10.2008
3. On Tantra, 9th March 2009
4. Rotledge, http://www.rep.routledge.com, 25.5. 2005
5. dalits@ambedkar.org
6. shuraisasai@rediffmail.com
7. www.ambedkar.org

Journals

1. EPW Research Foundation(1994): Three years of Economic Reform in India, Bombay
2. World Buddhism, Colombo, November 1961
3. Young East, Tokyo, Summer 1962
4. Minayef ed. Journal of Pali Text Society

Letters

1. Loknath's letter to Babasaheb Ambedkar, 1936
2. Ravikant Shinde, An Open Letter to Rajdeep Sardesai, 31st October, 2006
3. President, Ambedkar Centre for Justice and Peace, from UN, 10th August 2001

Articles

1. Sankrityayan, About Ambedkar, Dharmayug
2. Dr. K. Jamanadas, Some Self Introspection on Future of Buddhism, November 7, 2001
3. An Overview of India's Buddhist Movement, Friday, October 6, 2006

Leaflets

1. Leaflet issued by All India Canara Bank, SC and ST Employees Union, Nagpur 1986
2. President, All India Buddha Gaya Mahabodhi Mahavihara Action Committee, Indora Buddha Vihara, Nagpur, India

Dictionaries

1. Shambala Dictionary of Buddhism and Zen
2. William Edward Soothill and Lewis Hodous, A Dictionary of Chinese Buddhist Terms

Encyclopaedias

1. The Balfour Encyclopaedia of India, vol. III
2. Whitaker's World of Facts, New Delhi 2007
3. E. Craig ed. Routledge Encyclopedia of Philosophy, London

Speech

1. Kausalyayan spoke at Morris College, Nagpur 1984

Dissertations

1. P.N. Aglave, Modernisation in the Social Life of Buddhist Community in Nagpur City, Nagpur University 1984

Newspapers

1. Free Press, Indore, 10.10.200

Conversation

1. Conversation with W. Rahula, World Buddhism, Ceylon 1969

Index